D0215509

University of Winnipeg, 515 Portage Ave., Winnipeg, MB. R3B 2E9 Canada

DISCARDED

The Politics of the Unpolitical

PT
289
C7313
1995

The
Politics
of the
Unpolitical

*German Writers and the Problem
of Power, 1770–1871*

GORDON A. CRAIG

New York   Oxford
OXFORD UNIVERSITY PRESS
1995

Oxford University Press

Oxford   New York
Athens   Auckland   Bangkok   Bombay
Calcutta   Cape Town   Dar es Salaam   Delhi
Florence   Hong Kong   Istanbul   Karachi
Kuala Lampur   Madras   Madrid   Melourne
Mexico City   Nairobi   Paris   Singapore
Taipei   Tokyo   Toronto

and associated companies in
Berlin   Ibadan

Copyright © 1993 by C.H. Beck'sche Verlagsbuchhandlung,
München. Originally published in German under the title
Die Politik der Unpolitischen: Deutsche Schriftsteller und die Macht 1770–1871
by C.H. Beck'sche Verlagsbuchhandlung, München, 1993

English edition copyright © 1995 by Oxford University Press, Inc.

Published by Oxford University Press, Inc.
200 Madison Avenue, New York, New York 10016

Oxford is a registered trademark of Oxford University Press

All rights reserved. No part of this publication may be reproduced,
stored in a retieval system, or transmitted, in any form or by any means,
electronic, mechanical, photocopying, recording, or otherwise,
without the prior permission of Oxford University Press.

Library of Congress Cataloging-in-Publication Data
Craig, Gordon Alexander, 1913–
[Politik der Unpolitischen. English]
The politics of the unpolitical :
German writers and the problem of power, 1770–1871 /
Gordon A. Craig.
p. cm.   Includes bibliographical references and index.
ISBN 0-19-509499-9
1. German literature – 18th century – History and criticism.
2. German literature – 19th century – History and criticism.
3. Authors German – 18th century – Political and social views.
4. Authors, German – 19th century – Political and social views.
5. Politics in literature.
I. Title.
PT289.C7313   1995   830.9′358 – dc20   94-33179

1 3 5 7 9 8 6 4 2

Printed in the United States of America
on acid-free paper

For
Eva von Freeden
and
Ingrid Kinzel-Amuser

felices manus sedulae

Acknowledgments

I should like to thank my friend and colleague James J. Sheehan for the happy thought of calling this book *The Politics of the Unpolitical.*

The idea of bringing my love for German literature and my interest in German history and politics together in a book like this has been on my mind for a long time. Almost thirty years ago I wrote a series of essays about writers and politics that kept it alive. For the present volume, I have re-worked those articles and in several cases expanded them significantly or introduced shifts of emphasis. Chapter 2 appeared in its original form in *The Journal of Modern History* XLI, no. 1 (1969), Chapter 3 in *The Proceedings of the American Philosophical Society* CXII, no. 6 (December 1968), Chapter 4 in *The American Historical Review* LXXIV (1969), Chapter 6 in *Studies in International History*, edited by Kenneth Bourne and Donald Cameron Watt (London, 1967), Chapter 8 in *Überlieferung und Auftrag: Festschrift für Michael de Ferdinandy* (Wiesbaden, 1972), and parts of Chapter 10 in *The Pacific Historical Review*, XLI, no. 1 (February 1972).

The chapters on Goethe, Hölderlin, and Heine were written expressly for this book and have not been previously published.

Menlo Park, Calif.   G. A. C.
August 1994

Contents

Introduction

Some years ago, Northwestern University held a conference, "Commitment in an Age of Anxiety," in which there was a "Panel on the Creative Mind," chaired by Hannah Arendt and including a number of well-known artists and writers. After several formal papers were read, there was a very free discussion during which, at one point, the intellectual historian H. Stuart Hughes began to reproach Saul Bellow for showing no political engagement in his writings. Bellow protested that he neither knew nor cared anything about politics and just wanted to be left alone to write his novels. Hughes refused to accept this. "It is your duty to show where you stand," he cried. "It is your obligation as a writer. Look at Thomas Mann!" At this point the chairman broke in. "Stuart!" she said in her deep voice. "Stuart! Don't mention Thomas Mann! He lived up there on top of his mountain behind the banks of clouds, and he let the world go by. But, unfortunately, the clouds would part now and then, and he would emerge and make a pronouncement. And, Stuart, he was always wrong!"

Whether in fact Thomas Mann was more frequently mistaken in his views than Hannah Arendt is beyond conjecture, but it is, even so, not difficult to think of occasions on which he was obstinately irrational, not least of all on the subjects that form the main themes of this book, namely, politics and power. In the middle of the First World War, for example, in *Betrachtungen eines Unpolitischen* (Reflections of an Unpolitical Man), a brilliantly wrong-headed and often ludicrous attempt to prove the superiority of German values to those of the West, he asserted that politics was an activity that was alien to the German spirit. "German humanity," he wrote, "basically resists politicization. And, in fact, the political element is missing in the German concept of *Bildung*."¹ This, he continued, was a good thing, since politics embodied revolt and disorder, destroyed traditional values, and contained the danger of "a complete leveling, a journalistic-rhetorical stultification and vulgarization."² Thirty years later, at the end of another terrible conflict and in another impressive but ill-balanced book, which dealt, somewhat obliquely, with the causes of the conquest and destruction of Germany by National Socialism, Mann took the curious course of demonizing power and turning it into a kind of magic force that had irresistibly led "a people that was originally honest and obedient to the law but all too docile, all too prone to live according to theory, into the school of evil."³

One can be forgiven for thinking that somewhere between these two positions logic deserted the great novelist. Should it not have been clear to him by 1945 that it was the pervasiveness of the "politics destroys character" stance that he championed in *Reflections*, rather than any spell or ensorcellment, that contributed to the German capitulation to National Socialism after 1933? In the real world, rather than that of fiction, one is victimized not by magic forces but by tangible and explicable ones, not least of all by one's own failings, and there is no greater failing than neglect of politics. Felix Gilbert has written that Machiavelli believed that the purpose of politics "was to keep society alive in the ever moving stream of history" and that in making politics a component of the historical process he demonstrated that "every situation is unique and requires man to use all his forces to probe all the potentialities of the moment."⁴ Thus, it is politics that both helps mankind to detect the great turning points in history and supplies it with the means of adjusting to them. But politics has another even more important function. It is the only weapon that we have at our disposal that has the possibility of controlling arbitrary power, that ever present threat in modern society. For there is nothing mystical or demonic about power. It is just something that is always there, to be used for good or for ill, which will become a weapon in the hands of evil people if it is not controlled and used by good. Politics gives us the ability to make choices about the uses of power. Failure to avail ourselves of it makes us all potential victims.

Doubtless there were lots of Germans in the Bismarckian and Wilhelmine periods who—for reasons too complicated to be gone into here but all having to do with the collapse of liberalism after the foundation of the Empire – felt the way Mann did ("I want no politics, I want matter-of-factness, order, and decency. If that is philistine, then I want to be a philistine. If it is German, then I want in God's name to be called a German.")[5] But there have been many fewer who thought that way since 1945, and, in middle-class society and among writers and men of science, there were many fewer who thought that way before 1870.

In a striking formulation, Robert Minder once wrote that in a general sense one could say that "in Germany the writer, the artist, is first and foremost the denizen of another world: in France, he is to a much greater extent a *citoyen*, he has been transformed into a citizen [*eingebürgert*]."[6] The contrast here is between someone who has neither political rights nor interests and someone who is deeply involved in the affairs of his own land. Yet this distinction was certainly not relevant to the greater part of the period covered by this book, in which all of the great German writers gravitated to politics in one way or another. Even Goethe is no exception, although it is true that, after years of public service, he became so alienated that he retreated to a world of his own devising and counseled his fellow artists to follow his example. Most of the others, however, those discussed here and others who might have been – Ludwig Uhland, Rahel Levin, Karl Varnhagen von Ense, Georg Büchner, Karl Gutzkow, Ludwig Börne, Karl Immermann, and Adolf Glassbrenner, among others – sought to be *citoyens* either by serving the existing state, as Goethe did as minister of state in Saxe-Weimar and Wilhelm von Humboldt as minister of education and ambassador in the kingdom of Prussia, or by seeking to change or improve it, as Georg Forster and Friedrich Hölderlin and Georg Gottfried Gervinus did in their various ways.

The impulse, of course, came from France, to which German artists had long been accustomed to look for example and inspiration. If the great revolution of 1789 terrified Goethe, it significantly broadened the hopes and ambitions of Forster and Hölderlin, just as the revolution of 1830 caused Heine to cry in ecstasy, "Sacred July days in Paris!" Even the ambitious and power-hungry Napoleon Bonaparte was greeted by many German intellectuals as a liberator. Heinrich von Kleist, it is true, surely one of the most interesting political writers of the time, regarded the emperor as a new Quintilius Varus and gave himself over to a search for a German Arminius who could put him down. But to Goethe and Johannes von Müller and Georg Friedrich Hegel and Heinrich Heine, Napoleon seemed to represent the rare combination of *Geist* and *Macht* that gave meaning to history; in their eyes, he was a true World Historical Individual; and the lives and careers of each of them were significantly changed by him.

Not the least important of the legacies of the French revolutionary and Napoleonic period to German intellectuals was the idea that power was a subject worth serious study. Schiller's searching examination in his historical plays of the different faces of power and its relationship to freedom, Wilhelm von Humboldt's important essay upon the limitations set by reason upon the power of the state,[7] a study that greatly influenced John Stuart Mill when he wrote his *Essay on Liberty*, and Heine's speculations about the berserker potential of a German nationalism that had been nurtured by philosophy rather than politics were all responses to that challenge. So also was Gervinus's disturbing question: whether a German liberalism that believed that power should be given precedence over constitutional rights in the objectives of the national movement, as F. C. Dahlmann had said in the Paulskirche in January 1949 and Heinrich von Sybel had admitted under the influence of the victory over France in 1870, could be trusted to lead the nation in the direction of democracy, which Gervinus believed was the only goal worth pursuing.

The years covered by this book were years in which German intellectuals received their apprenticeship in politics and their first hard lessons in the difficulties of prevailing against the manipulators of power. The fact that so many of them lost heart and withdrew from the conflict in the subsequent period gives us no reason to forget these pioneers of commitment, who refused to believe that indifference to politics was a mark of moral or intellectual superiority or that, as Goethe's student jeered in Auerbach's tavern in Leipzig, a "political song" should automatically be considered a "nasty song."[8]

The Politics of the Unpolitical

1

Goethe as Statesman

In March 1828, in the course of a discussion with Eckermann about the relationship between genius and energy, Goethe declared,

> There is no genius without productive power that continues to work. Further, it doesn't matter what one's business, art, or *métier* may happen to be. It's all the same. Whether one shows genius in science, like Oken or Humboldt, or in war and statecraft like Frederick, Peter the Great, or Napoleon, or whether one writes a song like Béranger, it's all the same and comes down to whether the thought, the *aperçu* or the deed has living force and will continue to live.[1]

It is well to remind ourselves as we read this that, although the old Goethe was not averse to expatiating in general terms about any subject that Eckermann suggested to him, he was speaking here about things he knew very well. For he too had written songs and distinguished himself as a productive scientist, and he too, although this is sometimes forgotten, had been a statesman. Indeed, he had had more practical political experience than any German writer of his age. Wilhelm von Humboldt was for a short time Minister of Education in Prussia and served later, during the last stages of the war against Napoleon, as ambassador to Austria,[2] and Gottfried Keller was State Secretary in Zürich for fifteen years. But that sort of thing was nothing to Goethe's record of service under Carl August of Saxe-Weimar, which extended for almost forty years.

Goethe was a dedicated and principled public servant who addressed himself to the duchy's problems with energy and realism and brought a healthy sense of perspective to the criticism of its external policy. But his experience in office was, on the whole, a disillusioning one and left him with a deep aversion to politics. In one of his last conversations with Eckermann, he said bitterly, "I hate all botched work like sin, but especially botched work in affairs of state, which brings nothing but evil to thousands and millions of people,"[3] and to Frédéric-Jean Soret he admitted that the thought of death concerned him less than "the importance that is now given to political matters at the expense of literature and science."[4] There is no doubt that the strength of his feelings on this subject helped to validate the antipolitical stance that many Germans adopted in the nineteenth century. Nietzsche once wrote that Goethe was not only a good and great man but a culture in himself; but, he continued, "Who would be able to point to any trace of Goethe in the German politics of the last seventy years?"[5]

I

That the author of such spectacular successes as *Götz von Berlichingen* and *The Sorrows of the Young Werther* should suddenly embark upon a political career is not as surprising as it may seem. As Wilhelm Mommsen pointed out a long time ago, Goethe's interests were too diverse and his opinion of his abilities too generous for him to regard himself simply as a professional writer, and he would almost certainly have entered the public service of his native city Frankfurt am Main had he not turned to that of the duchy of Saxe-Weimar.[6] He was, after all, a member of Frankfurt's patrician class and a trained jurist and solicitor, and he must always have regarded a political career as the most likely means of providing him with the security and the material resources necessary for the development of his genius.

When the invitation from the young Duke came to him in 1775, there is no doubt that he was intrigued and flattered. He may also have considered it providential, for he had been wrestling for some time with the conflict between his love for the beautiful Lili Schönemann and his fear that marriage and its obligations would be restrictive and frustrating. The offer from Weimar freed him from this dilemma, and, on 30 October 1775, he wrote in his *Tagebuch*, with the relief of one whose *Daemon* had settled the issue for him, "Lili, adieu! . . . It has been decided—we must play out our roles separately."[7] What kind of a role his would turn out to be, he had, of course, no way of knowing, but he was clearly touched by the young Duke's evident desire to have him at his side as adviser and friend, and from the beginning he expected his position to be more than that of a glorified tutor. On 22 January 1776, he wrote his friend Johann Heinrich Merck:

> I am now involved in all court and political business, and it will be almost impossible now to disengage myself again. My condition is advantageous enough, and the duchies of Weimar and Eisenach a big enough stage on which to see whether a part in the affairs of the world suits me. . . .[8]

and, a few days later, to his friend Johann Caspar Lavater in Zürich, in language typical of a hero in a *Sturm und Drang* drama, "I am now wholly embarked upon the waves of the world—fully determined to discover, to win, to struggle, to be wrecked, or to blow myself with the whole cargo into the air."[9]

Nor was he as entirely self-centered and intent on his own aggrandisement as these statements made him appear. He had been reading Justus Möser's *Patriotische Phantasien*, with its strong emphasis upon upon the social obligations and opportunities of princes. He had discussed Möser with Carl August at their first meeting, and it seems likely that the positive response that he had sensed then led him to hope for a collaboration that would bring benefits to the Duke's subjects.[10] Later, in *Torquato Tasso*, he was to write:

> Es ist kein schönrer Anblick in der Welt,
> Als einen Fürsten sehn, der klug regiert,
> Das Reich zu sehn, wo jeder stolz gehorcht,
> Wo jeder nur sich selbst zu dienen glaubt,
> Weil ihm das Rechte nur befohlen wird.[11]
>
> [There is no fairer sight in all the world
> Than a prince who rules his subjects with intelligence
> Or a realm where men take pride in their obedience,
> Believing that they only serve themselves
> Because it is only the law that is enjoined on them.]

That he might help to educate such a prince must certainly have touched his mind when he decided to go to Weimar. The fact that he occasionally expressed it cynically—"A strange aspect of the governance of this world is trying to keep a head filled with such political and moral lice even halfway clean and in order"[12]—does not mean that he did not feel it deeply.

There is no doubt that his appointment brought him other gratifications, despite his pained discovery that no one likes court favorites and that, in his first days in Weimar as he confided to his diary, he found alienation where he had expected friendship. In an early note about his new occupation, he added so many exclamation points after the word *Regieren* (governing) that one senses a certain disgust with the bureaucratic backbiting that had filled his first months of service,[13] and indeed Carl August had to come down heavily upon some of the old hands who resented the intrusion of this inexperienced outsider.[14] Nevertheless, he did not become discouraged. He was ready for all challenges, unafraid of any assignment, however technical, and apparently tireless. Despite the grumbling of the veteran civil servants, the Duke did not hesitate to give him an extraordinarily wide range of duties. In addition, he insisted that Goethe accompany him on an incessant crisscrossing of the duchy, inspecting state installations and mines and alms houses and prisons by day and going to village festivals by night where they drank the local wines and played games and kissed and danced with the village girls. It was all very strenuous and at times exciting, and Goethe rejoiced in the adventures, particularly the putting out of fires, of which there seemed to be a great many, and the night-rides through the mountains, and the long talks by the fireside. "Early today," he wrote to his intimate friend Charlotte von Stein from Ilmenau in September 1780, "we had all the murderers, thieves, and receivers of stolen goods brought before us and interrogated them and brought them face-to-face with witnesses against them. At first I didn't want any part of this, because I avoid unclean things," but, he added, perhaps with a reference to the theories of his friend Lavater, "it is a great way of studying humanity and physiognomy." It was a busy time, and there always seemed to be too much to do, but he was learning to savor every minute. "It is the greatest gift, for which I thank the gods, that I can divide such a busy day, through the speed and diversity of my thoughts, into a million parts and make a small eternity out of it."[15]

He supplemented his official trips, as time passed, with explorations of his own, on which, under an assumed name and pretending to be a painter, he inspected favorite projects and listened to the opinions of people in inns and markets, doubtless deriving pleasure from this Hārūn ar-Rashīd activity. Sometimes in the course of these wanderings he remembered that he was a poet and then, as he wrote, "while I think that I'm sitting on my nag and riding my dutiful stations, the mare under me suddenly assumes wings and a noble form and with irrepressible desire carries me off from there."[16]

But such literary excursions came seldom. Christoph Martin Wieland was correct when he predicted in June 1776 that Goethe was too conscientious to slight his official duties for the sake of art. As a public servant, he wrote to Lavater, the newcomer

> will do much good and prevent much evil, and that must, if possible, comfort us for the fact that he will be lost from the world as a poet at least for many years. For Goethe does nothing by half. Now that he is entered upon this new career, he won't rest until he has reached his goal, to be as great as a minister as he was as an author.[17]

Goethe himself confirmed this prediction, also in a letter to Lavater, when he wrote, "I take too much upon myself, and again I cannot act differently. The person who is assigned to affairs of state should dedicate himself to them completely, and I shouldn't like it to be much different in my case."[18]

It is not easy, given the state of the surviving records, to give a very precise picture of what Goethe's duties were at any given time. What is abundantly clear was that Carl August, who had assumed independent rule of his possessions on 3 September 1775, at the end of his eighteenth year, was anxious to inaugurate his regime by getting rid of his mother's conservative ministers and starting a new dispensation,[19] and that his admiration of Goethe was so great that he wanted to involve him immediately on every level of administration. Thus, in June 1776, he made his new friend and adviser a member of the three-man Privy Council, which generally met with Carl August three times a fortnight, when the Duke was in Weimar, to discuss problems of the day and to make recommendations for the Duke's decision.[20] In addition, as time passed, Goethe became head of the commissions on war, highways, and mines and at various times was called on to prepare reports on commercial activities, church affairs and finances,

currency, taxes, and the internal affairs of the University of Jena. He
was also employed occasionally in negotiations with neighboring
states, as in May 1778 when he traveled with the Duke to Berlin and
Potsdam for talks about recruiting and the possibility of war in
Bavaria,[21] and in August 1784 when he acted as the Duke's private
secretary during negotiations in Braunschweig concerning the possibility of organizing a league of smaller states (*Fürstenbund*).[22] Finally, since Carl August was actively interested in cultural affairs, he
found himself inevitably charged with the job of satisfying the Duke's
latest enthusiasm. So he tended to be very busy, although perhaps not
quite as much so as Johann Gottfried Herder (whom he had been
instrumental in bringing to Weimar in 1776 as General Superintendent of the Evangelical Church)[23] said in a caustic letter to Johann
Georg Hamann in July 1782:

> He is . . . at the present time Working Privy Councillor, President
> of the Chamber, President of the War College, Superintendent of
> Construction, including road-building, in addition *Directeur des
> plaisirs*, Court Poet, arranger of beautiful festivities, court operas,
> ballets, masked balls and pageants, inscriptions, art works, etc.,
> Director of the Drawing Academy, in which he last winter gave
> lectures on osteology, himself everywhere the leading actor, dancer,
> in short the factotum of Weimar and, if God wills it, soon the major
> domus of all the Ernestine castles to which he will make proces-
> sions in order to be adored.[24]

What distinguished Goethe as a statesman in an age when theories
of cameralism sometimes caused more difficulties than they solved
was his gift for seeing problems in their own terms and seeking
commonsense solutions to them. His guiding principles were order
and economy, and he strove to do what he could to bring into balance
the finances of a state whose outlays regularly exceeded its revenues
without resorting to tax increases.[25] His success in recommending
and securing lower expenditures on non-productive government activities and services was undeniable, most notably in the case of the
armed forces, where he managed, although only after many struggles
with his ducal patron, to abolish the *Garde du Corps*, the militia
(*Landregiment*), the artillery corps, and half of the infantry.[26] These
savings—which have led Nicholas Boyle to call Goethe one of the few
defense ministers in history who have voluntarily halved their own
budgets[27]—compelled Carl Albert henceforth to do his professional

military training in Prussian maneuvers as a Prussian general instead of working with his minuscule force at home, and in the long run this had unfortunate results, but it also enabled Goethe to persuade the Estates to fund the national debt and to reduce taxes. This had the further beneficial effect of improving the lot of the cloth-workers in Apolda, particularly the so-called *Fabrikanten*, spinners and weavers who worked in their own homes for entrepreneurs and had been unfairly taxed.[28]

Public works Goethe took with great seriousness, and, if his attempts over the years to revive the silver mines at Ilmenau came to nothing in the end, they doubtless had the effect of temporarily relieving unemployment. Even more ambitious were his plans, after he became commissioner of roads in 1779, to replace the duchy's narrow, heavily rutted routes, often completely impassable because of washouts or fallen trees, with a modern system of metaled roads. At a cost of 11,000 thaler, the road from Weimar to Jena was transformed into a broad *chaussée*, and simultaneously the existing road from Weimar to Erfurt was resurfaced and plans were made for a highway from Weimar to Auerstädt, which, it was hoped, would attract commerce from the highway that ran from Erfurt over Buttelstedt to Eckartsberga. Earnest efforts were also made to bring the roads in the Saale valley near Jena into better order. As Fritz Hartung has written, there is no question about the importance of these improvements in stimulating the economy in the hard times of the early '80s.[29] Unfortunately, the pace that Goethe set in 1779 could not be sustained because of lack of resources, and one of his last official acts before leaving for Italy in 1786 was to write a long memorandum (9 June 1786), complaining that current resources were only sufficient to maintain the improvements already made and that, at the present rate of progress, it would take generations to complete his original plan.

Goethe was generally attentive to the needs of the people he met in the course of his constant traveling about the duchy, particularly those with special problems. In September 1780 he wrote to Charlotte von Stein, "One should do what one can to save individuals from destruction."[30] He sought wherever possible to find jobs for them or to devise community projects that would give employment to people like them. He was particularly sensitive to the needs of farmers and carried on a personal campaign against the laws that protected wild boar, which ruined their crops, and tried to persuade the duke, an inspired patron of the chase with a penchant for this particular prey, that "Estate owners, leaseholders, vassals, domestics, the huntsmen themselves – are all united in the desire to see these unwelcome guests exterminated."[31]

In matters affecting religion, Goethe had progressive views, and in the controversy in 1777 over the question of the church's right to maintain obligatory public penance for sins of the flesh, perjury, blasphemy, and immoral conduct, he took a more liberal position than either the High Consistory or General Superintendent Herder. Herder wished to retain penance in order not to increase the tendency towards indifferentism in religious affairs; Goethe believed it should be reduced to a private encouragement to repentance and improvement.[32] In most other questions, he tended to be conservative; in 1783, for example, during a controversy over the appropriateness of the death penalty for the killing of newborn children by their mothers, he wrote a memorandum that argued the social advantages of maintaining the traditional punishment.[33] This was true of most of his political views. Unlike his servant Philipp Seidel, who sympathized with revolution wherever it took place, he was opposed to fundamental change and was a supporter of the corporative state, an admirer of the upper nobility, about whom he was both uncritical and ill-informed, and a stickler for ceremonial and puctilio, insisting, even after decades of intimacy, in addressing Carl August with the utmost formality.

In September 1783, in his great poem "Ilmenau," Goethe apostrophized Carl August in terms of unlimited affection and praise.

> So mög', o Fürst, der Winkel deines Landes
> Ein Vorbild deiner Tage sein!
> Du kennest lang' die Pflichten deines Standes
> Und schränkest nach und nach die freie Seele ein.
> Der kann sich manchen Wunsch gewähren,
> Der kalt sich selbst und seinen Willen lebt;
> Allein wer andre wohl zu leiten strebt,
> Muß fähig sein, viel zu entbehren.
>
> So wandle du – der Lohn ist nicht gering –
> Nicht schwankend hin, wo jener Sämann ging,
> Daß bald ein Korn, des Zufalls leichtes Spiel,
> Hier auf den Weg, dort zwischen Dornen fiel.

Nein! streue klug wie reich, mit männlich steter Hand,
Den Segen aus auf ein geackert Land;
Dann laß es ruhn: die Ernte wird erscheinen
Und dich beglücken und die Deine.[34]

[So may, oh prince, this corner of your realm,
Be exemplary for your life.
You have long known the duties of your estate
And bit by bit restricted your own freedom.
That man can grant himself many an indulgence
Who is cold to anything but his own desire.
But he who strives to be a good leader for others
Must be capable of much self-deprivation.

So go not hence — the reward is not a small one —
Like an unsteady sower with faltering steps
Whose seed is but the merest play of chance,
Falling here on the path, there amid thorns.
No! Richly and cleverly with steady, manly hand,
Cast the blessed seed upon the well-tilled soil.
There let it lie. The harvest will appear
And bring joy to you and your progeny.]

The praise was well-deserved, and the confidence of future development seemed justified. With self-discipline and hard work, Carl August had transformed himself from a somewhat willful and stubborn youth into a ruler with a genuine interest in the well-being of his subjects and a conscious regard for how he was regarded in the world of ideas.[35] For this change, Goethe was in large part responsible, for, he had, with great delicacy and understanding, shown the Duke the obligations that came with his station and had not hesitated to reproach him for behavior that threatened to diminish the respect with which he was held in the land.[36] Even so, as time passed he was forced to recognize that his influence was diminishing and that Carl August was becoming more resistant to his recommendations. He began to notice reversions on the Duke's part to youthful self-indulgence and extravagance. On 10 March 1781, he wrote to Charlotte von Stein:

It is really wonderful how sensible he can be, how much insight he has, and how much he knows. And yet, when he wants to gratify himself, then he has to do something foolish, even if it's only to crush all the candles in his hands. Unfortunately, one sees that that sort of thing lies in his deepest nature and that the frog is made for the water, even though he can also get along well for a time on the land.[37]

At the end of the same year, complaining of Carl August's squandering of public funds on "sponging noblemen . . . who don't even thank him for it," he wrote with exasperation, "God knows when he will learn that fireworks at noon are not impressive."[38]

More serious was the fact that, as Carl August reached maturity, his political ambitions began to grow beyond the confines of his own realm. His "strong demonic personality"[39] required wider possibilities for self-expression than were provided by welfare policy in Saxe-Weimar. He began to interest himself in foreign policy and to dream of exercising influence in German affairs, either as the leading figure in a league of small states balancing between Austria and Prussia or, increasingly, as an ally of Prussia. Goethe, as a follower of Justus Möser, had a strong sense of the important contribution that small states made to the national culture and of the extreme dangers posed by any transgression of their natural limits. He tried to persuade Carl August that an effective foreign policy could not be launched from a base as small as Saxe-Weimar, but the Duke was not to be deterred and, indeed, after the death of Frederick II in 1786, was to make an alliance with his successor, take over the command of a Prussian regiment, and participate in the campaign in the Low Countries.[40] The intensity of Goethe's distress can be detected in the 1783 dramatic fragment *Elpenor*, in which he portrayed a situation similar to his own, that of the counselor seeking the good of his prince but disregarded by him.[41]

Growing dissatisfaction with the tendencies of Carl August's policy, as well as unhappiness about the way in which domestic projects were curtailed or jettisoned because of the diversion of revenues to unproductive purposes, eroded the deep satisfaction that Goethe had derived from his ministerial services in his first years. At the same time, he was conscious of a growing tension between his official duties and his desire to get back to his literary and scientific interests. He was beginning to feel perpetually guilty and, by the summer of 1786, knew that he must get away. "I'm now almost as overripe as the princely fruit," he wrote to Charlotte von Stein.[42] At the end of August 1786, without telling anyone of his intentions, he slipped away to Italy, where he was to remain for almost two years. From Jena, on his way, he wrote to Carl August, "I am going in order to improve all kinds of deficiencies and to fill up all sorts of gaps. May the healthy spirit of the time stand by me!"[43]

II

This is not the place to talk of Goethe's Italian journey and the effect that it had upon his intellectual development, but it is worth noting that it diminished his desire to resume the miscellaneous duties that he had performed in his first years as minister. Consequently, when he began to think about his return to Weimar, he wrote to Carl August in March 1788 about his future assignments. He assured the Duke that he was ready to serve in any capacity that would be congenial to him ("I can only say: Lord, here I am. Make of your servant what you will"), but he made it clear that his principal interest now was that of the artist and that he hoped "that you will employ me not directly and not on mechanical tasks."[44]

The Duke responded generously to this and to Goethe's assurances that he would be prepared to collaborate when needed with his successors in economic affairs and other branches of the administration. He sharply curtailed his ministerial functions, while leaving him in charge of mining activity, in which Goethe had a special interest, the theater, which he was to direct until 1817, and connected and expanding activities in the fields of the arts and sciences. Moreover, although Goethe no longer attended the regular meetings of the Privy Council, this did not exclude his being consulted by it on important issues, as he was during the student troubles at the University of Jena in 1792 and when he was asked for a report on currency questions in the following year.[45] All of this amounted to an appreciable diminution of his political functions. It was balanced, however, by a sharp increase in his preoccupation with politics, for the events in Paris in 1789 set all Europe in an uproar, and not even artists were allowed to detach themselves from the problems they posed.

Unlike his contemporaries Klopstock, Wieland, Forster, Hölderlin, Hegel, and Schelling, Goethe never showed the slightest enthusiasm for the French Revolution and, from the beginning, saw it as a force that would bring social upheaval and distress to all classes of society. Thus, in the "Venetian Epigrams" (1789), he wrote of

> Frankreichs traurige Geschick, die Großen mögen's bedenken!
> Aber bedenken fürwahr sollen es Kleine noch mehr.
> Große gingen zu Grunde: doch wer beschützte die Menge
> Gegen die Menge? Da war Menge die Menge Tyrann.[46]

> [France's sad fate, the great have reason to ponder it!
> But in truth the small even more.
> Great ones were ruined: but who protected the crowd
> From the crowd? The crowd became the crowd's tyrant.]

How long these troubles would last, he knew no better than anyone else, and in 1792, when the old Europe armed to extirpate the revolution, he joined the allied forces at Longwy at the request of Carl August, who commanded a Prussian Kürassier regiment. The Duke believed he was on the way to a triumph in Paris; Goethe went along with some foreboding, while writing to his friend Christian Gottlieb Voigt that he would at least have the opportunity to learn something about the conduct of war under a great commander (the Duke of Brunswick) and, at the same time perhaps, about the French nation.[47] His worst fears were realized: the campaign was badly managed; Brunswick was outmaneuvered by Dumouriez and Kellermann; and the allied armies, disorganized and short of food, were forced to withdraw before the French guns at Valmy. Thirty years later, Goethe recalled having said, "Here and today a new epoch of world history begins, and you will be able to say that you were there."[48] Whether or not he used those words, he apparently felt that way, and he had little faith that much could be done to alter the new situation. A few days after Valmy, he wrote to Voigt, "I have noted with distress that the Privy Council has unconditionally declared this war to be a *Reichskrieg*. We too, therefore, will plunge into destruction with the crowd — Europe requires a thirty years' war to appreciate what would have been sensible in 1792."[49]

Goethe left the army on 14 October and, after visits in Koblenz, Düsseldorf, Pempelfort, and Münster, returned to Weimar in December. His remarkable ability to detach himself from the hopes and fears caused by the recent events and to busy himself with literary projects astonished and shocked some of his friends, and one of them — Huber, the intimate of the Georg Forsters — wrote to Theodor Körner that, since the Italian trip, he no longer believed in Goethe's capacity for "enthusiasm for a higher goal."[50] In reality, Goethe was deeply moved by what he had seen and experienced and, as the war rumbled on in the Low Countries and French armies besieged Mainz, he tried to define his position with respect to the French Revolution. In 1793 he made two efforts to do this in dramatic form, in a one-act play called *Der Bürgergeneral* (The Citizen General) and a longer "political Drama" called *Die Aufgeregten* (The Agitated Ones). The former was a rather exaggerated parody of the inflated rhetoric of homegrown revolutionaries, which made the point, in a not very sophisticated way, that, in a land where the prince could be approached by every subject and where there were no impediments set to any legitimate activities on his part, there was no reason for party strife, and the influence of inflammatory foreign doctrines should be resisted. *Die Aufgeregten*, a much more effective piece of writing, told the story of a countess who, on a visit to Paris, has recognized both the ideals that animated the revolution and the crimes committed in its name and who returns to Germany resolved to institute reforms on her estates in collaboration with the local citizenry. When she does so, she is assailed both by the ultras and by mobs inflamed by agitators. In 1824 Goethe told Eckermann that the play was his "political testament of that time," showing that he was "no friend of the French Revolution" but "just as little a friend of arbitrary rule." He recognized that governments rather than peoples caused revolutions and that, if the former were just and vigilant and instituted necessary reforms before they were forced upon them, such bloody events could be avoided. But when he was writing the play, he added, he could not close his eyes to the fact that "there were people in Germany who tried to inspire *artificially* scenes like those that in France were the consequences of bitter necessity."[51]

By 1794, his mood was becoming darker and more resigned. Germany seemed to be divided among the anxious, the indifferent, and those who took pleasure in the misfortunes of others. "For my part," he wrote to Friedrich von Stein on 14 August, "I find nothing more advisable than to play the part of Diogenes and stick to my tub."[52] A month later, in reply to an appeal from Hans Christoph Ernst von Gagern to use his pen to unite the German people against the threat from abroad and against divisiveness and anarchy at home, he said that he was doing what he could in his own community, but that he felt that partisanship was already so prevalent that a writer who tried to appeal to the whole would go unheard. Few people, he suggested, recognized the extent of the danger, but "unfortunately, one must for the most part remain silent in order not to be regarded, like Cassandra, as mad when one predicts what is already before the door."[53]

This mood was reflected in his writing. In *Hermann und Dorothea* (1796–1797), Goethe sought to write a bourgeois idyll in the classic manner which would hold up a model of order to revolutionary violence and destructiveness. Goethe's message was that the individual cannot control destiny but is capable, in his own sphere, of choosing and acting freely and, if he is energetic, of mastering circumstance.

> Nicht dem Deutschen geziemt es, die fürchterliche Bewegung
> Fortzuleiten und auch zu wanken hierhin und dorthin.
> "Dies ist unser!" so laß uns sagen und so es behaupten![54]
>
> [It is not seemly for the German to transmit
> The terrible movement and also to vacillate here and there.
> Let us say, "This is ours!" and maintain it!]

But the faint optimism implicit in this story had disappeared by the time Goethe wrote the drama *Die Natürliche Tochter* (The Natural Daughter) in 1803. In this grim tale, Eugenie, the illegitimate daughter of a duke, is on the point of being received in court society, and beginning a brilliant career. Suddenly, through no fault of her own, she is sentenced to banishment and taken with one companion to a port city whence she is to be transported for life. Her stubborn, eloquent, and untiring attempts to win sympathy and assistance are defeated by a mysterious paper with a royal seal whose contents are unknown to her but have the power to turn the potential good will of those to whom she appeals to denial. In the end, her resistance exhausted, she is allowed to escape by foreswearing all of her titles and claims and disappearing into the anonymity of bourgeois marriage.

Goethe's contemporaries, on seeing the play, would have recalled the *lettres de cachet* of the *ancien régime*. Modern readers, without the intended sequel, which would have strengthened the French revolutionary setting, are more likely to think of the totalitarian regimes of our own century and to admire the poet's power to transcend his own time and to speak so intimately and poignantly to us of the kind of political persecution that has been so much a feature of our times and of the indifference with which it has been accepted.[55]

Verbannung! Ja, des Schreckensworts Gewicht
Erdrückt mich schon mit allen seinen Lasten.
Schon fühl' ich mich ein abgestorbnes Glied,
Der Körper, der gesunde, stößt mich los.
Dem selbstbewußten Toten gleich' ich, der,
Ein Zeuge seiner eigenen Bestattung,
Gelähmt, in halbem Traume, grausend liegt.[56]

[Banishment! Yes, the weight of that word of terror
Crushes me now with all its heaviness.
I feel already like a limb that has gone numb.
The healthy body casts me off,
And I resemble a self-conscious corpse
That, witness to its own interment,
Lies, half in dream, paralyzed and shuddering.]

It seems likely, however, that, when he wrote the play, Goethe was more intent upon emphasizing the radical separation between the private world of deprivation, humility, lack of ostentation, and security (from which Eugenie tried to escape and which in the end was her refuge) and the public world of politics and power and glamor and danger. Eugenie stands for the ideal of individual striving and refusal to give up what her inner nature tells her is due to her. But Goethe himself—now apparently convinced that revolution in particular and politics in general were natural processes before which the individual was powerless, the victim of secret forces that he could neither control nor understand—had opted for *Entsagung*, or resignation. The ideals that had animated him in his first Weimar years he had now given up. The political state of the world had driven him back into his own home where he could draw a circle around himself and where nothing could get in except love and friendship and art and science.

III

But the world of politics and power would not let him go entirely. Ever since the summer of 1805, mutual recriminations between the Emperor Napoleon and Frederick William III of Prussia had indicated that the Peace of Basel was disintegrating. As rumors of war began to spread, Carl August was once again aflame with military ardor and went to Berlin to offer his services to the Prussian king, making much of his special knowledge of the terrain of Thuringia and Franconia. In the months that followed, with conflict becoming ever more imminent, Goethe seems to have tried to find some way of dissuading the Duke from a course that he sensed was pregnant with disaster. In his *Jahresbericht*, he wrote: "What anxious letters I exchanged with my loyal and always unforgettable professional friend, the minister of state von Voigt, it would be difficult to describe, and even more so the pregnant conversation with my prince in Headquarters at Niederroßla."[57] Carl August was in no mood for cautionary preachments. In October 1806, after the Prussians had fortified Erfurt and begun to move troops towards Jena, he appointed Goethe quartermaster in charge of the victualing and supply of troops in the advance guard at Weimar. Observers noted that the poet did not seem overjoyed by the honor, one of them writing, "Goethe is a handsome man, marvelous eyes; yet his mood seemed depressed by the critical circumstances."[58] In fact, Goethe was not impressed by the Prussian officers here, or in Hohenlohe's headquarters in Jena, and he later wrote:

> It was surprising to me that, with all the great confidence in Prussian power and aptitude for war, I picked up warnings here and there that one should try to hide the best things and the most confidential papers. Under such circumstances I was bereft of hope and cried, among all the early larks and gaiety, "Well, if the heavens fall, many of you are going to end up as prisoners."[59]

Goethe's sole political success during the brief campaign, aside from seeing to it that the troops were fed, was to dissuade Hohenlohe's headquarters from sending a needlessly provocative piece of propaganda to Napoleon.[60] This did nothing to avert the disaster that came on 14 October, when the Emperor destroyed the Prussian armies at Jena and Auerstädt.

Carl August, who had dreamed of winning glory on the front line, had been posted to a command in the Thuringian mountains and may, because of this, have escaped the kind of death that befell Prince Louis Ferdinand at Saalfeld near Jena. Nor was he forced to see the destruction of that town by fire and the plundering, rapine, and random violence caused in Weimar by the retreating Prussian troops and the French squadrons that pursued them. The Duke was, in fact, a remarkably lucky man. His agitations for war before 1806 were well known to Napoleon, who is supposed to have referred to him as "*le prince le plus remuant dans tout l'Europe*," and he might very well have been punished for them by the loss of his territories. He was saved from this, however, by the personal intervention of Queen Luise of Prussia, whom Napoleon admired and to whose wishes he deferred.

He did not, however, escape the bitter and lasting reproaches of the friend and adviser of his youth. It was no accident that, in sending off manuscripts to the publisher Cotta for the fourth volume of his collected works, Goethe now made a point of including the unfinished drama *Elpenor*, which he had earlier refrained from printing because of the recognizable parallel between its protagonist's willingness to sacrifice his country's well-being in order to satisfy his fascination with war and Carl August's longing for military glory.[61] Despite his deep affection for the Duke, he no longer attempted to spare his feelings. The publication of *Campagne in Frankreich* (The Campaign in France) in 1822 was not only a justification of Minister of State Goethe's doubts about the wisdom of the Duke's judgment in 1792 but, in its conclusion —

> Und wie wir auch durch ferne Lande ziehn,
> Da kommt es her, da kehrt es wieder hin;
> Wir wenden uns, wie auch die Welt entzücke,
> Der Enge zu, die uns allein beglücke[62]
>
> [And, though we also travel through distant lands,
> Now in one place and then soon in another,
> We always turn, however the world delights us,
> To the narrow place which alone makes us happy] —

an argument against adventurism and unrealistic foreign policy. Finally, as Katharina Mommsen has demonstrated,[63] the second part of *Faust*, completed after the Duke's death, was in a real sense Goethe's political testament as stateman, and in it the poet catalogued what he considered in retrospect to have been the Duke's salient weaknesses, particularly in the scenes at the Emperor's court, in the battle passages in act IV, with their obvious references to Jena and its consequences, and in the Philemon and Baucis episode, in which Faust as ruler sacrifices his humanity to the greed of power.[64]

As the years passed, there was no change in Goethe's fundamental political position. His fear of revolution was his strongest impulse, and this was, as Nietzsche once remarked, closely linked with his readiness to accept any situation that would give him the peace and security he needed to pursue his scientific and artistic work. After the famous meeting in Erfurt in 1808, at which Napoleon talked intelligently with him about *Werther*[65] and made him a member of the Legion of Honor, he happily convinced himself that the Emperor was the guarantor of the kind of order that would benefit small states like Saxe-Weimar and creative individuals like himself; and he wore the red ribbon of the Legion quite un-self-consciously for the next five years, as Wilhelm von Humboldt noted with irritation when he visited Weimar during the campaign of 1813.[66] When Napoleon's star fell, it did not take him long to recognize in Metternich, whom he met after the battle of Leipzig, the best assurance of peace and order,[67] and by 1822 he was telling Eckermann that "nothing was ever discovered that was greater and more beneficial for mankind" than the Holy Alliance.[68] It was clear that he preferred integrated international systems to ones that were too loosely organized to prevent unilateral aggression by member states.

As for politics—by which he seemed to mean the organization and contention of parties—his aversion increased with the years. In a very real sense, he continued to support the corporate state as he had in his youth. He believed in status and clung to the belief that society worked best when most people remained in the condition in which they were born, under wise governors with a sense of social responsibility. The chance of the latter condition being true was in his view greater than that of popular sovereignty working for the general good. Party politics always seemed to him to be a threat not only to the existing but to any tolerable order, and political ambition a form of presumption. Thus, he could speak of the "*delusion* of the young people who want to have a hand in the most important matters of state."[69] Popular movements always filled him with alarm, and his reaction to the July Revolution in 1830 was no different from his attitude in July 1789.

Above all, and here his views were in sharp contrast to those of contemporaries like Georg Forster, he believed that politics should be no concern of practitioners of the arts, not because they would not be effective in that role but rather because it would change their nature and diminish their talents. He was angry when he discovered that Ludwig Uhland, a distinguished and much loved poet, had become a liberal politician and a member of the Württemberg parliament. To Eckermann he spoke with some vehemence about the case.

Just you watch, the politician will swallow up the poet. To be a
member of the Estates and to live in daily conflict and agitation is
not for the tender nature of a writer. It will be all up with his poetry,
and that is certainly to be deplored. Swabia possesses men enough
who are adequately educated and well-meaning, competent, and
eloquent enough to be members of the Estates, but it has only one
poet like Uhland.[70]

It did not occur to him to ask why Uhland should wish to sit in
Parliament or what he wished to accomplish there.

2

A German Jacobin: Georg Forster

Among the intellectual leaders of the German states during the period of the French Revolution, the political geographer and natural philosopher Georg Forster occupies a special place. As one who spent a third of his brief life outside Germany—living in England and travelling through the Russian steppes and the vast reaches of the South Seas—he was the least parochial of German thinkers, a fact apparent on every page he wrote. In his political views, he was perhaps the most consistent and certainly the most extreme of his generation, arriving, indeed, in the end, at the unfashionable conclusion that thought unaccompanied by action to implement its conclusions represents a mere waste of energy. These qualities of mind would in themselves make Forster worthy of attention by students of his period. The reaction of his contemporaries to his political activism, however, makes his case not only interesting but significant and illuminates characteristic attitudes of German intellectuals that, in Forster's own age and the century and a half that followed, slowed Germany's progress toward democracy.

In his own country Georg Forster has generally been without honor. There is no complete edition of his works, and the nineteen-volume one that was promised by the Academy of Sciences of the German Democratic Republic three years before the Berlin Wall went up was, after many delays and interruptions, still incomplete three years after it had come down. Most of the recent writing about Forster is superficial, apologetic, or romanticized, and only in 1987 did a major biography appear, by Klaus Harpprecht, which was based upon exhaustive research, balanced in its judgments, and clearly and vigorously written.[1]

In a country that has always honored its great minds, this is curious, particularly since there is no doubt about Forster's stature as a thinker and a writer. He was a pioneer in the field of political geography and comparative cultural history and must be regarded, in this respect, as the teacher of Alexander von Humboldt; his views on the relationship between social conditions and the arts profoundly influenced the young Hegel; his essays on literature, philosophy, and occasional subjects were read with enthusiasm by Goethe and Lichtenberg and eagerly solicited by Friedrich Schiller for his journal *Thalia*; and he was described by no less an authority than Friedrich Schlegel as one of Germany's classical writers. "It is virtually impossible to lay down any of his writings," Schlegel wrote in 1797,

> without feeling that one has been not merely enriched and moved to reflection by it but that one's mind has been stretched as well. In other German writings, even the best, one feels the stuffy air of the study. But with him one seems to wander happily in fresh air under a cheerful sky with a healthy man, now down into some charming valley, now up to some free summit from which one has an open view.[2]

This is high praise from a master critic, but Forster has been little read, and most literary and political historians have had little or nothing to say about him.

The reason for what is almost a conspiracy of silence is not far to seek. Georg Forster was not content to remain a *Dichter* and a *Denker*. He entered the world of practical politics, thus flouting two German prejudices that were well established even in his day—the belief that politics is apt to have deleterious moral effects upon its practitioners ("*Die Politik verdirbt den Charakter!*") and the assumption that a writer who addressed himself to the politics of the day need not be taken seriously any longer,[3] his status automatically declining from *Dichter* to *Literat*.[4] To make matters worse, Forster professed a kind of politics that was both revolutionary and antinational and was thus a hissing and a reproach to the conservatives who dominated German scholarship in the nineteenth century.

I

Georg Forster was born on 26 November 1754 in Nassenhuben, near Danzig. His father was a parson who was, however, more interested in the natural sciences than in the Gospel and who seized upon the first opportunity to flee from his pastoral duties. A choleric, vain and irresponsible man, who stormed through life under a heavy cloud of debts and personal resentments, Johann Reinhold Forster neverthe-less possessed great energy and undeniable scientific talent, and this was soon recognized by others. In 1765 he was commissioned by the Empress Catherine of Russia to go to the Saratov province on the Volga and assist in the drawing up of plans for new settlements there. In 1767 he was Joseph Priestley's successor in the so-called "Dis-senters' Academy" in Warrington in Lancashire, where he taught natural sciences. In 1772 the Admiralty appointed him scientific adviser to Captain James Cook, who was preparing to embark upon his second voyage of discovery. On each occasion Georg Forster was at his father's side as amanuensis, cataloguer of scientific data, and general assistant. It was a hard apprenticeship, for his father was an exacting taskmaster, but it was rewarding. The authority with which Georg Forster wrote later of the processes of nature and of the relationship between man and his environment and of the customs, manners, arts and literature of other peoples was made possible by his work with his father and the travels of his youth.

Later in his life, Georg Forster wrote that the three-year voyage with Cook, which took him around the Cape of Good Hope and into the polar seas, to New Zealand and through Polynesia and Melanesia, and to Easter Island and Tahiti, had determined his whole fate;[5] and, in the sense that it gave him a wider perspective than that of the ordinary intelligent European, there is no doubt of this.[6] It also launched him on a career of his own, for, when the journey was over, he wrote an account of it, which appeared in 1777 under the title *Voyage around the World* and was shortly thereafter translated into German and widely read in the German states. A year later, when Georg Forster went to the continent seeking to find a post for his father, who was once more unemployed and—as was not unusual with him—threatened with debtors' prison, he found himself famous. In Paris he met and talked about his voyage and about politics and philosophy with Benjamin Franklin; in Germany he was lionized as the man who had been to Tahiti, which was to the romantic imagina-tion something as remote and enticing as the mysterious blue flower.

This attention helped to bring the young man into touch with the leading minds in Germany and to promote his career as a German writer, and it also opened the way into the academic profession. In 1778 Forster was appointed professor of natural sciences at the Collegium Carolinum in Kassel, and in 1784 he moved with the same title to the new university in Vilna in Poland. After the high excitement of the Pacific voyage, this new life proved, however, to be disappointing. Neither at Kassel nor at Vilna did Forster find students who were capable of doing more than elementary work, and he was never provided with the financial support necessary to make possible serious scientific work of his own. He was, moreover, perpetually debt-ridden, for until his father received an appointment at the University of Halle in 1780 he was compelled to contribute to the support of his parents, and after 1784 he had a demanding wife and a growing family of his own. During these years he established himself as a writer of distinction, but the financial returns from this activity were exiguous, and the essays that elicited the admiration of Goethe and Schiller had to be sandwiched in between mountains of potboiling translation for the Berlin publisher Voss. This kind of existence continued after he moved to Mainz in 1788 to be the director of the Kurfürst's library, for this position proved to be as humdrum and as financially unrewarding as the earlier ones. In November 1791, Forster wrote his friend Friedrich Heinrich Jacobi: "I have perhaps in my whole life never found myself in a more oppressive situation than now. I have worked without let-up for the whole year, with iron discipline and great spiritual exhaustion. My energies are drained. . . . Nothing works for me. The more I do, the more I hope to gain, the more everything runs out between my fingers. . . . *Siehe da ein deutscher Schriftsteller.*"[7]

Within a few months of that despairing cry, Georg Forster's spirit and energies were restored, and he had launched himself on a new career, that of revolutionary politician. In October 1792, the French Revolution came to the Rhineland, and a French army under Custine occupied the town of Mainz. In the weeks that followed the Kurfürst's librarian became the leading spirit in the local Jacobin Club, an unofficial but trusted adviser to the French Commander, a popular and successful agitator in the rural districts outside the town, and eventually the dominant voice in the National Convention that met in Mainz at the beginning of 1793. It was he who drafted the decrees that declared the area between Speyer and Bingen a republic and abolished feudal privilege in this new creation; it was he who carried through the resolution favoring union with France as the only means of preserving the liberties proclaimed;[8] and, in March 1793, he was one of three commissioners sent to Paris to lay that request before the French National Assembly.

This proved to be the circumnavigator's last voyage, and it was one without return, for in mid-1793 the Allied Powers counterattacked and reoccupied Mainz. Cut off from his home, Forster remained in the French capital, performing occasional tasks for the republican government, until January 1794, when his health, always fragile, finally gave way and he died, as he wrote in his last letters, "without a home, a fatherland, or a friend."[9]

II

In December 1792 Schiller wrote to Georg Körner: "Forster's conduct will certainly be criticized by everyone, and I can see in advance that he will derive shame and regret out of this business."[10] This was an accurate prediction. The plunge into revolutionary politics was universally reprobated. As a result of it, Forster's marriage, which had always been a troubled one, broke down completely, although he continued to write to his wife, and to explain his motives, until his death. His closest friends from the days in Kassel—Jacobi, Nicolai, Sömmerring, and Lichtenberg—were hopelessly alienated by his radical course.[11] Wilhelm von Humboldt, a friend of the family for years, was shocked by what he considered to be Forster's ingratitude to his benefactors. "Despite my partiality for the French revolution," he wrote in December 1792, "I still can't forgive Forster for having, at this moment and so openly, gone over to the French party. . . . It strikes me as immoral and ignoble to the highest degree to be disloyal to the Kurfürst, to whom he owes many favors, at a time when he is in difficulties."[12] Forster's publisher, Voss, wrote to say, in effect, that the reaction in Berlin to his politics was so unfavorable that, as far as the book trade was concerned, he was a dead man;[13] and, a little later, this was underlined by the editors of the *Allgemeine Literatur-Zeitung*, an influential paper which had had a high opinion of Forster's literary talent but which now announced that he was "a sophistical and brooding mystagogue," a "wild enthusiast," and a writer who was "intolerable because of his bombast, his nauseating affectation, and his tasteless distortions of language."[14]

What was generally missing from any of these reactions was any understanding of why Forster had decided to take the road he took in 1792. In general, those people who knew him best seemed to assume that his decision was determined not by political but by personal factors—by impatience, disappointment, frustration, resentment. Goethe, for instance, appeared to regard Forster's action as that of an impetuous and immature man, and his 337th *Xenien*, written after Forster's death and clearly referring to him, was entitled "Unfortunate Haste" and read:

> Ach wie sie Freiheit schrieen und Gleichheit,
>   Geschwind wollt ich folgen
> Und weil die Trepp mir zu lang deuchte, so
>   Sprang ich vom Dach.[15]

> [Ah, when they shouted "Freedom!" and "Equality,"
>   I wanted to follow swiftly
> And because the stairs seemed too slow for me
>   I jumped from the roof.]

Thérèse Forster, on the other hand, upon whom the letters of her husband seem to have made no impression, let it be known that if Forster had only had a secure position in which he was respected, he would never have been interested in the revolution at all.[16]

Most of the historical writing that has dealt with Forster has taken the same line. Thus, in a variant of the Goethe explanation, Kurt Kersten has written that Forster never got over his voyage around the world, that he was continually yearning for new adventures, and that when the French Revolution opened before him he couldn't resist and hurled himself into its labyrinthine depths without reflection, thus destroying himself.[17] Reinhold Aris tends to agree with Forster's wife and holds that lack of stable circumstances and economic troubles were the principal goads to his action.[18]

Now there is, of course, something to be said for these psychological and economic explanations. It is doubtless true that Forster was frustrated by the nagging cares of his life and that, once he had made the plunge, felt an exhilarating sense of release. It is true also that his commitment brought to the surface once more the adventurous romantic side of his nature. If one reads the speeches that he made during the meetings of the Mainz Convention, it is impossible not to note the sharp contrast between their sentimental and undisciplined rhetoric and the taut intellectuality and unadorned simplicity of Forster's other writings.[19] He wrote these speeches, as Kersten rightly says, "as if the figure of Karl Moor was standing before him, as if Bürger's verse and the rebellious speeches of the men of the *Sturm und Drang* were ringing in his ears, as if Don Carlos were speaking with the Marquis von Posa."[20] There can be little doubt that he derived a high excitement from his brief career as a revolutionary agitator. This rings through every line of the letter of 27 February 1793 in which he describes how he drove the counts of Leiningen out of their estates at Grünstadt.

> I called upon them to join our cause with all their servants. They protested, formed cabals, stirred up the merchants and the peasants; one of my soldiers was attacked and wounded. I summoned more men and, when they arrived, took possession of both castles and placed their proprietors under armed guard. Today I have sent them as prisoners to Landau. Their women cross the Rhine tomorrow. So must everything that opposes the good cause be overthrown.[21]

The chance to exercise military command even on this small scale obviously delighted Forster, and he made the most of it.

It is nevertheless a mistake to place too much emphasis upon these aspects of Forster's behavior and to assume, as Reinhold Aris has done, that he was, "in truth, not politically minded."[22] The opposite is true. Far from being a frivolous or impetuous action, Forster's decision to work actively for the revolutionary cause was the result of long reflection over political matters and conscientious and pro-tracted self-examination.

Forster's views on politics at the time of his return to Germany in 1778 were typical of those of most German intellectuals of his time. He was a cosmopolitan and a rationalist and a believer in progress, which he saw exemplified in the liberties that had been won by the English middle class and were now being demanded by the American colonists. The guarantor of freedom was the force of reason, and Forster was inclined to believe that nothing could prevent it from triumphing over vice and stupidity. Like his fellows, he placed his faith in enlightened princes who would provide for the happiness of their subjects and grant them, sooner or later, the equivalent of the liberties that Englishmen already had. "Beneath the morning rays of enlightenment," he wrote in his essay *Cook the Discoverer*, "the obscurantism of men will pale. Toleration and freedom of conscience will announce the triumph of reason and open the way for freedom of the press and the unrestricted investigation of all the relationships that are, in the cause of truth, important to mankind."[23]

At the same time, Forster always had a more critical mind and a keener awareness of the real relationships in life than most of his German contemporaries, and he could not long remain content with this comfortable philosophy. He had neither the Olympian detachment of Goethe nor the *spießbürgerlich* selfishness of Gleim;[24] he noticed things. He was, for instance, aware of the fact that the Collegium Carolinum in Kassel was, like Lady Milford's jewels in *Kabale und Liebe*, paid for by the sale of Hessian troops to Britain. Johannes von Müller, who began his career as the historian of the Swiss confederacy and ended it as a slavish admirer of princes, could ignore this unpleasant fact and, at the Carolinum's inauguration, praise the elector of Hesse as "a benefactor of the citizens";[25] but Forster could never forget this or other hard realities. "There is no place on the round earth," he wrote, "that has so much poverty and *splendida miseria* in it as Kassel. . . . Virtue does not reign at our court."[26] When he went on to Vilna his cold eye again noted the contrast between the pretensions of princes and the results of their neglect of the needs of their subjects. Vilna, he said, was "a sad, empty, devastated place . . . where I have misery and barbarity and indifference constantly before my eyes."[27] He was revolted by the spectacle and struck by the thought that all this was perhaps not merely the result of inadvertence or even inefficiency; perhaps men were being treated like animals on principle. This suspicion was to grow and to find its fullest expression in one of his last writings, the essay "On the Relationship of Statecraft to Human Happiness."

Reprobation of despotism was a typical attitude in the eighteenth century, but it was usually coupled with the reassuring belief that the spread of the enlightenment was on the way to eliminating it. As a trained observer and a collector of data, Forster could see nothing to justify this faith. Not only did the dominion of despotism remain unchanged in size, but its influence was all-pervasive, affecting the arts, the sciences, and the world of the intellect in general. In an essay that impressed the young Hegel[28] and was published by Schiller, *Die Kunst und das Zeitalter* (*Art and the Epoch*), Forster compared ancient and modern art, to the disadvantage of the latter. Modern art had lost its inspiration because despotism had destroyed the condition of freedom that was indispensable to it, and its decline had been accompanied by a general degeneration of aesthetic and moral standards. As a result, Forster wrote, the salient features of the modern age were "bestial lasciviousness," "egotism," "scholastic fraud," and "idle metaphysical introspection," while "the road to experience and perception remained untrod and the darkness of prejudice drew its thick veil around the best minds." All of the noble passions that are associated with art on the one hand and virtue on the other shrivel under the cold breath of tyranny. This is true, Forster added, even of patriotism, which "cannot inspire a man who has no fatherland but only a master."[29]

Art and the Epoch appeared in the same year that the French Revolution burst upon the world, electrifying the German intelligentsia and inspiring Hegel, Hölderlin, and Schelling to plant a liberty tree in Tübingen and to dance around it singing revolutionary songs. In view of Goethe's poem about Forster's impetuosity, it is interesting to note that he showed little sign of sharing in the revolutionary rhapsodies of people like Klopstock and Wieland. His first reaction was warm but cautious. "What do you think about the revolution in France?" he wrote to his father-in-law on 30 July 1789, going on to predict that it would probably cause a change in the power relationship between England and France and expressing his admiration that "so great a change has cost so little in blood and destruction."[30] Two weeks later he wrote enthusiastically about the events of 5 August in Paris,[31] but he was still reserved in September, when Wilhelm von Humboldt arrived from the French capital with an eyewitness account of what had been going on there; and he agreed with Humboldt that what was happening was the beginning of a long and complicated process that would have to be studied with care.[32]

There was no suggestion in anything that Forster wrote in the three years that followed the fall of the Bastille that he wanted anything of the sort to happen in Germany. In the spring of 1790, with the dramatist Iffland and the young Alexander von Humboldt, he journeyed down the Rhine, through the Low Countries, and then to England and France, passing through Paris on the first anniversary of the beginning of the revolution. The remarkable book that resulted from this trip, *Views of the Lower Rhine*, is filled with glowing descriptions of the benefits of freedom, as seen in England and Holland and in Paris, but the eleventh chapter of the first volume, which is an extended discussion of the antinomies of politics, the contrast between liberty and despotism, and the relationship between law and power, has no very specific references to German politics aside from the general statement that "the crimes of a country's constitution can be removed without a powerful convulsion if one uses the proper means in time" and that "wise regents" will be able to perceive this.[33] It was in such princes, rather than in the people, that he put his trust. As late as the winter of 1792 he was still of the opinion that Germany was not ready for revolution. "Our poor, uneducated people are capable of rage," he wrote to Voss, "but not of constituting themselves." Improvement in Germany could only come from above, from enlightened rulers who profited from the French example. In this way, "the French volcano could save Germany from the earthquake."[34]

But the "wise regents", instead of doing as he hoped, opted for war against France. When the first suggestion that this might happen reached Mainz, Forster wrote in alarm to Heyne that this would mean that the revolution would become uncontrolled in France. "For the life of the royal family I wouldn't give a groschen. The passion of the Jacobins is capable of anything, and they are defiant in their power. If the crisis is driven to the highest point, they will surely attain the ascendancy. . . . Everything is going to end in violence . . . and who knows what limits of madness will be reached?"[35] Aside from that, he asked, will not a declaration of war against France signify that despotism has triumphed in Germany, and will that not force lovers of freedom to take their stand on the French side? Disgusted with the behavior of the *émigrés* in Mainz[36] and by their influence in German councils of state, Forster, by June 1792, was writing that he "was rather for than against the Jacobins, however much people may rage against them."[37]

He still kept these views to himself and a few correspondents, but he was too consistent a thinker to do so for long. He had always been impatient with thinking that remained in the realm of theory and had once written, in the Vilna days, that "we are here more for action than for speculation."[38] Now the opportunity for action had arrived, and he hesitated only momentarily before grasping it. The war came, as he had feared, and it came to Mainz, which was occupied by French forces on 20 October 1792. A week later Forster wrote to Voss that he had refrained from any engagement up to this point, but that "this neutrality is awkward; the crisis is here, and one must take a side." All the local notables, including the Kurfürst and the clergy, had fled the city, abandoning their fellow citizens. This showed the bankruptcy of the old order and indicated which way the choice would have to be made.[39] Two weeks later he wrote to say that he had been asked by a group of professors to go to General Custine and ask if he could authorize the payment of their back salaries out of sequestered funds, and that he had decided to help them. This mission had led to his involvement in arrangements to provide for the provisioning of the town; and it now looked as if he would be asked to serve in the provisional government. If so, he added, "I consider it my duty to refuse to turn down any assignment, whatever it may be, if it puts me in a position to help my fellow citizens."[40] Voss wrote in alarm that he must go slow and try to be a good Prussian. Forster answered that he was being so by doing what he could for the people of Mainz, adding, with a sudden burst of passion in an otherwise patient letter, "*Allein, um Himmelswillen*! If people would only realize what the mood of our time is, how the destiny of this moment has been prepared years ago, and how flatly impossible it is to prop up the rotten dams against which the waves of freedom are beating. This is one of the decisive epochs in the history of the world, this age in which we live! Since the coming of Christianity there has been nothing like it!"[41]

There were a few German intellectuals who were inclined to agree with this last point—Hegel, for instance, and Goethe, who said much the same at Valmy—but they were not going to do anything about it. Typical was the attitude of Johannes von Müller, the historian of Swiss liberty, who returned to his home in Mainz in November, talked with Forster and Custine, expressed the warmest sympathy for the cause of liberty and the republic, and then disappeared with all his books and furniture.[42] Wordy professions of this kind were commonplace now, but, faced with political reality and the necessity of choice, German intellectuals as a class were retreating *en masse* from the world of politics, back into the safe world of *Innerlichkeit* and aesthetic education. And because Georg Forster's consistency had demonstrated the hollowness of their principles, they cast him off in anger. "They cannot understand a man," Forster wrote to his wife in January 1793, "who can . . . also act, and they find me detestable because I have really gone to work to apply the principles that they applauded—as long as I only wrote about them."[43]

III

The unanimity of his colleagues' reaction could not help but trouble Forster and make him wonder on occasion whether his critics might not, after all, be right and whether he might not have made a mistake. During the first months of 1793, while he was working to establish the Rhenish Republic and was often on the go from four o'clock in the morning until midnight,[44] he was generally too exhilarated to suffer more than momentary doubts, but after March, when he went to Paris, his bouts of self-examination were frequent and anguished. The months that Forster spent in France were those in which the execution of the King brought England, Holland, and Spain into the war, when Dumouriez sold out to the enemy and anti-republican risings erupted in the Vendée and in Lyons, when the struggle between the Mountain and the Plain reached its climax and was resolved by the institutionalization of the Terror. It was a time of violence, passion, and ugly grasping after power, and it shook Forster to the depths of his being.

Paris, he wrote to his wife on 13 April 1793, was "a nauseating labyrinth" that made him wonder "whether I have devoted my utmost energy to something monstrous and worked with honest zeal for an ideal that no one honestly believed in and was nothing but a disguise for the most brutish passions. . . . It takes courage to withstand this thought and . . . to go on believing in humanity and truth."[45] Two weeks later he mentioned the difficulty he was having in finding employment now that his original mission was executed and complained: "Scientific knowledge and even capacity for business are of no use here. The people who rise to the top grab the rudder and hold on until someone else, momentarily stronger, forces them from the helm. If one cannot persecute, denounce, and guillotine others, one doesn't count for anything. For the first time in my life all my expedients fail me, and I stand like an abandoned child who doesn't have the power to feed himself."[46] In June he wrote: "Never in history has tyranny been more shameless and exuberant than here, never have all principles been so spurned, never has calumniation ruled with such unbridled power."[47] "The bloody tribunal is the shame of the Revolution; I don't want to think about it."[48] "If I had only known," he wrote in one low moment in August, "ten months ago, or eight months ago, what I know now, I would undoubtedly have gone to Hamburg or Altona and not into the Jacobin Club."[49]

But Forster did not abandon himself completely to these moods, nor did he collapse under the strain of the dreadful things he had to witness, like his fellow commissioner from Mainz, Adam Lux, who virtually committed suicide by writing and circulating a defense of Charlotte Corday, who had assassinated Jean Paul Marat.[50] As far as possible he busied himself with practical political work, making his services available to whatever group was in power and, in the last months of 1793, going on various official diplomatic missions along France's borders.[51] At the same time, he thought about what was happening around him, about passion, about power, about the revolutionary process.

The results of this reflection are to be found in his last letters, in two unfinished works (one of them a brief history of the revolution in Mainz and the other a series of "Parisian Sketches"), and a longer essay entitled "On the Relationship of Statecraft to Human Happiness." In these he argued that, while one must not forget or condone the crimes committed in the name of the revolution, one should not try to pass a final judgment on them. It was necessary to remember that the revolution was neither accidental nor the result of a conspiracy, but the outgrowth of a long chain of antecedent causes, and particularly of the abuses of despotism. The practitioners of power, the rulers of Europe, while claiming that their statecraft was dedicated to the promotion of their subjects' happiness, had always sought to hold their peoples under control by means of war, a corrupt church and a sycophantic educational system, the persecution of truth and reason, the toleration of misery and squalor, and the systematic brutalization of the human spirit.[52] That was the real cause and the justification of the Revolution. That it had come in France was perhaps accidental, and certainly less important than that it had come.

It had, to be sure, been accompanied by passion, violence, and crime. Revolutions, once started, were hard to control. "The Revolution is a hurricane; who can bridle it? Galvanized by its spirit, human beings find it possible to commit actions that posterity, out of sheer horror, will be unable to comprehend."[53] The "moving force" in the revolutionary process is "the raw power of the crowd,"[54] and—as Forster had written two years earlier in the eleventh chapter of *Views of the Lower Rhine*—"the excesses of the *Pöbel* are incalculable once they have been aroused and have taken as their motto the word 'Freedom', so easily interchangeable in their minds with the word 'License'."[55] The lover of liberty should, however, not flee from these scenes of violence, but do what he can to check ugly passions, working for his fellow men, appealing to their common humanity, and holding on to his faith that, in the end, free men will overcome their violence and greed and lust for power. "It would be madness," Forster wrote, "to give men freedom if one thought that they would remain savages." "The only reason that political liberty is worth having" is that it does eventually and inevitably help men become "*morally* free beings"; "for I believe that it is irrefutable that only in free states can virtue become universal."[56]

Meanwhile, men were doing horrible things in Paris. "But I stand by my belief that one should not regard the revolution merely from the standpoint of the happiness or unhappiness of individuals, but see it as one of the great instruments used by destiny to effect changes in the human race."[57] This was not merely a French revolution, but "the greatest, the most important, the most astounding revolution in the moral education and development of the whole human race."[58] It might almost be said that the French people were, "perhaps as a punishment, chosen to be martyrs for the good that the revolution will bring in the future—in much the same way as the Germans of Luther's time had to be martyrs for the common good when they accepted the Reformation and when they defended it with their blood."[59]

These reflections buoyed up Forster's sometimes faltering spirit and convinced him that he had taken the right course. In letters to his publisher Voss and to his wife's lover Huber, in which he commented on all that he had lost personally as a result of his entrance into active politics, he said, just about a month before his death; "The greatness of our time is a giant greatness . . . and for that very reason it demands extraordinary sacrifices."[60] "Despite the losses that fate has exacted from me, I am, with my whole heart, reconciled and gay. I know that one has to suffer for one's happiness, but to the man who has made any real moral progress in his life, the only true happiness is the awareness that he has *acted* on the basis of his convictions."[61]

IV

In October 1914, Kurt Hiller, Alfred Wolfenstein, and Rudolf Kayser met in Berlin and chose the word *Aktivismus* as the name for a new movement of intellectuals that they hoped to organize for purposes of antiwar agitation and promotion of a democratic revolution. Although they did not do so, they might appropriately have claimed Georg Forster as their patron saint. He was the first modern German activist, and the movement of 1914 was merely a belated attempt to challenge a philosophy that he had challenged a century before. The tradition of *Innerlichkeit* which regarded the external world and its works as being of no legitimate concern to intellectuals and which made aesthetic contemplation and the formulation of theory ends in themselves, he rudely rejected, with the argument that moral and spiritual progress was possible only in conditions of political liberty, and political liberty would never be achieved unless the intellectuals— the men of spirit and theory—led the fight to attain it.[62]

Having made that argument, he acted upon it. Forster, wrote the historian Gervinus in the middle of the nineteenth century, "was a man who made the hard transition from the idea to the deed, from the principle to its implementation, from knowledge to action; he represents a point of view that our people are yet hardly even beginning to grasp and understand"; "he acted on principles that, as is our way here in Germany, we prefer to leave in their intellectual state, rather than to carry them into action."[63] Gervinus was, of course, seeking to encourage the political instinct in his own generation by invoking Forster's example, but he did not succeed.[64] In the period of reaction that followed the failed revolution of 1848, German intellectuals were increasingly determined to have nothing to do with any form of politics except those undemanding ones that involved supporting the establishment, and few things contributed more to the tragic course of German history in the modern era.

3

Friedrich Schiller and the Police

It is sometimes assumed that the political instinct was not very highly developed in Friedrich Schiller. Unlike many German intellectuals and writers of the generation that reached maturity in the 1780s—one thinks of the brothers Schlegel, of Georg Forster, of Wilhelm von Humboldt, and even of Heinrich von Kleist, all of whom left the world of scholarship and the arts at least for a time to play an active role in public life during the revolutionary and Napoleonic period—Schiller remained aloof. He spent the first years after the fall of the Bastille as a professor of history and philosophy at the University of Jena; during the bloody events of the Terror in Paris, he was drafting his *Letters on the Aesthetic Education of Mankind* (1795); and in the years between the Treaty of Basel in 1795 and the dissolution of the Holy Roman Empire, years in which French power systematically destroyed the political liberties of his country, he was devoting his energies exclusively to literary production.

This apparent passivity in times of tumultuous change makes it understandable that Schiller should have been criticized in his own day for retreating from contemporary realities into the security of a remote past, and it explains why he has so often been labeled as an idealist and a romantic, with all the connotations of unfocused intellectuality that go with these terms. It makes understandable, moreover, why bourgeois critics of the nineteenth century found it easy to transform Schiller into an icon for self-improvement, as Friedrich Theodor Vischer did in a notable address in which he praised the poet for teaching human beings that they should be educated to "inner

37

harmony with themselves" before they grappled with the problems of
the real world, that "in the beautiful and in art one should seek the
road to goodness and justice," and that "it was only worth the effort to
be free when freedom bore the fruit of purely harmonious *Bildung*."[1]

In fact, nothing could be more inaccurate than these charges. Schiller was an intensely political man. If he left the emotional satisfactions
of activism to others, he was no less engaged than they. No member of
his generation reflected more deeply on the political tendencies of his
age or had such chillingly accurate intimations of their future consequences. It is this that accounts for the continued relevance of his
insights into the political process and excuses Benno von Wiese's over-
generous description of Schiller as "the only example of a great
political writer among the Germans."[2] In 1943 when Hans and Sophie
Scholl wished to convince their fellow students in Munich of the moral
necessity of resistance to Hitler, it was to Schiller that they turned,
distributing copies of a lecture on the nature and consequences of
totalitarianism that he had given in August, 1789.[3] Similarly, in our
own day, much that is written about the way in which bigness of
government leads to the erosion of freedom and the reification of the
individual, as well as a lot of what is said about the problem of
alienation, was anticipated in Schiller's *Aesthetic Education*,[4] a work
too little read by political scientists, perhaps because of its title.

It was in his plays—and particularly in the historical dramas of his
last period—that Schiller's political thought became most explicit. As
his life wore on, the poet came to the conclusion, as he once wrote to his
friend Goethe, that he had a special talent "for giving life and warmth to
historically defined subject matter and, at the same time, for making it
open out."[5] This form of drama, moreover, by the requirements of
authenticity that it imposed upon him, helped to restrain the fantasy and
wilfulness that had marred his early plays, and this enabled him to
write about the great issues of politics objectively and with an eye to
their universal significance. There was no doubt in Schiller's mind that
he had a responsibility to deal with such themes. The theater, he had
written as a young man, was a moral institution, "the common channel
through which the glow of wisdom flows·from the intelligent, superior
part of society and spreads itself in gentle streams through the whole
state."[6] The dramatist should be a preceptor of his people, and this was
what Schiller set out to become. The great dramas of his last period—
from *Wallenstein* to *Wilhelm Tell*—entertained and excited audiences,

University of Winnipeg, 515 Portage Ave., Winnipeg, MB. R3B 2E9 Canada

as they were meant to do, but they were also pedagogically inspired. Through them Schiller hoped to educate a future generation of free men; and he sought to do this, for the most part, by teaching them about power, its legitimate and illegitimate forms, its uses and limitations, its ability to corrupt, the evil consequences of lusting after it on the one hand and refusing to take responsibility for using it on the other, the moral ambiguities in which it involved those who tried to use it conscientiously, and the relationship between all of this and individual and collective freedom.[7] For the age in which Schiller lived this was an appropriate, indeed almost inescapable, theme, as the poet pointed out in the prologue to his finest drama.[8]

> Und jetzt an des Jahrhunderts ernstem Ende,
> Wo selbst die Wirklichkeit zur Dichtung wird,
> Wo wir den Kampf gewaltiger Naturen
> Um ein bedeutend Ziel vor Augen sehn,
> Und um der Menschen große Gegenstände,
> Um Herrschaft und um Freiheit wird gerungen,
> Jetzt darf die Kunst auf ihrer Schattenbühne
> Auch höhern Flug versuchen, ja, sie muß,
> Soll nicht des Lebens Bühne sie beschämen.

> [And now at the century's solemn end,
> When reality itself becomes literature,
> When the struggle of powerful natures for
> A worthy goal plays out before our eyes,
> And the fight for mankind's mighty objects,
> For power and for liberty, is waged,
> Now must art too upon its stage of shadows
> Seek a sublimer flight, indeed, it must,
> Lest it be put to shame by the theater of life.]

When considered in the light of this didactic purpose, all of the plays that Schiller wrote in his last period assume new interest. So do those he did not finish and even those that he did not even start. It is one of the last that concerns us here.

I

Among the dramatic fragments left after Schiller's death was a rough sketch and some scattered notes for a tragedy to be called *Die Polizei*

(*The Police*).[9] These have not aroused much curiosity among Schiller scholars, and those among them who have shown any interest have generally focused their attention on the way in which the original concept was transformed into a more detailed outline for a radically different play, which was to be called *The Children of the House* and was apparently meant to be a kind of modern nemesis play, using the technique of Sophocles' *Oedipus Rex*.[10] Virtually nothing is ever said about the original idea except that Schiller abandoned it[11]; and this is a pity, for the notes bearing on it are highly suggestive politically.

Schiller seems to have become interested in writing a drama about the police immediately after the conclusion of his *Wallenstein* trilogy in 1799,[12] and the play he planned bore some resemblance to the one just completed. Both dealt with forms of institutional power: *Wallenstein* with the army, the guardian of the state security against external threats; *Die Polizei*, with its domestic counterpart. In each case, the protagonist was a real historical figure: in the former, the Austrian Emperor's commander-in-chief during the Thirty Years War, Wallenstein, the Duke of Friedland; in *Die Polizei*, the French King Louis XIV's lieutenant-general of police, Marc-René de Voyer de Paulmy, Marquis d'Argenson.

In the eighteenth century, d'Argenson's name and fame spread far beyond the boundaries of France, partly because of the eulogy delivered after his death by Fontenelle, more perhaps because of the awe inspired by his reputation for sinister omniscience, pitiless efficiency, and systematic ruthlessness. He directed the police of Paris from 1697 until 1720 — a time of foreign war, domestic privation, intermittent famine, crime and civil unrest — and during it was given full authority to maintain public order and promote the general welfare in the King's capital city. He discharged his responsibility by means of a calculated policy of terror, carried out with the aid of thousands of secret agents who infiltrated every section of society. Saint-Simon, in a passage in his memoirs that was written in 1718, describes the chief of police as a man

> with a frightening countenance that recalled the faces of the judges of hell . . . [who] imposed such a state of order upon the innumerable multitude of Paris that there was not an inhabitant whose day-to-day behavior and habits he did not know, exercising an exquisite discernment in the force or delicacy of his intervention in every

case that arose, always bringing his pressure to bear upon the weakest parts in a way that made even the most innocent tremble before him: courageous, tough, audacious in time of *émeutes* and, because of all that, the people's master.[13]

A modern French historian is blunter. D'Argenson's predecessor La Reynie, the man who had created the police force, had, he writes, exercised his functions with a light hand; but "d'Argenson, goaded on incessantly by a nervous Louis XIV . . . , proceeded to make Paris groan under the weight of the suspicion, the fear, and the informing that are the sad appanage of police states."[14]

It was this Minos-like dispenser of justice to the people of Paris and the force of gendarmes, agents, spies, and informers that served him that were to be the subjects of Schiller's play, and the notes he left on them stress the darker aspects of their work rather than the redeeming features mentioned by Fontenelle. They speak—and I quote them now—of Paris as "a prison . . . in the power of the monarch [who] holds a million people there under lock and key." The King's appointed watchdog is d'Argenson, a man whose experience in office has made him "skeptical of good and tolerant of evil," who "has seen too much of men from their shameful side to be able to entertain a noble view of human nature," who can say sardonically to a poor devil who is pleading that "a man has got to live," "I don't see why"—this, apparently, an authentic remark by d'Argenson which Schiller found in Mercier's *Tableau de Paris*—a man, in sum, to whom human beings appear as "a species of wild animals who are to be treated accordingly." As for his instruments, the police, they are "the parts of an enormous machine in motion" and "their realm of activity [*Spielraum*] is the night."

> They work as power and are armed in order to carry out their decisions. They must often go secret ways and cannot always observe forms. They must often tolerate evil, yes, encourage and at times practice it, in order to do the good or avoid the greater ill. . . . The innocent can suffer at their hands, and they are often forced to use evil tools and evil means.

It is by doing so that they convince others that "not even the ring of Gyges could escape discovery by their all-piercing eyes," and it is this that invests them with their fearfulness. They are hated by the populace, but more feared than hated. In a demoralized and fragmented society, they are the power and the reality. "The only unity," Schiller wrote, with reference to the dramatic action he planned, but surely also to the social situation in which it was to take place, "the only unity is the police, which supplies the impulse and at last prompts the action."[15]

II

We need not concern ourselves with the plot of this projected tragedy, for Schiller never worked it out in any detail.[16] But we can ask why he should have considered doing a play with this somber setting at all. The answer is, in the first place, that the police was not an inappropriate subject for reflection by European intellectuals at the end of the eighteenth century, for this was a time of heightened police activity. In January, 1796, the French Directory created a new police force which was to win European notoriety, the Ministry of General Police; and in 1799, just as Schiller was beginning to play with his theme, Joseph Fouché became minister of that new force—the man of whom Balzac later wrote that his extraordinary genius at his job "struck Napoleon with a kind of terror,"[17] who imitated and improved on d'Argenson's methods, and whose famous 2d Division (the secret police) extended its power outward from France into Germany, maintaining an agency at Altona that in time coordinated French secret police operations in more remote centers like Stockholm and Berlin.[18] At roughly the same time, the Austrian Emperor Francis established a new centralized police administration and placed at its head Josef Anton Graf Pergen, whose zeal for his job and imitation of French methods, particularly in the development of the security police, led an Austrian observer, at the end of the 1790s, to write that his country had assumed a *Polizeicharakter* "of a kind never before seen in a great state."[19] This, incidentally, was the force that astonished foreign delegations to the Congress of Vienna (1814–1815) with the insistence of its surveillance[20]; and in the subsequent period it was instrumental in imposing thought control over large parts of Germany.

It seems unlikely that these developments—and similar ones in Prussia and in some of the lesser German states—were unknown to Schiller and without influence upon his literary plans. He could not but have been sensitive to them, because he was always aware of the way in which organized political power, so necessary to the well-being of society, tended in subtle ways and with plausible justification, to narrow the area of freedom. In his lectures at Jena on the legal codes of Lycurgus and Solon, he had argued, in language that was to be echoed by his friend Wilhelm von Humboldt in a famous essay on the limits of governmental power,[21] that "the State is never an end in itself; it is only important as a condition in which the purpose of humanity can be fulfilled, and that purpose is the development of all of the capacities of man."[22] But he was all too conscious of the fact that the whole tendency of eighteenth-century politics had in fact been to make the State an end in itself. "The new spirit of government," he had written in the sixth of the *Aesthetic Letters*, has tended to destroy the condition "in which every individual enjoyed an independent existence" in favor of "an ingenious clockwork in which, out of the piecing together of innumerable but lifeless parts, a mechanical kind of collective life" will ensue. Increasingly, the relationship of men to their society is ceasing to depend "upon forms which they spontaneously prescribe for themselves; . . . it is dictated to them with meticulous exactitude by means of a formulary which inhibits all freedom of thought."[23] And this development, Schiller felt, with that pessimism which had always clouded his political thought and which deepened in his last years,[24] was facilitated by two others that had been apparent since 1789: the increasing strength and efficiency of the instruments of state power, and the fact that men, by their fear of, or their abuse of, freedom, invited its destruction by those very instruments.

If his intention was to warn his contemporaries of the consequences of failing to appreciate this perilous situation by means of a dramatic representation of d'Argenson's police state, Schiller did not fulfill it. There is some evidence that he continued to revert to the idea of a play about the police until his death in 1805,[25] but he gave priority to other projects—notably to *Wilhelm Tell* and to the last play that he worked on, the powerful fragment *Demetrius*. It is possible, even so, to argue that the themes and contents of these last dramas give some indication of what might in the end have been the didactic thrust of *Die Polizei*. *Wilhelm Tell* is a romantic idyll in which the defenders of freedom triumph over the representatives of totalitarian state power—but we should not forget, as Schiller's contemporaries would certainly not have forgotten, that the freedom celebrated in the drama had in fact already been destroyed before the play was written. As for *Demetrius*, it is a shattering picture of a world in which liberty has disappeared completely and politics has been reduced to an endless succession of tyrants, successively hailed by an atomized society that derives emotional satisfaction from submission. In his last years Schiller seemed to agree with Wallenstein's belief that *"dem bösen Geist gehört die Erde, nicht dem guten."*[26] With what has been called his devastatingly disturbing insight into the dynamics of power and freedom,[27] he sensed that, given the tendencies of his age, the expanding potentialities of the modern state, and the ambiguity of the ordinary man's attitude toward force and liberty, the future might well belong to the Pergens, the Fouchés, and the d'Argensons.

4

Johannes von Müller:
The Historian in Search of a Hero

It has often been remarked of our discipline that it is grounded in terminological confusion, the word "history" referring both to the process with which it is concerned and the product of that concern. No similar ambiguity exists with respect to the term "historian." It is generally understood that a historian does not make history (in the way a general or a politician does) but writes about it after it has been made. At least, this is generally understood by the lay public. It is the historian who occasionally grows restive with the distinction. Why, he has been known to ask, should he be relegated to the sidelines when great events are taking place? Does not his profession both qualify and oblige him to play a role in national policy, since his knowledge of the past gives him an incomparably wider view than the ordinary politician and, when great decisions are to be made, enables him to supply a necessary sense of perspective? Is not, in fact, the proper place of the historian at the side of the prince, performing whatever services are assigned to him and retiring in the evening of his days to record what he has observed?

Since the growth of history as a professional discipline, there have been many historians who have felt this way and who have acted in accordance with their feelings. All too often, however, they have discovered that the princes they have sought to serve are neither impressed by their qualifications nor interested in their motives, and that, when they have been employed, it has not been in the interest of sound policy or historical truth but—as Herbert Lüthy once wrote, "in order to publish [the princes'] own glory, to justify their claims, to strengthen the loyalty of their subjects."[1] Sometimes this has been managed so delicately that the historian has never quite realized what is happening to him; but in most cases he has, sooner or later, awakened to the realities of his situation, and the experience has been chastening.

The career of the man discussed here is an excellent illustration of this.

Johannes von Müller has, of course, other claims upon the attention of an audience of historians. A member of the remarkable group of German intellectuals who reached the height of their powers during the period of the great French Revolution, he was the friend and correspondent of Herder and Goethe, of Georg Forster and Alexander von Humboldt, of Madame de Staël and Friedrich von Gentz, of Stein and Hardenberg; and his collected letters, which reflect most of the political and cultural currents of his day, comprise a treasure trove that deserves more attention from students of the period than it has received.[2] In his chosen vocation, he was the first German historian who had the feeling that he was writing for the ages, like Thucydides and Tacitus,[3] with whom, indeed, he was compared;[4] and in one sense at least he succeeded in doing precisely that, for it was he, more than any other person, who created the myth of the Swiss people, so that even today, when we think of Switzerland, we think unwittingly in his terms and his images. Nor was this the only way in which he transcended the limits of his own time. Writing in an age which, until Napoleon disabused it, clung to cosmopolitan values and utopian schemes of world harmony, he had an instinctive sense of the demonic qualities of power, and implicit in all his work was an insistence upon the importance of learning to face and control it. Finally, at a time when Europe was still the lever that moved the world, he anticipated the cultural pessimism that has had so profound an influence in German thought, and it is not too much to say that his life and writings were strongly affected by a sense of the passing of the European age and the coming transference of mastery to the emergent empires that lay beyond the Carpathians and the Atlantic.

For all of these reasons Müller is an interesting figure in the intellectual history of his time. It is, however, only of his political ambitions that I will speak here and of their disappointment.

I

Johann Müller (the patent of nobility came later)[5] was born on 3 January 1752 in Schaffhausen, Switzerland, where his father was pastor and teacher in the Latin School. He attended the local Gymnasium and, when he was eighteen, travelled to Göttingen with the intention of studying theology. Here, however, he fell under the influence of August Ludwig Schlözer,[6] who inflamed his already well-developed interest in history and persuaded him to attempt an account of the wars of one of the ancient Germanic tribes. The resultant study, written in Latin under the title *Bellum Cimbricum*,[7] showed mastery of the sources and skill in their use and won the approbation, not only of Schlözer, but, later, of so stern a judge as Niebuhr.[8] It also confirmed Müller in his choice of a career. Returning to Switzerland, he plunged into archival research, supporting himself meanwhile, through the good offices of a well-connected friend,[9] by a series of undemanding jobs as tutor and companion. In 1778 he aroused public attention with a series of spirited lectures on universal history, and in 1780 he published the first volume of the work which, when complete, was to be called *The History of the Swiss Confederacy*.[10]

This work brought Müller a degree of fame not usually accorded to scholars in his time, and it was deserved. No previous history of Switzerland was based so solidly upon historical records; and, whatever later historians might say about the frailties of Müller's critical method,[11] Friedrich Gundolf was correct in writing in 1923 that, thanks to his archival researches, Müller had succeeded in presenting "the first substantial and detailed account of the medieval period, of which until his time only vague unstructured notions, mostly about knights in armor, were current."[12] Moreover, it was the first historical work in German that had any literary distinction. It was constructed like a novel or epic and, in a series of dramatic scenes and brilliant characterizations and in a purposefully archaic style designed to enhance its verisimilitude, told the story of a freedom-loving people battling to preserve its birthright against external aggression.[13] Here half-forgotten figures—like Rudolf of Habsburg and Ludwig von Erlach—took on flesh and blood; here the oath on the Rütli was sworn again and the heroic form of Wilhelm Tell entered the popular consciousness (without Müller's history, Schiller's play would have been unthinkable);[14] here the clashes of arms at Morgarten and Sempach were turned into political symbols for a divided people that knew little of its past and was fearful of its future. This was a new kind of history, written with a verve that left few readers unmoved and may very well have inspired Goethe's famous statement that "the greatest gift that history has to give us is the enthusiasm it can arouse."[15] The success of Müller's first volume was unexampled, not only in his own country, but in France[16] and in the German states, where the author was hailed as "the Klopstock of German history."[17] Overnight he was raised to the first rank of European historians and could count on a secure and respected future in a university chair.

But this was not the career that Müller envisaged for himself. He was not interested in teaching, and even the private lessons he had given in Switzerland had bored him: "My lectures are killing me!" he wrote to his friend Bonstetten in 1779. "It is intolerable to have to cater four times a week to the tastes of a dozen youngsters!"[18] It was not an academic career but the world of politics that attracted him. In 1772, when he finished his book about the Cimbri, he had sent a copy to Emperor Joseph II with a plea—never answered—that he might be taken into his service. "To read, to witness, to admire great deeds and to do none myself," he wrote, "to write the annals of humanity and to deserve no place in them—Sire! for me that is impossible!"[19] These feelings were unaffected by the success of his Swiss history. He hoped, indeed, to use that success to fulfill them, not in Vienna this time, but in Potsdam.

II

In February 1781, thanks to a letter of recommendation written by the French philosopher d'Alembert, Müller was given an audience with King Frederick II of Prussia. It was a tremendously exciting experience for the young scholar, one that remained a source of inspiration to him and a dominant influence on his thinking for the next twenty five years—for almost all (but, as we shall see, not quite all) the rest of his life. He stumbled from the royal presence in a state of near ecstasy. "Oh, Frederick! Frederick!" he wrote in a letter to his closest friend. "I shall never forget you as I saw you in this divine moment! If I should live a hundred years and never see you again, I would always remember that I had seen Caesar and Alexander! *Je suis amoureux du roi!*"[20] He had no doubts now about what his career should be. He wanted to serve the King, as his historian and perhaps as one of his advisers.

Between those who admire power and those who wield it understanding is adventitious. Frederick had no need of a historical adviser, and he had, in any case, made little of this garrulous young man with his bad Swiss French. "Your Mr. Mayer has been here," he wrote to d'Alembert, "and I confess that I found him tedious. He has done research on the Cimbri and the Teutons, for which I give him no credit, and has also written an analysis of universal history in which he has studiously repeated what others have written or said better than he. If he only wants to copy things, one will increase the number of books *ad infinitum* and the public will gain nothing from it. . . . But our Germans suffer from the disease called *logon diarrhorea*. . . ."[21]

Müller, therefore, received no call from Berlin, but he did not return to Switzerland. Instead, he accepted an appointment at the Collegium Carolinum in the capital of Prussia's ally Hesse-Kassel where he gave lectures on diplomatic history to the young military officers who formed its student body, where he was employed on occasion as an adviser on foreign affairs, and where he was, he hoped, conveniently positioned in case the King changed his mind.[22] The job in Kassel was the first of a series of such positions that Müller was to occupy from now until his death, posts of marginal political importance, but always with duties onerous enough to interfere seriously with his historical researches, so that, in the end, none of his major works was completed. Frequently, Müller complained about this himself, and threatened to put the world of politics behind him.[23] He never succeeded in doing so.

It would be less than just to him to believe that this was only because of his personal ambition and his belief that one day he would be given the kind of political position he deserved. He was, in truth, a vain man, but there was more to it than that. To a large extent, his attitude was determined by a fundamentally pessimistic view of the times in which he lived and by his conception of the duties of the historian in such times. He had long felt—and had already said so to his old teacher Schlözer in 1774—that "Europe [was] sinking back into the night of tyranny" and that his age was "gravid with great changes."[24] Now, in 1782, in two remarkable letters to his friend Bonstetten and to the critic Jacobi, he elaborated on this theme. With obvious reference to Montesquieu and Machiavelli, whom he also claimed as his teachers,[25] he argued that the diversity of cultures and contitutional systems that was the basis of European civilization could only be maintained if governments showed restraint in their ambitions and peoples remained valorous in the defense of their freedoms. But the plain evidence was that popular virtue was being sapped by luxury and political energy by internecine strife — witness the growing divisiveness in Switzerland — while on the other hand military despotism and hegemonial ambition were everywhere rampant. The partition of Poland in 1772 was a warning that the liberties of Europe were threatened[26] the death of Frederick of Prussia, when it came, would doubtless bring other ominous changes in its wake. In all the world, the only happy sign was the revolution in America,[27] but this new birth of freedom could not save Europe from imminent death if she would not save herself. The times, then, were dark; but "what a time for a historian, when all the passions are on the move . . . and the dénouement of everything that has been preparing itself for three hundred years is at hand! What a time . . . and what obligations it imposes on us!"[28] For who could more effectively define the peril than the historian, or more persuasively show that, if Europe was to be prevented from falling under the sway of a single power, it must find new spirit and new leadership — another Gustavus, perhaps, or a William III? And if Europe's death was unavoidable, then surely it was the duty of the historian "to make clear the origins and the evolution, the interrelationship and the effects, of the great aberrations through which we have become what we are, and to do so truthfully and freely . . . as a warning to coming generations in the new world!"[29]

In either case, this meant that the historian must stay close to events, and this is what Müller did. If the world was on the move, he wrote to his brother, "do you think I could stay quiet in Geneva, giving lectures?"[30] And so, after four years in Kassel, he moved in 1786 to Mainz, entering the employment of the Archbishop-Elector, first as court councillor and librarian,[31] and later as one of his most influential advisors on foreign policy.[32] When the expansionist phase of the French Revolution brought a French army to Mainz in 1792,[33] he fled with the Elector to Vienna and soon transferred to the Austrian service, where he remained for ten years, working as curator in the Imperial Archives, as political pamphleteer and, on occasion, as confidential diplomatic agent for the government.[34] Insofar as he could, he continued to work on his history of Switzerland, bringing out a revised first and a second volume in 1786 and a third in 1796, but generally this was subordinate to his political activities.

As the years passed, his pessimism with respect to Europe's future deepened. In Mainz, under the inspiration of that *Fürstenbund* which Frederick II had formed as a barrier to Joseph II's Bavarian ambitions, he wrote his most extensive political essay—an eloquent plea for the elaboration of that association and for a political balance of power based on cooperation between Austria and Prussia which would secure the peace of Europe and establish the conditions necessary for its moral regeneration[35]—but within a year of its publication he was forced to admit that the spirit of the *Fürstenbund* had died with its author and that all his hopes were illusory.[36] In 1789 he greeted the fall of the Bastille in Paris as "the most beautiful day since the downfall of the Roman empire"[37] and expressed the hope that the events in France might have an electrifying effect in the German states, arousing new vital forces there; but before long he was expressing disgust over the "*Freiheitsschwindel und sophistische Gottlosigkeit*" in Paris,[38] abhorrence at the "fools and monsters"[39] there, to whom "the spectacle of the guillotine has become a necessity,"[40] and bitter disappointment over the failure of an effective political or military response on the part of the central European powers to French expansionism.[41] Thinking of this inadequate response to the external threat, he came increasingly to believe that Europe was suffering from failure of leadership. "The world is going to pieces more and more," he wrote to his brother. "The 149th Psalm is right. 'Put not your faith in princes!' "[42] If only Frederick were alive, this process of barbarism and decay would be impossible. "By the power of his scorn, by the flame of his great eyes, by the force of his command, the inciters [of these troubles] would be cast asunder and would stand naked and bare in their mediocrity and childishness, like our first parents after the eating of the apple. God be thanked for the twelfth of February 1781! Then I saw a king!"[43]

But where was the new Frederick to be found? Not in Vienna, where, since the death of Müller's first patron Kaunitz, qualities of leadership were regarded with suspicion at court. Must one wait patiently, until the right man came, one who would know how to assess the sorry state of Europe and would have the necessary internal fire to inflame the masses to save it?[44] Or should one admit that "the role of Europe is finished, and that the noblest among us must be saved across the ocean or in Asia?"[45] It was this mood of discouragement and doubt that oppressed Müller when he received yet another offer of employment and made his way back to the capital of his hero Frederick.

III

At the end of 1803, the Austrian minister Cobenzl wished to establish a secret means of communication with the Russian Foreign Office which would bypass the Russian ambassador in Vienna, the tendency of whose policy he distrusted. Cobenzl asked Müller to travel to Dresden and see if he could arrange this with a correspondent of his who was Russian councillor of legation there. Müller was glad of the opportunity to get out of Vienna for a while—he was tired of the political infighting, he was having trouble with the censor,[46] and he had just been involved in a rather messy court case that had thrown embarrassing light upon aspects of his private life—so he accepted the mission and executed it successfully. From Dresden he went on to Weimar, was entertained by Goethe and had private conversations with the Grand Duke, and then continued to Berlin. He was received graciously by the King and a few days later was invited to enter the Prussian service as *Geheimer Kriegsrath*, historian of the House of Brandenburg, and member of the Berlin Academy.[47] He accepted immediately.

After the cloying air of Vienna, he wrote to Friedrich von Gentz, the "free spirit" of Berlin was exhilarating;[48] and, indeed, once he had settled in, he had a spurt of literary activity in which he finished the fourth volume of his Swiss history and wrote a number of historical papers that were read before the Academy.[49] But the real excitement in Berlin was political, and Müller was soon caught up in it. He lived in a garden house on the Schiffbauerdamm, writing by day and, in the evenings, dining with Hardenberg and Struensee, with the brothers Alexander and Wilhelm von Humboldt, and on occasion with his young admirer Alexander von der Marwitz.[50] In the latter months of 1804, he became a regular member of the circle surrounding Prince Louis Ferdinand, whom he greatly admired as the embodiment of the

Frederician spirit and whom he may indeed have regarded, with his penchant for heroes, as a *Fredericus redivivus*.[51] The prince was a person of consequence in Berlin in 1804. Earlier than others, he sensed the threat posed by Napoleon's assumption of full power in France. He felt that the policy of drift being followed by King Frederick William III was suicidal, and he attracted to himself all those who felt the same way. Stein was one of his frequent visitors, and the new Austrian ambassador Metternich also belonged to his coterie, which developed into a pressure group working for an Austro-Prussian alliance that might discourage new French aggression in Central Europe. Müller was cordially received by these activists, who remembered or had heard of his *Fürstenbund* essay of 1787; and he, in turn, lent his pen to their cause. In a series of articles he attacked the "persistent antagonism of the two great German states" with a vehemence that delighted Gentz in Vienna,[52] and it was probably he who drafted the memorandum that Louis Ferdinand sent to the King at the end of the year, urging speedy accommodation with Austria.[53]

None of this had any effect upon the King, who was resolved to do nothing that might involve his country in war. Prussia remained aloof from the diplomatic maneuvers of the spring and summer of 1805 and from the short and shattering war that followed, leaving Napoleon the virtual master of the continent. The news of Austerlitz plunged Müller momentarily into the depths of depression—"Now Europe is done for: the most beautiful lands in the civilized world . . . the center of all scholarship, the hopes of all humanity—all done for!"[54]—but only momentarily. It is indicative of his euphoric mood in these days in Berlin that he concluded that the containment of Napoleon, which he had formerly believed possible only by means of an Austro-Prussian alliance, could now be effected by Prussia alone, and that once the Prussian army took the field, the spirit of Frederick would triumph.[55] In 1806 he was heart and soul with the patriotic party, as bellicose as Stein and Prince Louis Ferdinand, and busily turning out new memoranda for the King's eye, urging mobilization measures and recommending that cabinet councillors known for their attempts to appease Napoleon be dismissed from the royal service.[56] For the first time since his diplomatic activity in Mainz, he had the feeling of participating in a meaningful way in the historical process. It was all very exciting and even, at times, gay; but it ended in a series of gray mornings in October, when the war he wanted really came and when he learned that his hero Louis Ferdinand was dead at Saalfeld and that Frederick's army had been utterly destroyed at Jena and Auerstädt.

One might have thought that no one had burned his bridges more completely than Johannes von Müller. He was known to be a close associate of Napoleon's most inveterate foes and, in dozens of letters to his friends, he had made clear his reprobation of the Corsican, his conviction that a Bonapartist triumph would spell the end of European civilization, and his personal determination to take exile in Kazan or Irkutzk rather than "bend a knee before this contemptible anti-Christ, this creation of cowardice and failure of vision."[57] And yet, of course, Müller was a historian, and historians must take long views. Within a week of Jena, he was writing with cheerful resignation: "I find in history that when the time has come for a great change, there is no point in being against it: the true wisdom is to recognize the signs of the time."[58] And, a fortnight later, to his brother:

> I recognize now that God has given him [Napoleon] the empire, indeed, the world. Nothing makes this more apparent than this war, which, conducted with inconceivable lack of foresight, has thrust a victory upon him that can only be compared with those ancient ones at Arbela and Zama. As long as the old, the untenable, the worn-out had sooner or later to disappear, it is the greatest good fortune that the victory was given to him and to a nation which, more than others, has civilized values and respect for learning. . . . And just as Cicero, Livy, and Horace made no attempt to hide from the victorious Caesar and Augustus their former opposition, I have not concealed the fact that, although formerly of another party, or rather of a different point of view, I have willingly abandoned it, now that God has decided, and am prepared, if I cannot cooperate in the great world revolution, at least to describe it, wholly objectively. It is an inexpressibly exalting labor of the spirit to lift one's gaze from the ruins of defeated Europe to the vast interrelationship of universal history, to search for the causes of things, and with temerity to lift the veil a little that covers the probable future.[59]

This was a reorientation with a vengeance, and it was not to stop here. On 15 November 1806 Müller wrote to his friend Karl Theodor von Dalberg, former *Koadjutor* of Mainz. He repeated the argument and much of the text of his letter to his brother, spoke of Napoleon as "a Hero whose equal is not to be found in the memory of the centuries" and — knowing Dalberg's influence with Bonaparte — suggested that he deserved "un historien du genre antique; vous savez que j'appartiens à ces anciens siècles."[60] Dalberg was not unmindful of the historian's past services in Mainz. Five days later, after Napoleon had entered Berlin, Müller was given an audience with the conqueror.

We have only Müller's record of this meeting,[61] and there is no reason to believe that it is any more accurate than his account of his audience with Frederick. It is clear enough, however, even from his description, that Napoleon who, like other men of power, realized that intellectuals have their uses (since they, after all, create the Camelots of this world), deliberately set out to bedazzle Germany's greatest historian. He praised his works; he demonstrated his own interest in history by ranging freely over the centuries; and he did not neglect to underline his concern for Europe's liberties and his desire to protect them by imposing a universal federation upon the troubled continent. The Emperor succeeded in his purpose. Once again Müller was reduced to a state of rapture. "Since my audience with Frederick, I have never had a richer conversation . . . and I must, to be fair, admit the Emperor's superiority in depth and comprehensiveness of knowledge; Frederick was somewhat Voltairian. . . . It was one of the most remarkable days of my life. By his genius and his unconstrained kindness, he has conquered me."[62] He was, indeed, ready to give public testimony to the conquest, and on 29 January 1807 in the Berlin Academy he did precisely that, by giving an address in French, "De la gloire de Frédéric," in which he contrasted the great king's glory with the abased state of his successors and then — turning to the French officers sitting in the front rows — cried: "Frédéric, tu verras la victoire et la grandeur et la puissance suivre toujours celui qui te ressemble le plus!"[63]

IV

To most of Müller's friends this was the ultimate betrayal. There were not many like Goethe, in whom political passion was not highly developed and who admired the Academy address as an exercise in rhetoric and proceeded calmly to translate it into German.[64] The common reaction was that of Gentz, who broke off relations with him in a letter in which he said that Müller's life was "a continual capitulation."[65] The historian had obviously made his position in Berlin untenable, and he cast about for new employment and was forced, most reluctantly and only because he needed the money, to accept a chair at the University of Tübingen. "The whole world is changing," he wrote fretfully to his friend Dalberg. "It is a little sad to have to view it all from the corner of a college."[66] From this dismal prospect, he was, however, reprieved. His journey to Tübingen was interrupted by a messenger from Napoleon with an invitation to become Minister and First Secretary of State of Jerome, King of Westphalia.

And so, at long last, he had acquired a post worthy of his talents and of the perspective of a historian. Or had he? Once installed, he rapidly discovered that he had no real control over policy, which was made in Paris and carried out locally by imperial prefects. His position, although time-consuming, was largely ceremonial.[67] In the mood of disenchantment that followed this discovery, he applied for a reduction of duties and was made Minister of Public Instruction. This was even worse; indeed, for a man who, his life long, had fled from involvement in the realities of academic life, it was a crowning irony. Placed in a similar situation some years later, Wilhelm von Humboldt was to say that dealing with professors was like being the director of a company of travelling players.[68] Müller would have agreed. In his charge he had not only the professors of five universities and the instructional staffs of fifty *Gymnasien* and three thousand primary schools, but their student bodies as well. The professors, usually concerned only about promotions and salaries,[69] were developing more complicated grievances under French control, and the students were dangerously unpredictable. Müller had never felt easy with the young, and in 1795 had written that "students think anything they do is permissible, and to me this attitude causes more concern than the weapons of the French."[70] Now their patriotic agitations threatened to turn those weapons against the freedom of the universities. In this situation, Müller found himself in an unenviable position. By discouraging all forms of political organization and activity in the universities, he sought to dissuade the French from their evident intention of closing down some of the university centers and centralizing the whole system of higher education in Westphalia. He succeeded neither in winning the support of the university communities nor in retaining that of the French; and in May 1809, King Jerome, tired of his complaints about political interference, informed him that he didn't "want any more scholars; [the University of] Halle should be burned down and the other university towns destroyed; all we want is soldiers and *Dummköpfe!*"[71] Müller rose to the occasion. "Today," he wrote the King, "in announcing that you wanted only ignoramuses and that you reserved a funereal fate for the university towns, you offered me my dismissal. Your will is my command; I accept."[72]

This gesture had no far-reaching effects. Napoleon, it is true, remembered the historian with whom he had talked in Berlin and wrote to Jerome: "I am annoyed that M. Müller is leaving you. The fact is that he was very flattered with his position, but I guess he wasn't given enough leeway to become happy with it."[73] The Emperor was really not very concerned. He had gotten what he wanted out of Müller, who had for a time lent a spurious air of respectability to the new regime in western Germany, and could now be let go. No one else had much sympathy for the historian, either, or took much notice when, worn out by his frustrations, he became ill of erysipelas and died at the end of May 1809.

V

Two years before, on the road to Westphalia, Müller had written to his friend Dalberg: "I am coming down in the world, from the position of one who has the reputation of having done well in his profession to that of a secretary of state who deals with details and ends up by being disgraced. Why can't I remain a historian! There is always an overabundance of secretaries of state, but there have been whole centuries without a historian."[74]

Nevertheless, he went on his way, and—if we look beyond the element of personal vanity that always played an important part in his decisions—we can see that he did so because of his view of the demands of his profession. The first historian of the modern period to write history, not for scholars, but, like the classical historians upon whom he modeled himself, for the nation, his purpose was always to inspire and instruct, to hold out examples that would help men lead better lives, and to give them guidance in their present perplexities;[75]

and his belief in the didactic purpose of history made it impossible for him to remain aloof from the great political questions of his day.

That Müller was ill-equipped for effective participation in politics the record of his junketing from court to court makes all too clear; and at bottom, I suppose, the reason was that he was a credulous man. In his archival research, which he loved with a passion that led him to say that he looked forward to death because it would open God's records to him, he was often so overwhelmed by the rapture of discovery that his critical faculties were immobilized. This capacity for simple wonder is, indeed, one of the most endearing qualities of Müller the historian, but it is clear that it was a grave impediment for Müller the man of politics. But here too we must be cautious in our judgement. Wilhelm Dilthey once wrote, in an early essay, that "the historians of a nation stand in a more direct relationship to its political life than any other group of pure intellectuals."[76] In an age in which all verities were challenged, in which political legitimacy had all but disappeared, in which universal monarchy and universal catastrophe seemed equally possible, Johannes von Müller had the misfortune of living in a land that was bereft either of an accepted historical tradition or a common body of political experience that could supply it with guidelines to action. It is surely not surprising that, in his attempts to prepare himself to be the preceptor of the German people, he should have reflected all of its inadequacies and ambivalences in face of the crisis with which it was confronted; nor is it unworthy of note that his own pathetic search for a hero prefigured the most salient characteristic of its political immaturity in the nineteenth and twentieth centuries.

5

Heinrich von Kleist and the Duel against Napoleon

In January 1949, Thomas Mann wrote to a correspondent: "I must acknowledge the arrival of your book on Kleist and assure you of my earnest attention to it. Of *loving* attention I cannot speak, since much about this writer, even in your incisive study, strikes me as really dreadful; and, after reading it, I find I can warm to his genius less than ever. . . . In the *Hermannsschlacht* . . . one can see what a hysterical – Goethe said hypochondriacal – spirit he was on the whole, and one recoils in horror."[1]

This was an understandable comment. Next to Schiller, Heinrich von Kleist is generally considered to have been Germany's greatest dramatist, and his short stories are masterpieces of the language. To Mann, however, the admirer of order and rationality, Kleist's peripatetic life and the somber fatalism of his work could not but seem anarchic and unhealthy, and the neurotic violence of his political writings must have appeared particularly painful to him in 1949, so soon after he had finished *Dr. Faustus* with its reflections on the dark forces of unreason that had destroyed his country.

Even so, his judgment is less than fair. With all his failings, Kleist is a more attractive figure than many of his contemporaries whose reputation for rationality is impeccable. He is also one of the most interesting of those German men of letters who became involved in the politics of the Napoleonic period, not least of all because his life illustrates that curious pendular swing from neutrality to engagement

59

that has been so notable a feature of the modern intellectual history of Germany and has had such mixed results.

I

Had Kleist remained true to his earliest inclinations, he might have had a greater claim on Mann's sympathies. Although a member of a distinguished family that had given the Prussian crown eighteen generals and two field marshals since the Thirty Years War, he had cast off family tradition, military career, and Prussian allegiance, refusing to admit that there was anything in the world as important as his own intellectual and aesthetic development or to commit himself to any cause external to the sovereignty of his own ego.[2] With pain and sacrifice, he had attained the kind of freedom that would enable him to be a professional man of letters and, in the course of doing so, had become the completely unpolitical man that Thomas Mann had once prided himself on being. But having done all that, he had turned back to the things he had abandoned, throwing himself into political activity with a passion that in the end consumed him.

How are we to account for this reversal? Michael Hamburger has written that it is to be explained by the peculiar position of the writer in German society: that, in contrast to their counterparts in England and France, German writers as such had no status and were consigned to a life of isolation and insecurity; that Kleist had voluntarily chosen this kind of existence for himself but was psychologically incapable of tolerating it for long; and that in the end he sought compensation for his loneliness in extreme nationalism and patriotic activity.[3] This is more accurate as a description of the general state of the arts in Germany than it is of Kleist's own motivation. It would be more accurate to say—as Eugene Anderson said in what is still the best introduction to Kleist's political thought[4]—that, in the first place, it was Napoleon who made Kleist a political activist and, in the second, it was his feeling of responsibility for the protection of the cultural tradition of the German people.

Even Anderson, however, underestimates the obsessional nature of Kleist's hatred of Napoleon, as he does the essential irrationalism of his politics in general. The poet had no feeling for historical causation, or reason of state and the diplomacy of great powers, or the complications of the political process. He saw everything in terms of personality, and the greatest, and to him the most evil, personality of his time was the man he called "the consul of all the world."[5] In moments of personal distress or frustration, he was apt to find in Napoleon the author of his woes.[6] Thus, in 1803, when his creative springs ran dry, he blamed this on the general uncertainty caused by Bonaparte's political ambitions and the deleterious effects of this on artistic effort; and this thought preyed upon him to such an extent that he decided to commit suicide by enlisting in the force that Napoleon was raising for the invasion of England—surely a curious way of demonstrating the menace of Bonapartism to literature.[7]

He recovered from that aberration, but not from his fascinated hatred of the French leader, which indeed grew rapidly in the next two years, particularly in 1805, when Napoleon's brilliant victories in the so-called War of the Third Coalition left him undisputed master of the continent. In a rather hysterical letter written to his friend Rühle von Lilienstern on the eve of Austerlitz, Kleist referred to Napoleon as "the evil spirit of the world" and wondered fretfully why the French *émigrés* had not been enterprising enough to put a bullet through his head. This letter marks a kind of turning point in Kleist's attitude to politics,[8] because, for the first time in years, he identified himself with the Prussian state and its future, bitterly criticizing Frederick William III's vacillations and his failure to throw in his lot with the Austrians and Russians and predicting that a continuation of this policy would lead to disaster. Why, he asked, referring to Napoleon's recent breach of Prussian neutrality, which had gone unchallenged, had the King not

> summoned his Estates and, in a moving speech (his sorrow alone would have made him moving), revealed his situation to them? If he had merely made an appeal to their own sense of honor by asking whether they wished to be ruled by a humiliated sovereign, would not this have aroused something of a national spirit? And, if this feeling had manifested itself, would that not have been an opportunity for declaring to them that this was no ordinary war but a matter of to be or not to be; and that, unless he could increase his army by 300,000 men, he had no recourse but to die for honor alone?[9]

Had the King been able to read this letter, it is doubtful whether he would have understood much of it and possible that he would have been appalled by Kleist's view of how he should have acted. In any case, he did not change his policy and, having failed to join the allies in 1805, he was forced to fight alone in 1806, when his armies were smashed at Jena and Auerstädt.

It has been suggested that, by that time, Kleist had lost interest in politics again and was so deeply involved in the writing of his tragedy *Penthesilea* that he was indifferent to this defeat,[10] and that this indifference might have continued indefinitely if his hopes to establish himself as a publisher and bookseller in Dresden had not collapsed in 1808.[11] If true, this would invite a comparison with another distinguished poet, Gottfried Benn, who after years of political neutrality became an activist in 1933 because he bitterly resented the German republic's failure to give him the financial rewards he imagined he deserved.[12] But Kleist's concern over the course of politics, while intermittent, was always stronger than Benn's; his commitment when it came was not as abrupt; and his motives were loftier. It seemed clear to him from 1806 onward that the Prussian defeat at Jena portended the extension of French rule over all of central Europe and that, once his conquests had been consolidated, Napoleon would be able to plunder the German states to his heart's content. "We are," Kleist wrote to his sister shortly after the battle, "the subjugated peoples of the Romans."[13] And, that being so, would not the enslaved be exposed to cultural, as well as political, imperialism? Would they not be expected to submit to French standards in morals, manners, dress, literature? Kleist feared so. "Who knows," he wrote in August 1808, "whether in a hundred years' time anyone in this locality will any longer speak German?"[14] If this was, in reality, the prospect, then surely a German artist could not stand idly by and watch it happen. Goethe and Alexander von Humboldt were capable of that kind of detachment; the distinguished historian Johannes von Müller and the publicist C. D. Voss were persuaded by the defeat at Jena to become Napoleon's servants.[15] But Kleist felt a duty to resist.

His old friend Rühle von Lilienstern, who was close to Kleist during the Dresden period, wrote in his memoirs that, after the Peace of Tilsit, "this noble spirit wasted away more and more in melancholy, thinking about the downfall of his fatherland";[16] and the poet's letters reflect his agitation. "What times these are!" he wrote to his cousin Marie von Kleist in the summer of 1807. "You have always considered me, because of the privateness of my life, as isolated from the world, and yet there is perhaps no one more intimately engaged in it than I."[17] There was at this time probably more aspiration than actuality about his engagement, although there is some slight evidence that, during the latter part of this period, Kleist was receiving secret dispatches from a group of patriotic conspirators in Berlin.[18] But, although his loathing of Napoleon was greater than ever,[19] there did not seem to be much opportunity for effective action against the Corsican while his armies stood invulnerable from one end of Europe to the other. "How bereft of comfort," the poet wrote, "is the prospect that opens before us."[20]

In the summer of 1808, however, the news of the French capitulation at Baylén in Spain and of Wellington's victory at Torres Vedras indicated that Napoleon was not unbeatable after all. This electrifying intelligence shook the whole structure of Napoleonic Germany and released the forces that brought the renewal of the war by Austria in 1809. It also presented Kleist with an opportunity for the direct involvement in politics that he had long desired and he seized it with enthusiasm and surprising militancy. The result was his patriotic drama *Die Hermannsschlacht* and the war poems and political essays written for the ill-fated journal *Germania*.

II

Of the play, one can only admit that, despite the splendid roll of its verse and the tension of its plot, it is singularly unpleasant. Ostensibly rehearsing the victory of Hermann the Cherusker over Quintilius Varus in the Teutoburger Forest in the year 9 A.D., it is a thinly disguised tract for the times in which Rome stands for France, Varus for Napoleon, his German allies for the members of Napoleon's Confederation of the Rhine, and his conquerors, Hermann and Marbod, for Austria and Prussia. It is informed throughout by a nationalism more brutal and uncompromising than anything written by a German patriot before the 20th century, with the possible exception of the wilder mouthings of Father Jahn. It is worth noting that, while Kleist was writing his play, Fichte was delivering his *Addresses to the German Nation* in Berlin. Fichte emphasized the necessity of a spiritual and intellectual regeneration as a prerequisite for German liberation;[21] in contrast, Kleist—through the mouth of his hero—

jeered at "prattlers" and "writers" who theorized about freedom[22] and called instead for an elemental outburst of savagery, a *furor teutonicus*, that would baptize the new nation with blood.

This was a remarkable transformation. In 1799 Kleist had put aside the sword in order to cultivate love of humanity, and, in 1801, he had bitterly criticized French citizens for refusing to acknowledge any guilt for the crimes committed in the name of France.[23] Now he appeared to argue that, in the fight for the fatherland, there could be no guilt and that any excess was permissible.[24] Hermann, who expresses this philosophy, is certainly one of the least attractive heroes in German literature. He is an intriguer, a systematic liar, and a breaker of treaties (one German critic, writing in 1905, said that Kleist had admirably prefigured Bismarck in his dealings with Napoleon III).[25] He invites Varus into his territory in the hope that the excesses of the Roman troops will arouse the Germans against them, and, when there are no excesses, he invents them.

> Ich aber rechnete, bei allen Rachegöttern,
> Auf Feuer, Raub, Gewalt und Mord,
> Und alle Greul des fessellosen Krieges!
> Was brauch ich Latier, die mir Gutes tun?
> Kann ich den Römerhass, eh ich den Platz verlasse,
> In der Cherusker Herzen nicht
> Dass er durch ganz Germanien schlägt, entflammen:
> So scheitert meine ganze Unternehmung![26]

> [By all the gods of vengeance! I counted on
> Fire and rapine, brutality and murder,
> And all the horror of unfettered war.
> What need I Romans who would do me good?
> If ere I break my camp I can't inflame
> Loathing of Romans in my people's hearts
> So that it rages through all Germany,
> Then my whole enterprise is done for!]

He pledges his assistance to Varus in a war against a neighboring tribe, the Suevians, and then falls treacherously upon the Romans from the rear, slaughtering them to the last man. After all, he explains to his wife Thusnelda before the battle, there is no good Roman but a dead Roman. When she protests that she has known good ones, he answers:

> Das sind die Schlechtesten! Der Rache Keil
> Soll sie zuerst, vor allen andern, treffen![27]
>
> [Those are the worst! Revenge's thunderbolt
> Should smite them first of all, before the others!]

Thusnelda is apparently convinced, for she promptly arranges to have the legate Ventidius, whose gallantries she had been rather enjoying, killed, and in large part eaten, by a bear.[28] All in all, a modern reader of the play is apt to find himself on the side of the Romans,[29] sympathizing with Varus when he realizes what is in store for him and says sadly:

> O Hermann! Hermann!
> So kann man blondes Haar und blaue Augen haben,
> Und doch so falsch sei, wie ein Punier?[30]
>
> [O Hermann! Hermann!
> So one can have fair hair and eyes of blue
> And be as false as any Carthaginian?][30]

The fanaticism of *Die Hermannsschlacht* was, if anything, exceeded by the political pieces that Kleist wrote after the Austrians had taken the plunge into war in the spring of 1809. Even before the actual outbreak of hostilities, he was writing eulogies of Emperor Francis I and Archduke Charles as the duumvirate who would lead the German nation to freedom[31] (once more allowing his tendency to dramatize politics to mislead him, since he appeared to ignore the fact that his two heroes detested each other—although this was well known—and that neither was particularly interested in German liberty), and he had also composed a "War Song of the Germans," which argued that the French must be exterminated like the bears and panthers and other ravening beasts that had once roamed the forests of Europe.[32] Once the fighting started, Kleist applied to the Austrian government for a license to publish a patriotic journal to be called *Germania* and, against the time of its arrival, went on writing with increasingly lurid imagery, producing the notorious poem "Germania to her Children" with its suggestion that the Rhine might assume new and beautiful sinuosity if it were dammed up, here and there, with French corpses,[33] and an odd "Catechism of the Germans," which was distinguished by a completely uninhibited attack upon his arch-enemy Napoleon, who is described, among other things, as "a parricidal spirit risen from hell, who prowls around in the temple of nature and shakes all the columns upon which it is built."[34]

All this frantic rhetoric was to no avail, and the journal for which it was written was still born. The sun that shone on Kleist's hopes at the time of Aspern was eclipsed by the gloom of Wagram. The poet sensed that defeat was coming and sought desperately to stave it off. In a brief but emotion-laden essay written between the battles and entitled "On the Salvation of Austria," he pleaded that the war could still be won if the Austrian government rose above dynastic interest and established some relationship with the masses of the German people. "First and foremost," he wrote, "the Austrian government must recognize the war it is fighting, not as one for the glory, or the independence, or even the existence of its throne, but . . . as a war for God, freedom, law, and morality, the improvement of a sunken and denatured generation—in short, for values beyond any estimation, which must be protected at any price, no matter what, against the enemy that attacks them." Once he has transcended mere self-interest, the Emperor must proclaim the establishment of the German Reich and call all Germans between the age of sixteen and sixty to arms, announce that any German caught with weapons in hand fighting against the national cause will be punished with death, and promise that, when the victory is won, a general Reichstag will be summoned to give the Reich a new constitution.[35]

This was not a workable program and the fact that Kleist took it seriously shows how remote he was from the reality of the situation in 1809. As Kleist's friend Dahlmann wrote later, Austrian politics was so complex and devious by this time that Emperor Francis I actually seemed to be more willing to accept defeat than to face the possible consequences to his own position of another victory by Archduke Charles like that of Aspern, and he certainly had no intention of risking the likely repercussions of a German *levée en masse*.[36] Austria, therefore, made peace and before long Napoleon was being received in Vienna as an ally and son-in-law of the Austrian ruler. It was a shattering blow to Kleist, and the taste of defeat was made more bitter by one of the ironies that occurred so regularly in his life. At the beginning of 1809 he had submitted his play *Die Hermannsschlacht* to the director of the Vienna Burgtheater in the hope that it would be produced and might help inspire the war effort. It was never performed. Instead, once peace was restored, the theater direction presented his *Käthchen von Heilbronn*, a politically innocuous fairy story about unconditional love; and any pleasure the author might have derived from the thought that at least his poetry was being heard publicly (a rare event in his lifetime) was destroyed by the fact that the play was presented as part of the festivities in honor of Napoleon Bonaparte, on the occasion of his betrothal to Archduchess Marie Louise.[37]

III

"I am completely at a loss as to how I am to pull myself together again," Kleist wrote to his half sister in the fall of 1809.[38] The temptation must have been strong to give up entirely, like the minstrel in the poem that he wrote after the defeat, who

> . . . singt die Lust, fürs Vaterland zu streiten,
> Und machtlos schlägt sein Ruf an jedes Ohr, –
> Und da sein Blick das Blutpanier der Zeiten
> Stets weiter flattern sieht, von Tor zu Tor,
> Schliesst er sein Lied . . . [39]

> [. . . singing the joy of combat for his country,
> Found that his call fell flat on every ear,
> And watching how the conqueror's bloody banner
> Fluttered, and multiplied itself, from gate to gate,
> Ended his song . . .][39]

He resisted this impulse and turned his eyes northward. Even in the essay "On the Salvation of Austria," there had been an intimation that a truly realistic response to the national emergency might arise more naturally in Prussia than in Austria, since royal authority there might prove more responsive to the patriotic passions of the people. In this hope, Kleist returned to Berlin, where he founded an exciting new newspaper, wrote his last and best play, and suffered the final frustration of his political hopes.

The newspaper was the *Berliner Abendblätter*, which Kleist began to publish in the fall of 1810 in collaboration with his friend Adam Müller. The first daily journal in Berlin's history, and one of the first in Germany, the *Abendblätter* deserves more attention than we can pay it here. It is still a pleasure to read for its vivid glimpses of Berlin life and crime (based upon official police reports) and its longer articles on cultural and scientific matters; and it includes some of Kleist's finest anecdotes, as well as his famous "Essay on the Marionette Theater." For our purpose, its importance is that Kleist intended it—as is made clear in the "Prayer of Zoroaster" in the first issue, and, more explicitly, in a declaration in the issue of 22 October 1810—"to promote the national cause in every possible way."[40]

This quickly involved the publishers in a series of disputes with the authorities. In 1810–11 the Prussian government, under the leadership of Hardenberg, was seeking to avoid anything that might offend Napoleon and cause him to intervene in Prussian affairs in such a way as to disrupt its program for the economic and military recovery of the country. It was not helpful to have a newspaper that delighted in making references to heavy French losses in Spain and Portugal, even when these items took the form of artful denials that such rumors were true, or that praised the efficiency of the French continental system by pointing out that it had doubled the price of everything in Württemberg. It was not helpful either when the new newspaper assaulted the King's favorite theater director Iffland for his unimaginative choice of plays for Berlin production, or criticized the new Berlin University for its addiction to cosmopolitan rather than national ideas,or charged that the government's fiscal policy was unrealistic in view of the needs of the times.[41] As Chancellor Hardenberg wrote reproachfully: "Despite the freedom that we give for impartial discussion of subjects related to the governance of the state, it simply cannot be tolerated that dissatisfaction with the measures of the government should be aroused in newspapers."[42] The government reacted by denying to Kleist those privileges—access to the police reports particularly—which had made his newspaper popular in the first place; and the official censorship subjected him to such a degree of harassment that he lost the will to continue the fight and ceased publication.[43]

In view of his difficulties with the censorship during the brief life of his newspaper, it is hard to understand how Kleist expected his second venture into politics in Berlin to receive a warm reception. This was the "*vaterländisches Drama*,"[44] *Prinz Friedrich von Homburg*, which he had worked on intermittently since 1809 and which he finished in June 1811, at which time he sent it to a printer and submitted it for approval, and possible support, to Prince William of Prussia.[45] To regard this superb work simply as a political play would, of course, do it an injustice, for it is—as its popularity in our own time clearly attests—much more than that: a play about the relationship of life and death, of dream and reality, of the problem of human existence, and of self-realization through self-understanding. But it did have a political dimension and, in its time, it was potentially a more effective propaganda piece than *Die Hermannsschlacht*.

Kleist's drama tells the story of a young cavalry commander in the army of the Great Elector who commits a gross infraction of discipline during the battle of Fehrbellin because, rapt in a dream of love, he is inattentive during the pre-battle briefing. Although his disobedience of orders assures the victory of Prussian arms, he is tried by a military court and sentenced to death. When he realizes that the verdict is seriously meant, the prince is overcome by abject terror and begs his sweetheart and the Electress to intercede for him. After they do so, the Elector informs the condemned man that, in sentencing him to death, he had believed that he was merely doing his duty and had expected his approbation. If, in fact, Prince Friedrich feels that an injustice has been done him, he need only say so and his sword will be returned. Given this means of escaping the grave, the prince comes to himself and in an eloquent speech, announces that

> Ich will das heilige Gesetz des Kriegs,
> Das ich verletzt', im Angesicht des Heers,
> Durch einen freien Tod verherrlichen![46]
>
> [It is my will that the sacred law of war,
> That I infringed in the face of the whole army,
> Shall be ennobled by my own free death!]

As he awaits execution, secure in the knowledge that he has conquered and realized himself—"Nun, O Unsterblichkeit, bist du ganz mein!"[47]—the sound of the dead-march is overcome by trumpets, the blindfold is removed from his eyes, a crown of bay is pressed upon his brow, and he is hailed by the assembled court as the victor of Fehrbellin.

The play represented a significant development in Kleist's political thinking. Increasingly in his later works—in *Penthesilea*, for instance, and in the story *Michael Kohlhaas*—he had been preoccupied with the idea of law, a fact shown both in their substance (the protagonists being compelled to yield to the law's demands) and their style (which, in contrast to the violence of the content, became progressively severe and disciplined). *Prinz Friedrich* marked the ultimate step in this, Kleist admitting through his hero that the freedom that he had sought throughout his life could only have meaning if it were reconciled with, and directed by, a higher authority. Personally, the play marked the completion of Kleist's private circle, and his return to the things he had fled in his youth: legitimate restrictions upon individuality, the Kantian sense of duty, the idea of service to the State.[48] Politically, it was designed to inspire the liberation movement, by presenting a picture of Prussia as the home of martial valor and enlightenment, of freedom secured by order, of law tempered by humanity, of discipline inspired by patriotic initiative.[49]

But plays cannot exert influence unless they are published or performed, and Kleist's was not. The printer rejected it, and nothing was heard from the Prince of Prussia. The drama was not performed in Kleist's lifetime, and even when it received its first productions — in Vienna in 1821 and in Berlin in 1828 — it was withdrawn almost immediately, in both cases for the reason given by Kleist's former hero Archduke Charles of Austria, namely, that "it must have a demoralizing effect upon the army when an officer begs so cravenly for his life."[50] This reaction, incidentally, was shared, later on, by Hegel,[51] and, still later, by Bismarck, who in 1889 confessed that he didn't like the play because he found the protagonist a "weak reed."[52]

There may have been other reasons for the official silence that followed Kleist's completion of his play, for it was not the prince's fear of death that made it a hot iron in 1811. Rather it was the scene in which Colonel Kottwitz, speaking for a group of officers who have been enraged by the news of Prince Friedrich's sentence, reproaches his ruler for standing on the letter of the law, and says insistently:

> Was kümmert dich, ich bitte dich, die Regel,
> Nach der der Feind sich schlägt: wenn er nur nieder
> Vor dir, mit allen seinen Fahnen, sinkt?
> Die Regel, die ihn schlägt, das ist die höchste!
> Willst du das Heer, das glühend an dir hängt,
> Zu einem Werkzeug machen, gleich dem Schwerte,
> Das tot in deinem goldnen Gürtel ruht?
> Der ärmste Geist, der in den Sternen fremd,
> Zuerst solch eine Lehre gab! Die schlechte,
> Kurzsichtge Staatskunst, die um eines Falles,

Da die Empfindung sich verderblich zeigt,
Zehn andere vergißt, im Lauf der Dinge,
Da die Empfindung einzig retten kann![53]

[I beg of you, what difference do the rules make
By which the foe is beaten, as long as he
With all of his proud flags lies at your feet?
That he be beaten is the only law!
This army stands by you with ardent love.
Will you make it a mere implement, like the sword
That's resting, dead, held in your golden sash?
Only the sorriest wight, alien to the stars,
Could hold such theory! This accursed,
Shortsighted statecraft! Because one time
Passion has proved to be unfortunate,
It forgets ten other cases, in the course of things,
Where passion is the only remedy!]

In the play, Kottwitz's argument is repudiated both by the Elector, standing for the Law and the State, and by the Prince. Even so, that point might well have been lost on a Berlin audience in 1811, and the speech taken for a political manifesto. For it mirrored with remarkable precision the views of that group of patriotic and potentially rebellious officers led by Neidhart von Gneisenau who opposed the cautious line of policy pursued by Hardenberg. It was well known that these firebrands resented the restrictions placed on them by "accursed, shortsighted statecraft" and that some of them were openly contemptuous of their sovereign for his failure to draw the sword. No one in government or court circles could have permitted their disaffection to be advertised by a representation of it on the stage.

The fact that Kottwitz's sentiments so closely resembled those of Gneisenau was hardly an accident. Temperamentally, Kleist and Gneisenau had been kin for a long time. In 1808, when the poet was composing *Die Hermannsschlacht*, the soldier submitted a long memorandum to his king, in which he not only invoked the name of the historical Hermann,[54] but called for the kind of war against Napoleon that Kleist's Hermann fought against Varus—

Einen Krieg, bei Mana! . . .
. . . der in Deutschland rasselnd,
Gleich einem dürren Walde, um sich greifen,
Und auf zum Himmel lodernd schlagen soll![55]

[a war, by Mana! . . .
. . . which, raging through all Germany
As through an arid wood, will devour all
It meets and throw its hot tongues to the heavens!]

And in 1811, when a sharp deterioration of relations between France
and Russia gave patriots new reason to hope that the tide might be
turning against Napoleon, he returned to the charge with a passionate
appeal for a *levée en masse* and an immediate declaration of war. The
King turned the proposal down with the written comment "Good, as
poetry," to which Gneisenau responded, "Religion, prayer, love of
one's ruler, love of fatherland—these things are nothing else than
poetry. There is no lifting of the heart that is not atune to poetry.
The man that acts only in accordance with cold calculation becomes
an inveterate egoist. Upon poetry is founded the security of the
throne."[56]

This had the real Kleist ring, and it makes it easy to understand why
Gneisenau became the poet's hero and his hope in the last months of
his life. Kleist too had been excited by the rumors of an imminent
break between France and Russia, and the thought that Prussia might
be allied with Russia in a war of liberation had moved him, through
the good offices of Marie von Kleist, to petition the King in September 1811 for the restoration of his commission as a Prussian officer.
Considering the numerous reasons he had for dissatisfaction with the
poet, Frederick William was more than generous. He promised that,
if war broke out, he would find a place for him, although he added
privately to Marie that he hoped that the occasion would never arise.[57]
Kleist was immediately aglow with enthusiasm; he had for some time
been in touch with members of the patriotic party; he had met
Gneisenau and had begun to do some writing for him, the nature of
which is not known; and he had dreams of a staff position in the
crusade that the general would lead.

But these hopes were dissipated almost before they were formed.
In the prospect of a Franco-Prussian war, Frederick William and
Hardenberg saw peril rather than opportunity. They had no illusions
about Prussian strength. Ringed about by the heavily armed states of
the Rhenish Federation and with a strong French garrison in Frankfurt an der Oder, Prussia's prospects as an ally of Russia were
hopeless. French troops would be in Berlin in two days, whereas it

would take the Russians ten days of uninterrupted marching to reach the Vistula.[58] From Vienna, no help was to be expected, and Prussia's ambassador in that capital, Wilhelm von Humboldt, warned against any Prussian alignment with Russia, since the Austrians might be unable to withstand French pressure for an alliance.[59] Nor were there any obvious signs in the country of enthusiasm for a popular insurrection; "Nobody will come," the King wrote laconically on Gneisenau's proposal of an appeal to the people.[60]

Since neutrality would also be a dangerous policy if war should break out, Hardenberg took the only course that was left to him; and in the third week of September it was rumored that the King was going to sign a military alliance with France.

> How this prospect affects me [Kleist wrote to his cousin Marie] you can easily imagine. My soul is stupified and apathetic, and there is not a single bright spot in the future to which I can look with any hope or joy. A few days ago I was with Gneisenau and gave him, as you advised, some essays I had worked out; but that all seems now, as the French say, *moutarde après diner*. Really, it is extraordinary how everything that I undertake goes to pieces now . . . Gneisenau is a wonderful man . . . I am certain that, if he had been given the position for which he feels himself trained and destined, I would have found mine somewhere in his entourage. How happy that would have made me, given my present mood! For it is a joy to be with an able man; energies which are no longer properly harnessed in our world can be awakened to new and joyful life in such a presence and under such protection. But from what one hears now, there is no longer any point to thinking about all that.[61]

The rumors of alliance with France were reliable; and Kleist was faced with a final irony. If war broke out now, he could be called to the colors, not for service against Napoleon, as he had hoped, but to fight on his side! This was the final blow. "The alliance that the King is concluding with the French," he wrote to Marie on 10 November 1811, "is hardly calculated to make me hold to life."[62] He had, in fact, been thinking hard about death for some weeks, but he was determined that it would not come to him, like a ludicrous mirror reflection of his suicide project of 1803, as a soldier of Napoleon. He would die in his own way, and on 21 November 1811 he did so, on the banks of the Kleiner Wannsee near Berlin.

IV

Heinrich von Kleist's political activity was not the happiest phase of his troubled life, and it is understandable that his admirers have generally regarded it as an aberration which distracted his energies, revealed him in his least engaging aspect, as blood-and-guts tub-thumper, patrioteer, and purveyor of national prejudice, and, in the end, contributed to the emotional anguish that led him to take his own life at the age of thirty-four. It did, of course, do all those things, but to think of it as a deviation from the poet's proper sphere would do less than justice to Kleist's seriousness of purpose and the earnestness of his engagement. To him, politics became as necessary a part of his self-fulfillment as writing. After having created for himself the isolation from affairs which he needed in order to make himself an artist, he became, perhaps a bit belatedly, aware that, in an age in which all Europe was caught up in an a relentless struggle for "mankind's mighty objects, for dominance and freedom,"[63] as Schiller expressed it, the artist dare not remain aloof, since his future – indeed, the future of all art – would be determined by the outcome. No one who has read Kleist's letters can be satisfied with Michael Hamburger's explanation that Kleist's politics was a psychological compensation for loneliness, let alone his description of Kleist as a reactionary.[64] The poet's activism was rather the result of a conviction that his age called for it. In one of his poems Bertolt Brecht has written

> Was sind das für Zeiten, wo
> Ein Gespräch über Bäume fast ein Verbrechen ist
> Weil es ein Schweigen über so viele Untaten einschließt?[65]

> [What times are these, when
> A conversation about trees is almost a crime
> Because it is mute about so much injustice!]

Repeatedly, in the letters written from 1805 onward, Kleist seems to be saying, "What times are these when one cannot write a page of verse without the shadow of Napoleon falling across it?"[66]

He was, of course, singularly ill-equipped, by training or by temperament, to play a political role or even to judge a political situation. He was impatient and uncompromising – a truly uncondi-tional man – and he was, above all, a dramatist, who wrote all his own scripts for the politics of his day and then expected the historical events and actors to conform to them. Hence the grotesque rhetoric of 1808, the idealistic but impractical prescriptions of 1809, and the excessive despair over the course of events in 1811 (events which, as more phlegmatic men like Hardenberg and Wilhelm von Humboldt realized, were moving with deliberate speed, if not with majestic instancy, towards the goal Kleist longed for).

It has often been said, particularly by critics of the modern school, that Kleist's dramas and the greatest of his stories were a century before their time. Something of the sort might be said of his politics as well. In all of his basic attitudes toward political questions, he seems more like a German intellectual of the twentieth century than a representative of the Napoleonic era; and perhaps the time has come to regard him, in this respect, as a precursor of the Expressionists of the Weimar period rather than as a member, or associate, of the romantic school, a connection that was never, in any case, very convincing.[67] Like Kleist, the Expressionists moved from neutrality to engagement, from contempt for the political process to violent intervention in it; like Kleist, they were essentially irrational in their approach to political questions, scorning the rules of reason and the compromises and cautionary precepts of the professionals in favor of simple and often catastrophic solutions; like him, they had an ineradicable faith that passion could solve all problems; like him, they dramatized politics and saw in every situation, large or small, a struggle for "God, freedom, law and morality, and the improvement of a sunken and denatured generation."[68]

This was a kind of politics—one hesitates to call it Kleistian; perhaps it should just be called German—that seldom had positive results and not infrequently was productive of great harm. But it had its own peculiar nobility, and every once in a while it inspired, or helped to inspire, a *Prinz Friedrich von Homburg*.

6

Wilhelm von Humboldt
as Diplomat

Some years ago, the *American Foreign Service Journal* received an article about Prussian and German diplomats in which the name Humboldt appeared. When they published it, the editors embellished the text with a photograph of Alexander von Humboldt, the explorer and natural philosopher.[1] This was a natural enough slip; Alexander von Humboldt was much better known in the United States than his elder brother Wilhelm, and the large number of American towns and counties that bear the family name are, like the Humboldt Current, named for him. Even so, it is a bit startling to find a professional journal devoted to diplomacy confused about which of the brothers was the statesman,[2] and this may be taken as symptomatic of a general lack of awareness and appreciation of Wilhelm von Humboldt's diplomatic talents and achievements. Even specialists on the Napoleonic period and historians of the Congress of Vienna have been guilty of this. In his work on Castlereagh, Sir Charles Webster makes no more than casual reference to Humboldt and is misleading with respect to his objectives and his relations with his superiors.[3] Sir Harold Nicolson, usually a shrewd judge of diplomatic stature, mentions Humboldt only five times in a three hundred page account of the Congress of Vienna, and in Henry A. Kissinger's rather longer book on the diplomacy of the period after 1812, Humboldt's name barely manages to get into the index.[4]

This is hardly generous treatment of one who has a right to be called the most formidable diplomatic talent in the Prussian service before Bismarck's day, and it would have seemed odd to Humboldt's contemporaries. During the negotiations in Vienna in 1814, on-lookers regarded him as one of "two great contending athletes [in comparison to whom] the other delegates seem[ed] to make little impression," (the second being Talleyrand).[5] Friedrich von Gentz said that the representatives of the assembled powers generally regarded him as the "most significant" figure in the deliberations, while Talleyrand, who had no reason to love his great antagonist, said that Europe possessed only three or four diplomats of Humboldt's stature and competence.[6]

These contemporary judgments are certainly not free of hyperbole, but a review of the relatively brief diplomatic phase of Humboldt's varied career tends to support them. It also throws light on some problems that have been endemic to diplomacy in general and Prusso-German diplomacy in particular.

I

Like his greater follower Bismarck, Humboldt came to the world of international statecraft late and reluctantly. He had turned his back on the world of practical politics in 1791 at the age of twenty-three, after a scant year's service as *Auskultator* (junior counsellor) in the Berlin city court, and, despite the storms and crises that affected his country for the next eighteen years, he remained intent upon his own aesthetic education and absorbed in travel and theoretical studies of literature, art, and language. His service as Prussian resident in Rome in the years 1802–1809 marked no break in this aloofness from politics, for his duties in the papal capital were few and encroached in no significant way upon his program of reading or his linguistic studies.

If he had had his way, he would have lived his life out in these pleasant circumstances,[7] but this design was frustrated by two men: Napoleon, who deprived Prussia of most of its Catholic inhabitants by the Tilsit settlement, and thus made it unnecessary for the state to maintain a mission in Rome;[8] and Stein, who, on the eve of his own dismissal from the Prussian ministry, offered Humboldt the post of minister of public instruction in a way that made it impossible for him to refuse it. This office, in which Humboldt rendered those services to the Prussian state for which he is usually remembered, proved to be a way station between the scholarly and diplomatic phases of his career, for in June 1810 he was surprised to hear from the lips of the new state chancellor, Hardenberg, that the king had appointed him ambassador to Vienna.

It cannot be said that he was overjoyed by the prospect. Indeed, he reacted to it with even less enthusiasm than Bismarck was to show when he was appointed envoy to the Frankfurt Diet in 1851. Even three years later, Humboldt could write to his wife that he detested drafting diplomatic notes,[9] and that, although he had got used to it, it was against his whole nature, which could also be said of

> all aspects of the ambassador's life. The indefiniteness of the work, the continual dependence upon foreign initiative, the stretches of idleness that so frequently interrupt business, and the protocol — all this thoroughly repels me. It is only the freedom that the occupation affords, as well as my love for foreign countries and my penchant for seeing my own from abroad, that could ever have led me into it.[10]

To make things worse, he found himself in the most awkward and exasperating of all possible positions for the working diplomat, that of being distrusted both by his own court and the one to which he was accredited. It is highly likely that the principal reason for his appointment was Hardenberg's desire to remove him from Berlin, lest his ideas on ministerial reform prove embarrassing. This design was facilitated by a rumour, which the chancellor made no effort to check, to the effect that Humboldt was a member of the *Tugendbund*, a kind of moral uplift society founded in 1808, which had gained an undeserved reputation for conspiratorial and revolutionary intentions and had, in Clausewitz's words, become "a chimera with which one keeps the people and court of Berlin in continual terror."[11] Unfortunately, the court of Francis I was just as susceptible to this kind of nonsense as that of Frederick William III, and, for some time after his arrival in Vienna, Humboldt found himself threatened with political ostracism.

This situation was not relieved by the fact that Hardenberg kept him imperfectly informed about developments in Berlin and, not infrequently, used special envoys to do business that should properly have fallen within the province of the embassy,[12] practices hardly calculated to raise Humboldt's prestige in Vienna. At a later date he described his position at the inception of his mission in language that could have been echoed by some of Bismarck's envoys (and, indeed, by some of John Foster Dulles's):

> Given the nature of my situation here – knowing nothing of the real intentions of the King and Your Excellency, receiving the disclosures of Count Metternich less as official communications than as friendly advice (and because of this receiving them all too late and unsystematically) and often not daring to make use of them in reports to my government – I could in no way work effectively for the King's service, and even as a simple observer had no confidence in [the effect of] my reports, which could only be understood if one kept this peculiar situation constantly in mind and regarded it from my standpoint. This situation was extremely painful to me.[13]

This was, perhaps, overstated. In the course of his first year in Vienna, Humboldt managed to overcome both the doubts of his superiors in Berlin and the suspicions of his hosts. His impeccable social background gave him the *entrée* to the great houses of Vienna, particularly those of political importance, and his light, unconstrained, and agreeable manner (which Callières had recommended to an earlier generation as the proper and effective attitude for the diplomat in society[14]) belied and in the end dissipated the rumours that surrounded him. More important was the fact that he gained Metternich's confidence, principally, one gathers, by giving no credence in his reports to gossip designed to weaken the Austrian chancellor's own position and by remaining aloof from the anti-Metternich *fronde* in Vienna. One of the earliest and soundest judgments that Humboldt made after entering the jungle of Austrian politics was that Metternich was shrewder than any of his rivals and would hold on to his post, a view not widely held in 1810.[15] Sensing this,[16] Metternich responded by opening as much of his mind to the Prussian ambassador as he did to any foreign representative.

Humboldt's relations with his own government changed markedly during the first eighteen months of his mission, and this was due primarily to the quality of his dispatches – despite what he was to say later on about the labors of drafting them. In them he did more than make a correct guess about Metternich's staying power. The critical question upon which the Berlin court needed information in 1811 was what the Austrian government would do in the event that the deterioration of relations between France and Russia should lead to war between those powers. On the basis of his conversations with Metternich and a shrewd assessment of Austria's financial and military resources, Humboldt supplied the right answer in a series of reports that infuriated the patriotic party in Berlin and removed the *Tugendbund* label, at least temporarily, from his own person.[17] In the event of a Franco-Russian war, he wrote, Austria could not be expected to withstand French pressure for an alliance, the more so because Russian policy in the Balkans had aroused the liveliest suspicions in Vienna.[18] The Prussian government must therefore guard against basing its own policy upon the expectation that Austria would try to remain neutral or experiment with armed intervention; and, whatever its own sympathies in the event of war, it must be careful not to commit itself to Russia too soon. This line of reasoning, repeated and elaborated throughout 1811, conformed to Frederick William's own prejudices, and his ambassador's reports had a not inconsiderable effect upon his decision, in February 1812, to yield to Napoleon's insistence and to conclude an alliance with him, which promised, at small cost, to guarantee Prussia's safety until the European situation was somewhat clearer. However much Humboldt may have personally regretted this step, the soundness of the reports that had induced it was demonstrated when the Austrian government concluded a similar alliance with France on 14 March 1812.

At the end of his diplomatic career, Humboldt wrote: "Nothing is as important in any political process as the ability to comprehend exactly how things are, whether one wants to leave them that way or to change them."[19] His own reports from Vienna exemplified this ability, and this was particularly true after the outbreak of hostilities between France and Russia. War reawakened the hopes of the patriots in Berlin, and, by the time Napoleon had received his first checks at Borodino and Moscow and had begun his great retreat, the most egregious expectations were being entertained about what the German powers might contribute to his discomfiture. Humboldt himself was not insensible to the enthusiasm of the moment, but he did not allow it to distort his judgment. The hatred of France that was so common in Prussia was foreign, he pointed out, to Metternich and the Austrian court. Metternich's "system" he had described at the outset of the Russian campaign as being directed not to the destruction of French power but to its containment within a just and equitable European order that would secure the independence of the major

Powers.[20] Napoleon's retreat from Russia had not changed the Austrian chancellor's views. Napoleon's enemies could expect no Austrian support if they fought a war of ideas rather than one of interest or if, in their zeal to overthrow Napoleon, they did so at the expense of the European balance that Metternich was seeking to reestablish. In any event, Austrian policy would continue to be tentative and vacillating in the months that lay ahead, and, if possible, the Prussian government would be well advised to avoid committing itself before the Austrians did. An alliance with Russia might have unfortunate results if the Austrian government decided to place its growing military resources at Napoleon's disposal.[21]

On this occasion, Humboldt's advice was powerless to check Prussia's drift toward war. As he himself recognized,[22] his country's policy could not be based on long-range estimates of Austrian intentions alone; the developing military situation could upset the nicest calculations and present the state with dangers or opportunities so urgent that its policy would in effect be made in the field. The advance of the Russian armies into Europe, the quasi-mutinous action of General von Yorck at Tauroggen, which committed Prussian forces to the Russian cause, and the enthusiasm with which this was greeted throughout East Prussia forced the king's hand; and in mid-March Prussia was at war with Napoleon.

II

This turn of events changed Humboldt's role and increased its importance. Till now he had been a mere reporter of conditions and prospects; now, as it became a vital concern of the northern courts to persuade the Austrian government to join the anti-French coalition, he became an advocate as well. From now until the collapse of the Prague conference in August, he was engaged in a continuous process of informal negotiation with Metternich, seeking by a variety of approaches to win a definitive commitment from him. At the same time he found that he had to devote an almost equal amount of his energy and his dialectical skill to combating the forces of impatience, on the one hand, and discouragement, on the other, within the allied camp. Although his work later at the Congress of Vienna is the only aspect of his diplomatic career that has attracted the attention of western scholars, Humboldt was probably correct in regarding his labors in 1813 as the most important part of his public life.[23]

Once again his task was complicated by Habsburg fears of revolutionary enthusiasm. The declarations made by Stein and his agents in East Prussia, the inflated rhetoric of some of the more unbuttoned soldiers in the Blücher-Gneisenau camp, and particularly the minatory references, both to the punishment that would be meted out to the German princelings who had collaborated with Napoleon and to the united Germany that would be erected at their expense, disturbed Emperor Francis and his advisers, and Humboldt was impelled to urge a moderation of language. In allied councils, he wrote, it was customary to talk about the liberation of Germany and Europe, but

> here one prefers to speak only of political systems and of great powers, and Germany is mentioned infrequently. I am far from approving of this, but I must say that, when I consider the spirit of the communications that come to us from the allied armies and think about our objective, which is to win the princes of Germany to our side, I am inclined more to the manner of regarding things that has been adopted here. I regard it as my duty here to minimize this difference and to prove that basically we are completely united with respect to our goals and objectives.[24]

In his conversations with Metternich, Humboldt sought to convince the chancellor that Prussia and Russia were also interested in establishing a viable balance of power in Europe, but that the only way that this could be assured would be for Austria to declare itself boldly on their side. To delay doing so unnecessarily would merely protract Napoleon's resistance and make it more difficult to establish the kind of equilibrium that would provide security for Austria and Prussia. In that case, he argued, posterity would take a dim view of Metternich's statecraft.[25]

Privately, Humboldt was perfectly aware that these arguments would not deflect Metternich from the delicate course he was pursuing. A shrewd judge of military facts, he had kept abreast of the buildup of Austria's armed forces, and he knew that within a few months the chancellor would have 150,000 men behind him. Metternich was not going to be foolish enough to make any agreements until that force was available to win him good terms, and there was little point in becoming irritated about his studied unreceptiveness to allied offers and his cynical trafficking with the French in the meanwhile. In a masterful dispatch of 1 May 1813, Humboldt wrote:

> I cannot conceal the fact that, if one examines all the details of the present conduct of the court of Vienna, one finds things either difficult to explain or capable of giving umbrage, but I would think that I was neglecting my duty if I overemphasized these and did not go ahead, asking myself always what are the essential facts about the position of Austria and what are the practical methods best calculated to work on the cabinet here and to lead to a more favorable result.[26]

It was unfortunate that Austria had not joined the coalition, but, he added with an oblique reference to the Empire's growing military strength, it did no good to be annoyed by this. The allies should remember that, when the time came for the reordering of Europe, the cooperation of all of the powers would be needed. In the meantime, it would be wise to maintain a close and sympathetic understanding with the Austrian government.

Until May Humboldt was forced repeatedly to urge the headstrong allies to be patient with the Austrians and to indulge in no defiant gestures; from then on, after the unexpected and disconcerting Napoleonic victories at Großgörschen and Bautzen, he found himself in the position of arguing against tactics born of panic. To plead frantically for Austrian aid now, he wrote, or to nag at Vienna because of nonfulfillment of promises which Metternich could probably prove that he had never made, would be equally bootless. Far better to make it clear to the Austrians that the recent setbacks were not critical and would not affect the allies' will to victory, and to use language that indicated that they were confidently assuming that, when Austria's military preparations were complete, her government would not hesitate to join them. "There is a way of expressing confidence," Humboldt wrote to Hardenberg, "which places an obligation upon him who receives it, and this is the mode that should be employed here."[27] At the same time, it would do no harm to intimate to Metternich that any attempt on his part to arrange a peace with Napoleon that did not accord with the interest of the allies would be rejected and that they would take up the fight without Austria, which might be awkward for the Habsburg dynasty in the sequel.[28]

In June 1813, the center of European diplomatic activity moved from Vienna to the boundary of Bohemia and Silesia. Hoping to exploit the allies' post-Bautzen discouragement in order to secure a settlement with Napoleon, Metternich and his sovereign moved north so as to be in close contact both with allied headquarters and with the French emperor's court at Dresden. Simultaneously, Hardenberg authorized Humboldt to hand over the embassy in Vienna to a *chargé d' affaires* and to join him at Reichenbach. In the king's entourage the ambassador found muddle and dissension, the Stein-Blücher-Gneisenau party demanding a policy of war *à outrance*, the king and his close advisers Ancillon and Knesebeck showing every sign of willingness to make peace on any terms. In this situation, Humboldt sided with the soldiers, repeating the advice he had sent on from Vienna. "Believe me," he wrote to his wife on 13 June, "I have not been idle and I have advised nothing but the strong line," so much so, indeed, that Stein "said to me today that I was like St. Elmo's fire that shows on the masts of ships when there is a storm."[29]

It was probably at this time that Metternich began to regret the confidence he had earlier placed in Humboldt and to regard him as an awkward colleague. The Austrian chancellor was relying on the influence of the faint-hearts at allied headquarters to help him get a compromise peace with Napoleon, and the armistice he arranged with Napoleon in June and its subsequent prolongation until 10 August were intended to strengthen their hand. But these tactics availed him nothing because Humboldt, with Hardenberg's backing, was successful in making allied assent to his arrangements conditional upon Austrian agreement to enter the war on their side if Napoleon did not, in fact, accept peace terms considerably stiffer than Metternich, left to his own resources, would have accepted. The infighting that went on during the complicated negotiations at Ratiborschitz, Gitschin, Opotschina, and Dresden in June and July 1813 is not well documented; but it is known that Humboldt worked persistently to weaken Metternich's influence at the Prussian court, persuading Hardenberg to tell the king that he would resign rather than sign a peace that did not give Germany security, and doing his best to get the congenitally pessimistic General Adjutant von Knesebeck replaced by one of the younger and more militant soldiers like Boyen or Grolman.[30]

At the beginning of July, after reading a memorandum of Knesebeck's in which the general showed a willingness to lower the price of peace by abandoning such war aims as the dissolution of Napoleon's

Confederation of the Rhine and the annexation of Magdeburg by Prussia, he wrote a devastating reply in which he once more demonstrated his awareness of the facts of power.

> In general it seems difficult to me when speaking of states [he wrote], to separate independence from power. . . . The present moment is doubtless the most critical in which the Prussian monarchy has ever found itself, and certainly nothing would be more criminal than to expose the welfare of the state to the most imminent dangers by false enthusiasm or exaggerated ambitions. But war is not the only thing that destroys states; peace often leads them much more surely to their destruction, by depriving them of the means of defence and leaving them vulnerable to their enemies.[31]

Rather than accept terms that would be dangerous, Prussia must be prepared, if necessary, to resume the war, with Russia as her sole ally. Torn between his desire for peace and his hope of increasing the strength and resources of his country, Frederick William III came down hesitantly on Humboldt's side, perhaps swayed by the ambassador's additional argument that firmness at this juncture represented no great risk, since the logic of events would bring Austria into the war as his ally.

The armistice came to an end in August at a conference in Prague in which Metternich served as mediator between Napoleon and his antagonists, having privately agreed to join the allied cause if the French emperor did not accept their terms.[32] Since, thanks to Hardenberg and Humboldt, the Prussian and Russian governments had remained true to the essentials of the program they had agreed on at the time of their alliance—namely, the complete destruction of the French position in Germany—Napoleon had no intention of making peace, although it took him some weeks to make this clear. By 10 August, however, there was no mistaking it, and relations with France were broken off. Whatever his hopes and fears, Metternich now had to declare war. As Enno Kraehe has written: "Any other course would have cost him his personal prestige, forever impaired his ability to negotiate, and invited a . . . peace at Austria's expense."[33]

Humboldt could not help but regard this result as in some measure a personal triumph. On 11 August he wrote to his wife: "I stand at the point I wished to reach. I have now carried through *one* important matter in my life, although, when I say that, I don't mean I really did it alone. Other people contributed just as much as I did, the circumstances more, and Napoleon most of all."[34] Two years later, in a letter to Hardenberg, he went a bit farther and ventured an appraisal of his diplomatic activity in the whole period from the time of his appointment to the Vienna post until the collapse of the Prague conference.

> When it was a matter [he wrote], of maintaining a just balance between unconsidered judgment and untimely zeal, and when one incurred just as much risk of arousing false expectations by encouraging confidence as of contributing to defeat by awakening distrust, I believe that I can say without boasting that without me the affair would not have succeeded, or would not have turned out as well.[35]

This seems fair enough. Humboldt had counseled patience with Austria when the opposite would have had no effect upon its position, and firmness when the reverse might have led to a disastrous peace. He had a right to claim a share in bringing it into the alliance on tolerable terms. But his success was bought at a price. His stubbornness in the matter of peace terms, and his campaign against the appeasers at court, had reawakened his own sovereign's suspicion of him and revived the *Tugendbund* myth,[36] while his hardheaded defence of Prussian interests had aroused Metternich's respect, but also his antagonism. The Austrian chancellor did not allow the memory of pleasant midnight walks with Gentz and Humboldt over the bridges and through the streets of Prague[37] to soften his resentment or his determination to deny Humboldt the opportunity to get in his way again.

III

The diplomats now moved into the field, and the months that followed were filled on the one hand with the clash of arms and on the other with bitter wrangling among the allies over political and strategic questions.[38] It was, to use the modern parlance, a time of hawks and doves, the former, represented by Stein, the leaders of the Silesian Army, and, in his optimistic moments, Alexander of Russia, wanting to liberate Germany completely and carry the war into France; the latter—Metternich and the commander-in-chief Schwarzenberg, Fre-

derick William III and Knesebeck, and Bernadotte of Sweden—
desirous of a speedy settlement with Napoleon and an end to hostilities short of the Rhine. Humboldt inclined to the former party. The
movement and the sound of battle exhilarated him; he was conscious
of being involved in a decisive development in history and was critical
of those who had no part in it (like Goethe, trying to cadge a medal
from Emperor Francis to replace the one Napoleon had given him,
and Alexander von Humboldt, sitting out the war in Paris); and his
head teemed with visions of the new Germany that could arise if only
a "soft peace" were avoided.[39]

This martial ardor, which was to be tempered at a later date, had
little effect upon the decisions taken by the allies during the winter
and spring campaigns. Metternich remembered Prague and had no
desire to have his policy of seeking peace handicapped by the exer-
tions of one whom the French were now calling "a passionate man"
and whom he himself regarded as "petty and difficult."[40] He tried to
revive Hardenberg's dormant suspicions of his ambassador by accusing the latter of intriguing for the state chancellor's post; he succeeded
in sidetracking Humboldt from the allied talks at Frankfurt and
excluding him from the important negotiations at Langres in January
1814;[41] and, when Hardenberg's health made it necessary to appoint
Humboldt as Prussian delegate to the Châtillon conference in February—a meeting that represented the Austrian chancellor's last hope
of a compromise peace—Metternich appealed to the Prussian government to issue explicit and binding instructions to his old antagonist.
"He has a way", he wrote, "of handling the whole business as a
joke . . . and I know Humboldt well enough to recognize that, if you
do not give him firm orders, he will maneuver and hold a back door
open for the northern and southern Jacobins."[42]

Thanks to Metternich's vigilance, Humboldt remained more a
spectator than an actor in the diplomacy of the spring campaign; his
advice, on the big issues, was unsolicited and, when offered, disregarded; and he was speaking the truth in April 1814 when, discovering
that he had the reputation in Paris of having blocked a compromise with
Napoleon, he described this as undeserved, adding, "I am firmly
convinced that,if I had never been present, things would not have
differed by a hair."[43] His time during the campaign had been spent for
the most part in performing petty administrative tasks and formulat-
ing plans for a new German constitution which were, despite their

eloquence, to remain unrealized.[44] The shrewdest diplomatic proposal that he made in this period—a suggestion to Hardenberg that it
might be a good idea for Prussia to negotiate a hard and fast agreement with its allies with respect to territorial and financial compensation before peace negotiations got under way—was let slip by the state
chancellor until it was too late to do anything about it.[45]

This proved to be a grave omission, as became clear once Napoleon
had been dethroned and the allies had begun the long process of
peacemaking that started in Paris in April 1814, continued in London
in June, and culminated at the great congress in Vienna in the
autumn. In Paris Humboldt watched disgustedly as his country's
allies competed for influence over the new Bourbon government and,
in the course of doing so, showed little concern either for the requirements of German security or for financial claims the legitimacy of
which the Prussian government had unwisely taken for granted.[46] It
was no satisfaction to reflect that this could have been avoided if his
advice had been taken. His bitterness grew during the talks in London, where the tsar flatly refused to discuss the question of territorial
compensation, while Metternich took refuge in equivocation; and he
looked with foreboding toward the gathering of the diplomats at
Vienna because it was clear to him that allied solidarity had broken
down completely and that there was no fundamental agreement on
any of the issues that were basic to a new European order.[47]

After the Vienna deliberations had begun, Humboldt raised the
complaint that was to be heard after each of the great wars of the
twentieth century.

> The evil results caused by the postponement of many things from
> one epoch to another are now coming to light; one cannot postpone
> them any longer and yet does not know how to get out of the
> embarrassment they are causing. During the whole war we kept our
> eyes only upon the problem of overthrowing Napoleon . . . seizing
> upon everything that seemed to make that goal yet more certain and
> pushing aside everything that might even momentarily have de-
> layed it. Therefore, we never reached a prior agreement with
> Russia about Poland . . . and we never used the right language
> toward Bavaria and Württemberg. That is all avenging itself now in
> the most shameful manner, and difficulties are springing up in
> places where, had we acted differently, we could have had a per-
> fectly smooth path.[48]

To the extent that these deficiencies could be repaired by technical expedients and administrative skill, Humboldt repaired them. The labors performed by him and the privy councillors of Hardenberg's chancery were prodigious. Humboldt himself provided the procedural plan that prevented the Vienna negotiations from becoming hopelessly complicated and spelled out the way in which the decisions of the great powers would be communicated to and enforced upon the others;[49] and his staff made almost all the statistical studies and calculations that served as the basis for the redrawing of the map of Europe. At times their industry depressed or annoyed the other delegations, and Talleyrand once pointed to the statistician Hoffmann and asked, "Who is that little man who is always counting heads and losing his own?"[50]

But the procedural plans, the statistical briefs, and the situation papers on every conceivable subject from the military importance of the Swiss-German frontier to navigation rights on international rivers had no power to solve the intractable problems that separated the powers. These were territorial, and the most difficult of them was that raised by Tsar Alexander's desire for all of Poland and the Prussian government's hope of annexing the kingdom of Saxony. It was this question that almost caused the congress to end, not with a European settlement but with another war, a conclusion that was prevented in the end only by a secret alliance between Austria, Britain, and France against the northern courts. In the sequel, Prussia was forced not only to suffer the disappointment of its Saxon ambitions but to watch the emasculation of its proposals for a new German constitution as well.

The historian Treitschke blamed this setback on the weakness of Prussian diplomacy at Vienna and pointed in particular to a memorandum written by Humboldt on 20 August 1814, in which the ambassador described Metternich's fears of Alexander's Polish design and his hope of forcing its modification by joint Austro-Anglo-Prussian pressure. Humboldt argued that Prussia's interests too were threatened by Alexander's plans and that the government should therefore give loyal support to Metternich in this matter. If they did so, they could expect him in return to support their claims on Saxony, despite the concern of certain Austrian soldiers over the prospect of Prussia controlling the passes in the Erzgebirge.[51]

Treitschke describes this as "a remarkable piece of writing, which shows with surprising clarity how grossly even a fine mind of decided

political talent can misread the political relationships of the moment,"
and he goes on to argue that Humboldt, misled by "Metternich's false
tongue," misled Hardenberg in turn, so that, instead of remaining
true to his Russian comrade in arms, he "led his state to a shameful
setback."[52] This argument is charged with all the power and emotion
of which the great Prussian historian was capable, but it does less than
justice to Humboldt's thinking, and its argument that complete loyalty
to Russia would have brought Prussia Saxony, Mainz, and whatever
else it wanted is hardly convincing. Humboldt had had enough
evidence of the tsar's volatility and his studied unreliability during the
spring campaign and the negotiations in Paris and London to distrust
him, and in any event he felt it time to do away with the client
relationship with Russia that had continued since the treaty of Kalisch
of February 1812 and to restore the independence of Prussian policy.
Far from being deluded by Metternich, he had correctly gauged the
extent of the Chancellor's concern over Russian expansion, and he
believed that, if Prussia helped to relieve it, it would lay the basis for
an effective Austro-Prussian collaboration in central Europe, which
would be reflected in a German constitution that would satisfy the
spirit of national self-consciousness inspired by the war and in a
viable European balance of power that would keep both Russia and
France within proper bounds. It is worth noting that such sound
observers as Gentz and Carl August of Saxe-Weimar were persuaded
that Metternich was willing to grant Prussia's claims on Saxony in
return for the kind of support Humboldt proposed; and Hardenberg, a
lazy but not a naïve man, entirely agreed with his policy and accepted
it as his own.[53]

There is no way of telling whether the Humboldt plan would have
succeeded. The most that can be said of it is that, before the Polish-
Saxon question had reached full crisis, Hardenberg had enlisted the
support of the British, and the combination envisaged in Humboldt's
memorandum seemed on the point of being realized. But Alexander
possessed an unbeatable weapon. Observers in Vienna had been
amused by the deference that the Prussian king paid to the tsar in all
matters, out of gratitude for his services to Prussia in 1812;[54] and this
misplaced loyalty confounded Humboldt's plans now. In the first days
of November, Frederick William summoned Hardenberg to his presence and forbade him to act further with Britain and Austria in the
Polish question. The state chancellor was astounded, but gave way;

Humboldt, more doughtily, fought back against this almost classic example of sentimentality in politics with a strong appeal to his sovereign, but this had no effect beyond angering the tsar, who told Frederick William that Humboldt had been bribed by the Jews.[55] The royal intervention immobilized Prussian policy, alienated the British, and freed Metternich from any commitments to Prussia. In consequence, the Austrian chancellor not only defeated its Saxon ambitions but, in the protracted negotiations over the German question that filled the last months of the congress, supported the South German states in their systematic and successful evisceration of Humboldt's constitutional plans.

By June 1815 all of Humboldt's hopes had been disappointed and, as the negotiations dragged to an end, he felt drained of energy.

> The war was the really great and beautiful thing [he wrote to his wife], and it was like a young and beautiful tree suddenly reaching toward the clouds. The Paris Peace put the first blight upon it, and the Congress more. . . . At no time in my life have I had fuller control over my energies, but equally at no time have I been so filled with a lively desire to retire from all these affairs.[56]

IV

Having seen his proposed line of policy at Vienna defeated by the romantic notions of his king, Humboldt was now, in his last important negotiation, to find his task needlessly complicated by the soldiers and to discover, as Bismarck, Bethmann-Hollweg, and Stresemann were to discover after him, how difficult it was to keep the German military within their proper sphere.

He suffered this experience at Paris, during the peace negotiations that followed the campaign of the Hundred Days and Napoleon's second defeat. Because Hardenberg was ailing, Humboldt played the leading part in the discussions that took place in the French capital in June and July 1815, and it was his hope that Germany would receive stronger frontiers than those drawn at Paris a year before and that, in view of the dominant role played by its army in the recent campaign, Prussia would be granted generous financial compensation, as well as

strongpoints on the Mosel and the Saar. He prepared his case carefully[57] and presented it with the authority and acerbity that had
characterized his confrontations with Talleyrand at Vienna.

It was clear from the outset that the other powers were hardly
enthusiastic about these claims, but Humboldt would probably have
received a more sympathetic hearing had it not been for the behaviour
of Prussian military authorities in France. The dissatisfaction of the
soldiers over what they considered to be inadequate diplomatic reward for their efforts had been growing since the first Peace of Paris,
and so had their tendency to indulge in political gestures. During the
London conference of 1814, the British were concerned over the
reluctance of Prussian forces to obey orders to evacuate the Nether-
lands;[58] and during the Congress of Vienna Talleyrand reported to his
king that the Prussian general Grolman had, without consulting his
government, actually written to Wellington to warn him that the
Prussian army would never consent to the loss of Leipzig.[59] But these
maneuvers were nothing to those indulged in by the military when
they moved into France in 1815. Prussian army commanders levied
contributions on the civilian population, superseded local authorities,
and made arrests without authorization from their government, and
Blücher's headquarters turned a deaf ear to Hardenberg's complaints
and admonitions. The Prussian high command was animated by a
spirit of revenge and rebelliousness that alarmed Prussia's allies and,
because of their alarm, made them unresponsive to Prussian diplomatic proposals.[60]

Humboldt, whose relations with the army chiefs, and particularly
with Gneisenau and Grolman, had always been cordial, was as worried as his allies. "In the army," he wrote to his wife, "they go much
too far . . . and so we have to defend things that we would rather
prevent, if we had the power,"[61] and again—after a summary of army
measures against civilians—"these things are useful neither to the
state nor to the army and simply give the French weapons against
us."[62] It was all very well for Blücher to complain that he could make a
better peace settlement than the diplomats; he did not realize that,
unless Prussia was capable of fighting all Europe for what it wanted
(and it did not have the resources for that), it must negotiate, and
negotiation generally resulted in getting rather less than one desired.[63] Humboldt tried to convince Gneisenau of this, and through
him the other army chiefs, but he was unsuccessful, and he concluded

that, thanks to the soldiers, the peace settlement would be worse from Prussia's standpoint than even the pessimists had thought. He was right, and the peace signed on 20 November 1815 satisfied few of Prussia's claims.

In February 1814, at Châtillon, Humboldt had written that peace-making was one of the most thankless tasks in the world. "In it we have the real conflict between what is desirable in itself and what is attainable under the circumstances, and one never escapes the reproach of having fallen short of the attainable."[64] This now proved true in his own case, and, ironically, it was the soldiers, who had done most to defeat his efforts, who now blamed him for lack of determination and courage. He was abandoned by those he had supported during the campaign of 1814, and even his friendship with Gneisenau now faded away.[65]

This was not his only loss. His performance at Paris, which had been marked, as he foresaw the defeat of Prussia's ambitions, by increasing bitterness and sarcasm, had completed the alienation of the tsar's sympathies, annoyed the British and the Austrians, and aroused the hostility of the Bourbon régime in France; and Humboldt soon discovered that this would have some unfortunate personal results. He had hoped that his next post would be in Paris, but he had now become *persona non grata* in that capital. In fact, except for some routine and very boring assignments in the next year, his diplomatic career was at an end and, thanks to the tsar's continuing influence over his master, his prospects in domestic politics were not bright either, as he was to discover during the constitutional crisis of 1819 that ended his public career.

V

Some thirty-five years ago James Joll wrote a book about intellectuals in politics in which he described "the difficulties and frustrations which confront the man of theory in the world of practice . . . where none of his intellectual concepts apply precisely" and where his sensibility is constantly offended by "the compromises, half-truths and personal sacrifices of political life."[66] Few people would deny Humboldt's qualifications as an intellectual, yet he remained, during his diplomatic career, singularly unaffected by these difficulties.

Between his scholarly proclivities and his professional duties no great conflict developed, and he confirmed Callières's belief that men of letters make good diplomats.[67] After some initial hesitation, he brought to the practice of diplomacy the same lively curiosity and intellectual energy that marked his work in linguistics and literature, and he soon made himself a superb technician in a profession at that time not richly supplied with technical talent. From his study of aesthetics he brought the habit of seeing things in their uniqueness, their consonance and their interrelatedness, which greatly contributed to the objectivity and incisiveness of his reports. From his travels and his reading and his life in the world, he brought a freedom from sentimentality that was as marked as Bismarck's was to be, and an awareness that life is largely a matter of compromises and half-truths and that rigid formulae and total solutions rarely work. All of this made him a good diplomat—although perhaps not, as he himself seemed to believe, the *only* good diplomat in the Prussian service in his time.[68]

Humboldt was never, like his greatest successor, in a position of complete responsibility. He was always a working diplomat in the second rank, sometimes busied with the most routine tasks and always subject to the frustrations from which the professional diplomat must suffer—of being imperfectly informed of matters relevant to his own work, of having to carry out instructions of which he does not approve, of seeing his own advice disregarded at subsequent cost to his country, of being criticized by the hawks for timidity and the doves for bellicosity, and of having to take the blame for the faults of others. Yet at the end of his career he could look back to some solid achievements. In the difficult years from 1810 to 1812, his accurate reporting of tendencies in Vienna had prevented his government from adopting policies that might have been dangerous; in the days after Tauroggen his patient pressure and his tactical prescriptions to his own government had played an important part in bringing Austria into the Grand Alliance; and during the long period of peacemaking he had made the most of the situations presented to him, forced as he was to cope, not only with the hardheaded representatives of other powers, but with a not entirely reliable chief, a timorous and sentimental king, and a group of greedy and insubordinate brasshats. All things considered, the years of diplomacy are not the least creditable phase of Wilhelm von Humboldt's extraordinary career.

7

Hölderlin and the Barbarians

In October 1989, in his inaugural lecture as Professor of Poetry at Oxford University, Seamus Heaney addressed himself to the problem of how poetry's existence at the level of art relates to the existence of the poet as citizen. The answer was to be found, he suggested, in "the redress of poetry," its capacity to provide society with a "revelation of potential that is denied or constantly threatened by circumstances." The poet must be helpful "in adjusting or correcting the world's imbalances"; he must be "a model of active consciousness"; his art must be able "to withstand as well as to envisage, and in order to do so it must contain within itself the coordinates of the reality which surrounds it and out of which it is engendered."[1]

This falls short of being a call for political engagement, being rather a reminder that the poet cannot be entirely indifferent to politics and that he is not exempt from the requirements of civic duty. Even so, this is not so modest a requirement as it might seem, and throughout history individual poets and, indeed, whole cultures have repudiated it. As we have seen, Thomas Mann insisted, in 1915, that the political element was missing in the German concept of *Bildung*.[2] Throughout the greater part of the nineteenth century, and even later, German writers generally shared this attitude with the majority of their fellow citizens, with the result that the men of power in German history had little to contend with in the way of opposition from the *Dichter und Denker*.

Friedrich Hölderlin was a conspicuous exception to this rule. "A writer in a barren time," as he described himself in his moving elegy

"Bread and Wine,"[3] he viewed his country as a cultural wasteland, sunk in feudal backwardness, in which "the barbarians who surround us tear our best talents to pieces before they can attain their full development. . . . *It is not so much that they are what they are but that they consider what they are to be the only thing possible and won't let anything else count*: that is the evil."[4] Hölderlin believed it to be the duty of the poet to lay bare the spiritual poverty of the times, and to challenge his fellow citizens to lift their eyes to new horizons of freedom. His ode *"Dichterberuf"* ("The Poet's Calling") begins with a bold assertion of the poet's function as the redresser of the balance in society—

> Und du, des Tages Engel! erweckst sie nicht die noch schlafen?
> [And you, the angel of the day, do you not wake them who still
>   sleep?]—

and ends by asserting the bond of community between him and his fellow man.

> Und gern gesellt, damit verstehn sie
>   Helfen, zu anderen sich ein Dichter,
>
> Furchtlos bleibt aber, so er es muß, der Mann
>   Einsam vor Gott, es schützet die Einfalt ihn,
>   Und keiner Waffen braucht's und keiner
>   Listen, so lange, bis Gottes Fehl hilft.[5]
>
> [A poet is glad—so they will know
>   How to help—of other company,
>
> But fearlessly, if he must, the man
>   Will remain alone before God, simplicity protects him,
>   And he needs neither weapons nor
>   Cunning, until God too absconds.]

In the society that he wished to save, Hölderlin found neither gratitude nor understanding, and posterity proved to be as unforgiving as his contemporaries. If the barbarians of his own time crushed his spirit by their indifference, their successors were to inflict even worse indignities upon his memory, which had to suffer the jeers of the midcentury philistines, the nationalist sacralization of neoromantics in the Wilhelmine period, and, after the dawn of a new age of barbarism, the brutal patronage and exploitation of Martin Heidegger and Josef Goebbels.[6]

I

Georg Lukács has written that Hölderlin's glory was that he was the poet of Hellenism, but he notes that his Hellenism had little in common with the arid academic classicism of the mid-nineteenth century.[7] If this is so, it was because it was informed from the beginning by his enthusiasm for the French Revolution, which erupted while he was still a student at the Tübinger Stift. To him, as to William Hazlitt, the Revolution was "the bright dream of [his] youth; that glad dawn of the day-star of liberty; that spring-time of the world, in which the hopes and expectations of the human race seemed to be opening in the same gay career as [his] own, . . . and when to the retired and contemplative student, the prospects of human happiness and glory were seen ascending like the steps of Jacob's ladder, in bright and never-ending succession."[8] Through the agency of the Revolution, Hölderlin believed, the cultural glories and the freedom of the Greece that he celebrated in his elegies and odes might have an opportunity to bloom in Germany. He was from the beginning therefore its partisan, not in the way that Georg Forster was, who founded Germany's first republic in Mainz and after its suppression went to Paris, where he died during the Terror, but as one who believed in its ideals, followed its fortunes eagerly, and wrote letters to like-minded friends, seeking information about favorite leaders.[9] During the Rhineland campaign of 1792, he wrote to his sister, "Believe me, my dear sister, we shall have bad times if the Austrians win. The abuse of princely power will be frightful. Believe me! and pray for the French, the defenders of human rights!"[10] After Valmy, he was enormously heartened, and, although the progress of the French armies did not live up to his expectations, he wrote to his half-brother in mid-1793, "Freedom must come in the end, and virtue will thrive better in freedom's warm and holy light than in the icy zone of despotism. We live in a time in which everything is moving toward better days."[11] Even the expulsion from power of the Girondins, who had been his heroes, and the coming of Jacobin rule and the horrors of the Terror could not discourage him. To his friend Johann Gottfried Ebel, who was living disillusioned and deeply unhappy in Paris, he wrote in January 1797,

> It is almost impossible to see the dirtiness of reality unveiled without being made ill by it oneself. . . . But I have one comfort,

namely, that every fermentation and dissolution must necessarily lead either to annihilation or to a new form. But there is no annihilation, therefore the youth of the world must rise again from our corruption. One can say with assurance that the world never looked so gay as it does today. It is a prodigious diversity of contradictions and contrasts. . . . One could recite their litany from sunrise to midnight without naming a thousandth part of the chaos of humanity. But so shall it be! The fact that the better-known part of the human race is like this is certainly the harbinger of extraordinary things. I believe there will be a future revolution of thinking and the imaginative faculty that will make everything that has happened before red with shame. And to that Germany can perhaps contribute a great deal. The more quietly a state grows up, the more magnificent it will be when it attains ripeness. Germany is silent, modest, there is much thinking there, and the people work hard, and in the hearts of the young lie great developments, which will not be dissipated in talk as elsewhere.[12]

But already the times were belying these hopes. The Terror had ended the first innocent enthusiasm for the revolution in Germany, and the Thermidorean reaction was greeted with relief and a general desire for accommodation. Among Hölderlin's closest friends at Tübingen, Schelling had already lapsed into reactionary conservatism, and Hegel had given up the radicalism of his years in Bern and was using the cunning of reason to come to terms with the changed spirit of the age, rather than to oppose it. Schiller, the idol of Hölderlin's youth, had turned his attention from the public stage to the private one, devoting his time during the Terror to the drafting of the *Letters on the Aesthetic Education of Mankind* (1795), and the implicit argument of both his long poem "The Song of the Bell" (1799) and Goethe's *Hermann and Dorothea* (1796-97) was that the individual would do well, in troubled times, to retreat to the security of bourgeois existence. This was an argument that Goethe underlined in his play *Die natürliche Tochter* (1803) and, indeed, in his own behavior, for his friend Knebel wrote to Jean Paul Richter that, during the aftermath of Prussia's collapse at Jena, Goethe showed no trace of interest in politics, being entirely engrossed in his study of optics.[13]

Hölderlin, in contrast, remained true to the ideals that he had acquired as a student. He was appalled by the attitude of the two great men of Weimar, who seemed intent upon retreating to a life of aestheticism while abandoning the country to the philistinism that was praised in "The Song of the Bell" and *Hermann und Dorothea*, and his feelings can be sensed from a fragment of a poem discovered in his papers:

> meinest du,
>
> Es solle gehen,
> Wie damals? Nämlich, sie wollten stiften
> Ein Reich der Kunst. Dabei ward aber
> Das Vaterländische von ihnen
> Versäumet und erbärmlich ging
> Das Griechenland, das schönste, zu Grunde.[14]
>
> [do you think
> It should happen
> As it did at that time? That is, they wanted to establish
> An empire of art. But when that happened
> What belonged to the Fatherland
> Was neglected by them, and pitifully
> Was Greece, the most beautiful, destroyed.]

Lukács's description of Hölderlin's efforts to prevent this from happening in Germany ("Unknown and unmourned, he fell like a solitary poetic Leonidas at the Thermopylae of invading Thermidoreanism"),[15] seems grandiloquent and exaggerated when one remembers the actual scope of Hölderlin's political activity. Apart from maintaining contact with small groups of dissidents, most of them literary men like himself, and playing a peripheral role in his friend Sinclair's plans to found a republic in southwestern Germany,[16] Hölderlin's political engagement was literary in nature and hardly calculated to influence large numbers of people. Still, he did what a poet can do, and, if his efforts were largely unnoticed in his time, they seem noble enough when compared with the neutrality of his more highly regarded contemporaries.

There is considerable evidence throughout Hölderlin's oeuvre of concern over the adequacy of his engagement. In poems like "Song of the German" and "To the Germans," he invoked the memory of ancient Greece as a model of what Germany might become and praised his country for those qualities of patience, hard work, and love that must be nurtured if it was to achieve this ideal, but he was constantly troubled by the powerlessness and inertness of his country, and wrote:

Spottet ja nicht des Kinds, wenn es mit Peitsch und Sporn
    Auf dem Rosse von Holz mutig und groß sich dünkt,
      Denn, ihr Deutschen, auch ihr sind
        Tatenarm und gedankenvoll.

Oder kömmt, wie der Strahl aus dem Gewölke kommt,
    Aus dem Gedanken die Tat? Leben die Bücher bald?[17]

[Don't make fun of the child when with whip and spurs
    on his wooden horse he thinks himself brave and great,
      For, you Germans, you too
        Are poor in deeds and given to thought.

"Or, as the lightning comes from the cloud,
    Will the deed come from the thought? Will books soon
      live?]

As David Constantine has written, "the division between the world of action and the world of reflection worried Hölderlin, and in defining Germany's predicament in those terms he was simultaneously defining his own."[18] In poems like "Death for the Fatherland" and "To Eduard," he enthusiastically embraced the road of action, and the result of the long debate between Hyperion and Diotima in Hölderlin's great novel in letters reflects the same choice.

There are, of course, various ways of reading this masterpiece of German prose style, and *Hyperion* has been interpreted as the most sublime expression of Hölderlin's love of classical Greece, as a call for a sick humanity to yield itself to the restorative power of Nature, and, on the personal level, as a eulogy of his lost love, Susette Gontard.[19] But apart from this, it is also a political novel, in part a lament for the lost revolution in France, in part an appeal to German youth to remain true to the ideals of the revolution of 1789. Georg Lukács has written that, in contrast to Goethe's educational novel, *Wilhelm Meister* (1795–1796; 1821–1829), which teaches adaptation to bourgeois reality, *Hyperion*, in calling for resistance to that reality, is "a novel of the citizen."[20] To put the matter more clearly, it is a novel of the education of the *citoyen*, who will be a member not of an acquisitive society whose subjects are reified and drained of idealism, but of a *polis* in which the free development of all members will be the guiding motive of each.[21]

In the novel, Hyperion, a young Greek of the last decades of the eighteenth century—and, we are led to believe, a poet[22]—longs to participate in the liberation of his country, which is under the domination of the Turks. He dreams of building a free society in which the powers of the State will be kept under strict limitation ("The rough husk around the kernel of life. . . . is the State. It is the wall that surrounds the garden of human fruits and flowers")[23] and the principles of humanity and civic duty will guide conduct ("the new church" that will emerge from the "soiled, outmoded forms" of the present).[24] How this is to be accomplished is not clear to him, and he is torn between the political activism represented by his friend Alabanda and the counsel of his loved one, Diotima, who urges him to create the commonwealth he longs for by works of peace and by becoming the educator of his people. The conflict is resolved by the outbreak of the popular rising of 1770 against the Turks, and Hyperion goes off to war, pleading, "A power is in me, and I do not know whether I myself am what leads me to this step," while Diotima, recognizing that she is powerless to stop him, acquiesces with the words, "Act as you must; I will bear it."[25]

The enterprise comes to nothing. The idealism that Hyperion believes inspires his troop of mountain dwellers vanishes after their first easy victories in the Pelopponnesus spread before their eyes opportunities for rapine and plunder, and, as they yield to the acquisitive instinct, the revolution collapses. Hyperion seeks death in a sea battle, after writing to Diotima to tell her of his intention. He escapes, however, although Diotima never learns of this, and when he returns home he finds that she has died of heartbreak. He becomes a lonely wanderer in a world of shattered hopes. At the end of the novel, Hölderlin has his rootless hero travel to Germany and, in a famous passage that clearly expressed his own views about the defeat of the French Revolution and the triumph of the Thermidorean Reaction, has Hyperion describe the Germans as

> Barbaren von alters her, durch Fleiß und Wissenschaft und selbst durch Religion barbarischer geworden, . . . in jedem Grad der Übertreibung und der Ärmlichkeit beleidigend für jede gutgeartete Seele, dumpf und harmonienlos wie die Scherben eines weggeworfenen Gefäßes, . . . ich kann kein Volk mir denken, das zerrißner wäre wie die Deutschen. Handwerker siehst du, aber keine Menschen, Denker, aber keine Menschen, Priester, aber keine Menschen, Herren und Knechte, Junge und gesetzte Leute, aber keine Menschen. . . . Deine Deutschen . . . bleiben gerne

beim Notwendigsten, und darum ist bei ihnen so viele Stümperarbeit
und so wenig Freies, Echterfreuliches. Doch das wäre zu ver-
schmerzen, müßten solche Menschen nur nicht fühllos sein für alles
schöne Leben, ruht nur nicht überall der Fluch der gottverlaßener
Unnatur auf solchem Volke.[26]

[Barbarians from ancient times, become more barbarous by diligence and science and even religion, . . . in every degree of their
posturing and poverty of spirit offensive to any good-natured soul,
dull and without harmony like the shards of a pot that has been
thrown away, . . . I can think of no people that is more riven than
the Germans. You see manual workers, but no human beings,
priests but no human beings, lords and subjects but no human
beings, young people and settled people but no human beings. Your
Germans . . . are happy to restrict themselves to what is necessary; that's why there is so much botched work among them and so
little that is free and truly enjoyable. Yet that could be forgotten if
only such people were not so completely bereft of feeling for
everything beautiful in life and if the curse of godforsaken unnatu-
ralness did not lie everywhere upon them.]

Here certainly was an example of what Seamus Heaney called "the
redress of poetry," and it may be considered the most forthright and
uncompromising appeal to the Germans to confront the nature of their
condition and make efforts to realize their potential that was written by
any German poet during the revolutionary period. Hölderin followed it
with his magnificent, if incomplete, poetic drama about Empedokles,
the Greek philosopher and leader of the democratic party in Acragas
(Agrigento) in Sicily in the fifth century before Christ, who was
expelled from his city because of his radical ideas of social reform and
his supposed violation of divine authority and who finally immolated
himself in the crater of Mount Aetna. Hölderlin took up this project at a
time when the Suaabian radicals were still hoping to found a republic in
southwestern Germany under French auspices, and Pierre Bertaux has
written that his *Empedokles* was intended to inaugurate the new Suaabian democracy and was left unfinished when that project foundered;
David Constantine is more inclined to believe that its ultimate failure
was rooted in Hölderlin's inability to relate the suicide motif with the
political story in a satisfactory way.[27] But even as a fragment, *Empedokles* is a sublime work—E. M. Butler once compared it with the
Prometheus of Aeschylus and wrote that "the second part of *Faust* is

pale beside it, and Shelley's *Prometheus Unbound* has not the same
reality"[28]—and its political passages are moving, as in the powerful
speech in which Empedokles berates the *Bürger* of Acragas for cravenly yielding to priestly authority in demanding his expulsion—

Ha geht

Nun immerhin zu Grund, ihr Namenslosen!
Sterb langsamen Tods und euch geleitet
Des Priesters Rabengesang! und weil sich Wölfe
Versammeln, da wo Leichname sind, so finde sich
Da einer auch für euch, der sättige
Von eurem Blute sich, der reinige
Sizilien von euch; es stehe dürr
Das Land, wo sonst die Purpurtraube gern
Dem bessern Volke wuchs und goldene Frucht
Im dunkeln Hain und edles Korn, und fragen
Wird einst der Fremde, wenn er auf den Schutt
Von eurem Tempeln tritt, ob da die Stadt
Gestanden.[29]]

[Ah, go then

To ruin, you nameless ones!
Die slow deaths to the accompaniment
Of the raven's song of the priest, and, because wolves
Gather where corpses are, so may there be
One there for you who will sate himself
From your blood and purge
Sicily of your kind; may the land stand barren
Where once the purple grapes gladly
Grew for a better people, and golden fruit
In the cool glade, and noble grain, and one day
The stranger will ask, when he comes on the rubble
Of your temples, whether the city
Had stood there.]—

and in his refusal, when they have relented and begged him to return,
to take the crown from their hands:

Dies ist die Zeit der Könige nicht mehr.
. . . Schämet euch,
   Daß ihr noch einen König wollt; ihr seid
Zu alt; zu eurer Väter Zeiten wär's
Ein anderes gewesen. Euch ist nicht
Zu helfen, wenn ihr selber euch nicht helft.[30]

[This is no longer the age of kings.
. . . You should be ashamed of yourselves
    Still wanting a king; you are
Too old; in your fathers' times it would
Have been different. You cannot be
Helped, if you do not help yourselves.]

It was too late, or too early, for such appeals to have any effect. Disregarded by the public, abandoned by colleagues who might have helped promote his work, his plan to found a literary journal aborted, his great hymns and odes misunderstood and unappreciated, his personal life a tragic failure, Hölderlin eked out a miserable life as a tutor until in 1806 his health broke down and his mind was clouded by madness, although he did not die for another forty years.

II

In the nineteenth century, Hölderlin was, as Georg Herwegh called him in an essay in 1839, "one presumed to be dead."[31] There was no collection of his poems until 1829, when Gustav Schwab and Ludwig Uhland made one, and even then they were little known. *Hyperion* always had its admirers (Bettina von Arnim claimed that it was her favorite book her life long) and of the first part of "Bread and Wine," published separately as "Night" in 1807, Clemens von Brentano said that he had read it a hundred times and never without deep emotion and renewed admiration. In a long essay called "Excursions with Hölderlin" in 1826, Achim von Arnim wrote the first appreciation and analysis of the hymn "Patmos," which he described as a work which had no model with which it could be compared: "What inspired him came from a long distance." But these were exceptions, and it was not until the end of the century that there was wide recognition of his work or his stature, despite his obvious influence upon Nietzsche's *Birth of Tragedy* and *Zarathustra*.

Certainly there was no recognition of Hölderlin's views of the civic duties of the poet. His conception of the *citoyen* did not fare well in Germany in the century after his confinement in the gatehouse in Tübingen, and by midcentury philistinism was so pervasive among the middle class that Ferdinand Freiligrath's mocking verses possessed a clear social authenticity:

So hab' ich's doch nach all den Jahren
Zu diesem Posten noch gebracht,
Und leider allzu oft erfahren,
Wer hier im Land' das Geld vermacht.
Du sollst, verdammte Freiheit, mir
Die Ruhe fürder nicht gefährden!
Lisette! noch'n Gläschen Bier!
Ich will ein guter Bürger werde.

Diogenes in seiner Tonne –
Vortrefflich! Wie beneid' ich ihn.
Es war ja keine Juli Sonne,
Die jenen Glücklichen beschien.
Was wär' ihm eine ewige Republik,
Daß sich die Leute toll gebärden!
Zum Teufel mit der Politik!
Ich will ein guter Bürger werden.[32]

[So have I after all these years
Attained this position,
And unfortunately all too often learned
Who in our land has money to bequeath.
You shall, accursed freedom, no more
Menace my peace of mind!
Lisette! Another little glass of beer!
I want to be a good citizen!

Diogenes living in his tub –
Excellent! How I envy him!
It was certainly no July sun
That shone upon that happy man.
What would he care for an eternal republic
Whose people acted like lunatics?
The devil take all politics!
I want to be a good citizen!]

Nor were the intellectuals immune to this feeling. Friedrich Theodor Vischer, the aestheticist and critic, wrote, "We Germans have allowed ourselves to be latecomers in politics because we have been working for our own and humanity's inner development."[33] He was not inclined to recognize, let alone praise, the political strain in Hölderlin, in whose poetry he found, in any case, only "a web of feeling in which no clear form is possible, a continuous fluctuation of mood that produces only immature shapes with dissolving and fading outlines,

sentimental in the worst sense." Hölderlin belonged among the pas-
sive, feminine geniuses, he continued, and, if he had any importance,
it was in the "history of fantasy."[34] Vischer's fellow exile in Zürich in
the '50s, Richard Wagner, who had at one time been proud of his
political radicalism, had become so bourgeois in attitude by the '70s
that the *citoyen* Hölderlin was neither recognizable nor congenial to
him. When Malwida von Meysenbug gave a copy of Hölderlin's
works to Wagner in December 1873, Cosima wrote in her diary, "R.
and I recognize with some concern the great influence that this writer
has had on Professor Nietzsche: rhetorical bombast, images falsely
heaped upon one another, . . . together with a beautiful, noble senti-
ment; only, R. says, he can't form a good opinion of these New
Greeks, because he is always expecting them to say suddenly: I am a
student at Halberstadt et cetera."[35]

From the disregard bordering upon contempt that was Hölderlin's
lot in the great bourgeois age, the poet was rescued only after the turn
of the century, when the dawning of a new sensibility and a new
aestheticism changed the standards of literary criticism and made
possible a reappraisal. When it came, however, it resembled more an
exaggeration of one aspect of his work than a measured assessment of
it in its totality, and out of it grew a sacralization of Hölderlin that
distorted his message. The pioneer in effecting this transformation
was Norbert von Hellingrath, born the son of a Bavarian general
in 1888, who from an early age devoted himself to the study of
Hölderlin, writing his dissertation on the poet's translations of Pindar
and going on to decipher and edit Hölderlin's late hymns, which had
been disregarded as the products of madness, and to plan a major
historical-critical edition of his works. Hellingrath had as little interest in Hölderlin's politics as Vischer and the other critics of the
naturalist age had had. To him, as he made clear in a private lecture on
Hölderlin in 1914,

> Hölderlin is more unique than Pindar or Sappho, is more human
> and fulfilled than any prophet, Platonist or Gnostic, wholly and
> exclusively herald, carrier, vessel of the gods. He occupies an office
> with which they have invested him, a mission, and that is all, is the
> whole thing: office, mission, embassy.[36]

Hölderlin's madness was, in this view, not a mere consequence of a
life of disappointment and frustration and illness, "not merely the

goal into which life empties. The madness is the secret that attracts one like a riddle and thrusts one away by its unanswerability, the tempting secret after which curiosity inquires,"[37] the mystery that challenges us to apprehend and understand the poet's meaning for our times and his role as prophet of the future.

Hellingrath's zeal was compelling enough to persuade Stefan George and Rilke, who became converts[38] and helped make a vogue out of Hölderlin's late poems, particularly among young people. The outbreak of patriotic enthusiasm after the onset of war in 1914 encouraged this. Hellingrath, who fell at Douaumont in 1916,[39] was not the only soldier who died with a copy of *Hyperion* or the poems in his pocket. Indeed, letters from the front testify that Hölderlin helped in dark hours to sustain the spirits of young trench fighters and strengthen their conviction that their cause was just. And in the postwar period, when many of the idealists of 1914 had become embittered enemies of the Weimar government, which they regarded as an agglomeration of traitors and profiteers, Hölderlin remained for them a symbol of the Germany that had been betrayed and a prophet of a new Germany that would arise. Thus was the lover of the French revolution turned into an enemy of democracy.

In his "Eulogy to Hölderlin," Stefan George praised him as the discoverer of a new language, as one who had penetrated to the very source of speech and come back with the "life-giving word." But this accomplishment, he continued, was only incidental.

> It is not that his dark, sprung meters became the model for inquiring students of verse. . . . They have higher meaning. Through a process of breaking apart and coalescence, he is the rejuvenator of speech and, at the same time, the rejuvenator of the soul. . . . With his unambiguous and irreducible prophecies [he is] the cornerstone of the next German future and the voice announcing the New God.[40]

But the New God who actually came to Germany was certainly not the one that Stefan George expected, for he never accepted him. The New God was rather the one that Hölderlin himself warned against in a passage in *Empedokles* that was carefully forgotten after his coming, a god who would turn a brave and civilized people once more into a race of barbarians.

Soll ein Volk vergehn,
So schicken nur die Furien einen Mann,
Der täuschend überall der Missetat
Die lebensreichen Menschen überführe.
Zuletzt, der Kunst erfahren, machte sich
An einen Mann der heiligschlaue Würger,
Und herzempörend glückt es ihm, damit
Das Göttergleichste durch Gemeinstes falle.[41]

[If a people is to pass away,
Then will the furies just send a man
Who, spreading deceit all over, will indoctrinate
The healthy people in crime.
At last, experienced in the art,
The sacred, sly strangler will fasten on one man
And, filling his heart with rebellion, succeed in making
The likest to God succumb to the most rotten things.]

III

Of the period after 1933, the shade of Hölderlin might well have sighed, "So came I among the Germans. . . . Humbly I came, like the homeless, blind Oedipus to the gate of Athens, where the grove of the gods received him and beautiful souls met him. – How differently it went with me!"[42]

He was, of course, made welcome. He was taken under the wing of Germany's leading philosopher, Martin Heidegger, who had responded passionately to National Socialism and, in 1933, when he was Rektor of the University of Freiburg, had called upon the university to rally to Adolf Hitler as a leader called by destiny and sanctioned "by the inexorability of that spiritual mission that the destiny of the German people forcibly impresses upon its history."[43] A thinker who prided himself on his repudiation of reason, science, and technology as being irrelevant to the primal realities of life, Heidegger thought he found in Hölderlin a kindred spirit, one who had escaped from the "alienation of being through reason" to the origins of things and whose thought was "more rooted in beginnings and therefore in the future than the pallid cosmopolitanism of Goethe."[44] Günter Grass once wrote of Heidegger that he had debauched the German language and rendered it unintelligible for any useful purpose. It is likely that most lovers of Hölderlin's poems, trying to read Heidegger's interpretations of them, will be inclined to agree. Of the late hymns, he wrote, "Hölderlin's turning is the law of the poet's becoming-at-home-in-himself as a result of the poetic passage of the un-at-homeness when abroad";[45] the delicate and moving poem *Andenken* ("Memory") he buried under 194 pages of exegesis, assuring his readers that "the poetized in the word of the essential poesy 'over-poetizes' the poet and those who hear it," and warning them against "mere admiration of the beauty of the poem."[46]

Other indignities waited on the poet in the land of the new barbarians. In 1939, on the occasion of the Führer's fiftieth birthday celebration, Hanns Johst read ecstatically from *Hyperion*; five years later, however, he had decided that the poet was outmoded. In an essay in the *Schlesische Zeitung*, he wrote:

> There are, of course, in Germany, as the home of superannuated culture, graybeards here and there aged twenty to ninety who believe that the language of poetry must be what they assume Goethe or Hölderlin would have written if they were still alive. But against these antiquated humanists stands the sound phalanx of National Socialist youth. In the struggle of our time the spirit is purifying itself on all fronts where the Germans are engaged: in Germany we will write with blood![47]

Others were not sure how this change was to be effected and found Hölderlin's "Death for the Fatherland" a useful means of encouraging German youth to fight Hitler's battles, disregarding the fact that the earlier version of this poem, "The Battle," had been inspired by the French Revolution and the cause of freedom rather than conquest. Still others felt that Hölderlin's work would be perfectly acceptable if it were only touched up here and there. Thus, in quoting the concluding lines of the great hymn "To Germany," —

> Bei deinen Feiertagen,
> Germanien, wo du Priesterin bist
> Und wehrlos Rat gibst rings
> Den Königen und den Völkern
>
> [On your festal days,
> Germania, where you are
> The unarmed priestess giving counsel
> To the kings and peoples]

they deleted the word *wehrlos* in the penultimate line.[48]

Books about Hölderlin written during the Nazi period did their best to portray him as a good National Socialist or at least an early supporter of its ideas and values, as the "seer of German folkishness,"[49] the creator of the myth now become reality under Adolf Hitler.[50] Their pages are replete with gaseous declarations like

> On the threshold of the folklore-discovering Romantic Movement and the folk-destroying century stands the extremely unfolkish Hölderlin as the savior of the picture of the chosen, of the 'loving' folk, as the purifier and herald of the figure—hinted at dimly in Herder—of the truly folkish youth.[51]

and

> How near stands now the renewal of our folkish thinking, the consciousness, grown so strong today, of the unity of our people based upon blood, that is, upon common origins—that thought of unity that was Hölderlin's![52]

Even the more objective Hölderlin scholars, who founded a Hölderlin Society in 1943, were constrained by the fact that their "protector" (*Schirmherr*) was Josef Goebbels and felt it necessary to indulge in this kind of bombast and to make other stylistic genuflections to current political orthodoxy.[53]

The thought of Hölderlin being interpreted by Martin Heidegger and protected by Josef Goebbels is, in any case, almost insupportable. One can, indeed, hardly think of a less congenial setting for this lover of freedom and of collaboration between nations, this believer that the state should be merely the external shell within which civic virtue will flourish, than Hitler's brutal totalitarianism, intent upon stamping out the last vestiges of independence and individuality in its subjects before plunging Europe into the most dreadful war in history.

"Was bleibt aber," as Hölderlin once wrote, "stiften die Dichter" ["What remains, however, the poets endow"].[54] His poetry survived Hitler, and so did his hope for his country.

> Schöpferischer, o wann, Genius unsers Volks,
> Wann erscheinest du ganz, Seele des Vaterlands,
> Daß ich tiefer mich beuge,
> Daß die leiseste Saite selbst

Mir verstummen vor dir, daß ich beschämt
Eine Blume der Nacht, himmlischer Tag, vor dir
Enden möge mit Freuden . . .[55]

[Creative spirit of our people, when will you,
Soul of our country, appear entirely
And humble me, so that
My music ceases before you

To the last note and shamed
Like a flower of the night before you, heavenly day,
I may end in joy . . .]

8

Lenau as Political Writer

It is easy to be misled by titles. The one above is not intended as a classification, for to describe Nikolaus Lenau as a political writer could be justified neither by the nature of his poetry nor by his own view of his calling. It is clear that the vast bulk of his work—*Das Posthorn* and the other lyrics that Theodor Fontane so greatly admired,[1] the songs of Hungary, the delicate *Schilflieder*, the *Waldlieder* with their rhythmical originality, and even the greater part of the epic poems—have no specific political content. Indeed, Lenau regarded politics as an unpleasant distraction from the artist's true concerns and had no respect for writers like those of the Young German movement who devoted the greatest part of their energies and talents to it. He was speaking from the heart when, on the eve of his departure for America in 1832, he wrote: "It will be good for a while not to be able to hear anything about that damned politics, . . . a disgusting business, especially when one can never shut one's ears to it, as here at home."[2]

And yet, however reluctantly, Lenau *did* write about politics. It is not too much to say that he was forced to do so, by the nature of his times and by his conscientious regard for his profession. His political engagement was never as direct or as continuous as that of the Young Germans, and he was criticized by them because of that. But what he had to say in his political verse was no less acute than their modish feuilleton pieces and, indeed, sometimes showed a deeper and more democratic commitment.

I

Franz Nikolaus Niembsch, Edler von Strehlenau, was born on 13 August 1802 in Csatád, a small garrison town in the Hungarian Banat. His father was an unsteady and luckless drifter who had been forced to give up his commission in the Austrian army because he had married below his class and who died in 1807, leaving his family in penury, a condition that does not seem to have been much relieved when his widow remarried in 1811. The future poet's early years were darkened by the family's financial insecurity and by a continuing dispute between his mother and his paternal grandparents, who wanted the boy to live with them so that they could direct his education. Eventually, he yielded to his grandparents' pressure and, when he had completed his courses in the gymnasium of the Piarist order in Pesth, moved to their home in Stockerau, near Vienna. Their attempts to persuade him to take up the study of law were, however, unavailing. When he went to the university, he changed his course of study frequently, moving from jurisprudence to philosophy and political economy and from there to medicine, without, however, bringing any of his programs to completion. As early as 1821 he was writing to his mother that his main interest was reading and the writing of poems,[3] and it was this passion that eventually dominated his life.

During the years in which he was groping his way toward his *métier*, he became aware for the first time of the political realities of Metternich's Austria, a country in which *quieta non movere* had been engraved at the head of the tablets of the law and in which novelty, movement, and change were reprobated. During his term at the University of Vienna he was given a striking example of the attitude of the state toward the spirit of free expression, when his teacher of philosophy, Leopold Rembold, was dismissed because of his efforts to inculcate critical standards in his students,[4] and soon he was having more personal acquaintance with this sort of oppression. Indeed, as soon as he began to write and to look for opportunities for publication, he learned the truth of what the Austrian refugee Charles Sealsfield wrote in 1818: "The Austrian writer is probably the most tormented creature in the world. He is not permitted to attack the government—any government of whatever nature—or any minister or bureau or the clergy or the nobility; he dare not be liberal or philosophical or humorous. In a word, he dare not be anything."[5]

In one of his more unbuttoned moments, Metternich once engagingly explained that thought was free in Austria and so was speech, provided it was restricted to conversation among individuals, but that anything printed fell under different regulations. "There," Metternich said, "the state must draw firm limits, which we call *Zensur*."⁶ From Anastasius Grun to Adalbert Stifter, no Austrian writer escaped the blighting influence of the apparatus of censorship that was built on this principle. In his autobiography, Franz Grillparzer tells of traveling in a railway coach from Hitzing to Vienna and falling into conversation with a court councillor from the censorship office whom he had previously met in Vienna. "He began the conversation," Grillparzer wrote, "with the question that was a stereotype at that time in Vienna: Why I didn't write more? I answered that he as an official of the censorship office must know the answer better than anyone else. 'Yes,' he answered, 'that's the way you gentlemen are! You always think that the censorship is in a conspiracy against you. When your *Ottokar* was held up for two years you probably believed that some embittered enemy prevented its production. Do you know who held it back? I did, who certainly am not an enemy of yours.' 'But, Herr Hofrat,' I responded, 'what did you find in the play that was dangerous?' 'Nothing at all,' he said, 'but I thought to myself: You never can tell!' "⁷

The young man from Csatád suffered from the censorship like the others. It was to escape its restrictions that he changed his pen name from N. Niembsch von Strehlenau to Nikolaus Lenau; and, when the disguise did not alleviate the situation, he was led to a graver decision. Ludwig Börne once wrote that the only redeeming feature of the Austrian system was that there was no dearth of shoe leather in the country which could be used to flee from it.⁸ Lenau availed himself of that now, although with a heavy heart, for he loved Austria. "The country!" he wrote, "The country is divine, even more so when one compares it to its people. Alps may tower here, cataracts plunge, avalanches thunder; the enfeebled heart of man trembles in the dust and cannot clamber up the proud cliffs to lofty thoughts and sensations. Certainly the people here were once different; once brave men and heroic knights lived here. But it pains us to remember those days. Every ruined castle in the land looks to me like the bitter laughter of time turned to stone, grimacing down from the gray promontory upon the desolate heart."⁹

It was this mood that inspired Lenau's first political verse. Even before his decision to leave Vienna, his notebooks were being filled with political fragments and sketches. The bitter attack upon Metternich, which begins by showing the Chancellor at the height of his power,

> Du führst im goldnen Glückeswagen
> Dahin den raschen Trott,
> Von keuchenden Lüften fortgetragen
> Und dünktest dich ein Gott
>
> [In golden chariots of fortune
> You ride off at a fast trot
> Borne by panting breezes
> And you fancy yourself a god]

and ends with him lying dead, while

> Das Vaterland mit Lachen und Singen
> Hält Wach an deinem Grab,
> Scheucht Tränen und Seufzer und Händeringen
> Fort mit dem Bettelstab—
>
> [The fatherland with laughter and song
> Holds watch at your grave,
> And drives tears, and sighs, and handwringing
> Away with the beggar's staff]

—a polemical poem infinitely more uncompromising than Anastasius Grün's portrait of Metternich in his *Promenades*[10] and with as much concentrated hatred as Shelley's and Byron's attacks upon Castlereagh[11]—probably had its origins before his departure.[12] Certainly written in this period were his first attacks upon the clergy and the nobility, short epigrammatic pieces that are remarkable in their recognition that injustice and lack of freedom were the result not of tyrannical governments alone but of the entrenched social interests that supported them.[13]

Nor was Lenau's concern over the threat to liberty caused exclusively by what he saw in Austria. The poet's political horizons were widening rapidly, and the events of 1830–1831, and particularly the Polish insurrection and its bloody suppression, inspired him to write a series of poems which, in their passionate intensity, are unequaled by any of his early works. These were at once a tribute to the gallantry of the Polish patriots and a reminder that the extinction of freedom in Warsaw threatened freedom everywhere.

> Haut die Gläser an den Tisch!
> Brüder, mit den rauhen Sohlen
> Tanzt nun auch der Winter frisch
> Auf den Gräbern edler Polen,
> Wo verscharrt in Eis und Frost
> Liegt der Freiheit letzter Trost.[14]

> [Beat the glasses on the table!
> Brothers, with rough soles
> The new winter is dancing too
> On the graves of brave Poles,
> Where buried in ice and frost
> Lies freedom's last consolation.]

The desire to find a place where men could breathe freely and the artist flourish seems to have influenced Lenau's decision, first, to take up residence in Stuttgart and then—although only briefly—to go to America. Neither experiment was entirely fortunate. After leaving Austria, Lenau made up his mind to settle in the principal city of Württemberg because he felt the need of intellectual stimulation and because Stuttgart was known as the center of the so-called Swabian Circle of poets. He was received warmly by them, but this was a mixed blessing. With the exception of Uhland, the members of the group were undistinguished, and their parochialism doubtless contributed in the long run to Lenau's persistent and ultimately tragic melancholia. Egbert Hoehl has speculated on what might have happened had Lenau chosen instead the more bracing intellectual atmosphere of Berlin, and it may well be that, had he done so, his life would have taken a happier course.[15] But these are questions that cannot be answered. Stuttgart became his temporary home and, after the American adventure, he continued to live there, although with frequent trips to Austria.

There can be no doubt that the voyage to America was in large part politically motivated, the poet hoping to escape from a world in which

> Das edle Wild der Freiheit scharf zu hetzen,
> Durchstobert eine finstre Jägerbande
> Mit Blutgewehren, stillen Meuchelnetzen
> Der Walder Heiligtum im deutschen Lande.[16]

[To harry the noble quarry of freedom
A sinister band of hunters ransacks
With bloody weapons and murderous nets
The sanctuary of the woods in the German land.]

and to find an Eldorado of material comfort and civic liberty. The song of farewell to Europe was almost ecstatic with expectation.

> Flieg, Schiff, wie Wolken durch die Luft,
> Hin, wo die Götterflamme brennt!
> Meer, spüle mir hinweg die Kluft,
> Die von der Freiheit noch mich trennt!
>
> Du neue Welt, du freie Welt,
> An deren blütenreichen Strand
> Die Flut der Tyrannen zerschellt,
> Ich grüsse dich, mein Vaterland![17]
>
> [Fly, ship, like clouds through the air.
> To the place where the altar of the gods burns!
> Ocean, wash away the gap
> That still separates me from freedom!
>
> You new world, you free world,
> On whose blossom-rich shore
> The tide of tyrants breaks,
> I greet you, my fatherland.]

Yet Lenau had done nothing to prepare himself for his confrontation with the new world and, in consequence, was surprised and appalled by what he found. Like other European travellers—Charles Dickens, for example—he found Americans unrefined in manner and preoccupied with the accumulation of material goods, while the land they lived in turned out to be too untamed for his taste. Before leaving home, he had written, "My poetry lives in nature, and in America nature is more powerful, more beautiful than in Europe,"[18] and he had looked forward with excitement to seeing the great falls of Niagara. But in fact it was all too overpowering,[19] and he found himself longing for the quieter German woods and for gardens filled with nightingales, which, he reflected, Americans neither had nor deserved.[20]

Worst of all, he neither found freedom in America nor escaped from his preoccupation with its loss in Europe. It is interesting to note that, of the half dozen important poems that he wrote about America, two have to do with injustices practiced against the native Indians,[21] a theme that was unusual among European travelers at that time. In a third poem, "The Log Cabin," he pictures himself, rather improbably, in a rude inn in the American wilds, drinking Rhine wine and reading Uhland, and thinking about home.

> "Uhland! Wie steht's mit der Freiheit daheim?"
>   Die Frage
> Sandt' ich über Wälder und Meer ihm zu.
> Plötzlich erwachte der Sturm aus stiller Ruh'
> Und im Walde hört' ich die Antwortklage.
> Krachend stürzten draußen die nacktgeschälten
> Eichen nieder zu Boden, die frühentseelten,
> Und im Sturme, immer lauter und bänger,
> Hört' ich grollen der Freiheit herrlichen Sänger:
> "Wie sich der Sturm bricht heulend am festen Gebäude,
> Bricht sich Völkerschmerz an Despotenfreude,
> Sucht umsonst zu rütteln die festverstockte,
> Die aus Freiheitsbäumen zusammengeblockte!"[22]

> ["Uhland! How is it with freedom at home?"
>   The question
> I sent to him over the woods and the sea.
> Suddenly, out of its silent peace, the storm broke,
> And in the forest I heard the answering lament.
> Outside, stripped naked and early deprived of life,
> The oaks came crashing to the ground
> And in the tempest, ever louder and more anxious,
> I heard freedom's magnificent singer raging:
> "As the howling storm breaks on the strong house
> So breaks the people's sorrow on the despots' joy
> And tries in vain to shake the obdurate structure,
> The blockhouse made from trees of freedom!"]

This was hardly a prospect that would encourage anyone to return to Europe, but there was nothing in America's inhospitable forests to deter the poet, and he went home.

II

Upon his arrival he found himself much in the public eye, for his first book had been published in his absence,[23] and the freshness of the poems of nature and the melancholy of those on love had charmed a wide audience. This first success was to be confirmed when his *Neuere Gedichte* appeared in 1838, including his sea poems and those about America. His popularity spurred him on to new experiments. In 1835 he published his epic poem *Faust* and, two years later, another called *Savonarola*. There was not much in these longer poems that was concerned with German or European politics, although Emperor Ferdinand and Metternich were burlesqued in passing in the former and one critic interpreted *Savonarola* as a veiled attack upon contemporary absolutism.[24] It is more accurate to regard these epics as extended reflections on human desire and limitations, the existential dilemma, and the relationship of the individual to nature and to God.

Meanwhile, Lenau had attracted the attention of the most prominent and certainly the noisiest literary coterie in Germany, the so-called Young Germans. Of the leading members of this group — Gutzkow, Laube, Mundt, Wienbarg[25] — Friedrich Engels wrote in 1842 that they had emerged from the confusions of a disturbed age and had won an easy victory over all contenders by declaring that the lazy old *Belletristik* of the past must give way to youth and that they represented the forces of modernity. Since, for a time, no one challenged them, they became overconfident and vain. "They regarded themselves as world-historical figures. When a young writer appeared, a pistol was immediately put at his breast, and unconditional surrender was demanded."[26] Gutzkow put this somewhat differently, while essentially admitting its truth. "We are the product of political agitation," he wrote. "We are still young, dazzled by the future. . . . Like amphibians, we live half on the firm land of politics, half in the waters of literature. . . . We are too much demagogues to become the *castrati* of art, and again too jealous of what Goethe and Schiller did to be exclusively demagogues. The consequence is half-solutions that make us most unhappy." "Literature," he said on another occasion, "was a game to me, because I regarded it only as a subordinate expedient for political goals."[27]

It is not difficult to divine from these examples of Young German self-importance that members of this coterie would not find Lenau congenial. They had several counts against him, not least of which was the dedication to his chosen art that had led him to say, "I believe I am myself poetry; my innermost self is poetry."[28] This was

no recommendation in their eyes, since they believed that prose was
the only appropriate vehicle for the man of letters in a revolutionary
age and that "verse scribblers" were slaves who were as ready
to submit to the restrictions of the Metternich system as they
were to those of the dactylic.[29] Gutzkow's opinion of lyric poetry was
the same as his views on music, which he once described as "the
unnatural use of a chance dexterity,"[30] and one of his disciples,
Alexander Jung, agreed so completely that he simply left Lenau,
Anastasius Grün, Herwegh, Freiligrath, and other lyricists out of
his *History of the Modern Literature of the Germans*, which appeared
in 1842.[31]

Also offensive to the Young Germans was the fact that Lenau
refused to accept Gutzkow's dictum that "the necessity of politicizing
our literature is undeniable"[32] and its corollary that all writers should
write for the press on the issues of the day. The best expression of his
contrary view is his "Die Poesie und ihre Störer," in which he
portrays Poetry walking in the woods and being disturbed by "a loud
swarm" who interrupt her meditations and demand her services with
the words:

> "Komm, komm mit uns, verding' uns deine Kräfte,
> Wir wollen reich dir jeden Schritt bezahlen
> Mit blankgemütztem Lobe in Journalen,
> Heb' dich zum weltbeglückenden Geschäfte!-
> Laß nicht dein Herz in Einsamkeit verdumpfen,
> Erwach' aus Träumen, werde sozial! . . . "
>
> ["Come, come with us, put your powers at our service,
> For every step we'll repay you richly
> With freshly minted praise in journals.
> Elevate yourself to work that will benefit the world!
> Don't let your heart grow stupid in isolation!
> Wake from your dreams, become social!"]

To this Young German harangue, Poetry replies coldly:

> "Prophetisch rauscht der Wald: Die Welt wird frei!
> Er rauscht es lauter mir als eure Blätter,
> Mit all dem seelenlosen Wortgeschmetter,
> Mit all der matten Eisenfresserei.
> Wenn mir's beliebt, werd' ich hier Blumen pflücken;
> Wenn mir's beliebt, werd' ich von Freiheit singen;
> Doch nimmermehr lass' ich von euch mich dingen!"[33]

["The wood rustles prophetically: The world is free!
The rustling is louder than your journals
With all their soulless verbal trumpeting,
With all their worn out swaggering.
When it pleases me, I'll stay here gathering flowers,
When it pleases me, I'll make up songs of freedom.
But I'll never let you tell me which to do."]

This attitude offended the democratic sensibilities of the Young Germans, who took to jeering at Lenau as the "baron from Hungary" and dismissing his poetry as idle *Schwärmerei*, as clumsy imitation of Goethe, a crime in their eyes whether clumsy or not, since Goethe was their detested father figure, and (in the case of *Savonarola*) as religious obscurantism. The fact that their deadly enemy Wolfgang Menzel had praised Lenau's poetry gave them an excuse for accusing him of being a tool of the system. Gutzkow seems to have acquired a special detestation of Lenau and to have become a specialist in attacks on him, which the poet answered in kind, for he came to regard Gutzkow as "the worst character and abomination in German literature" and wrote that his most pronounced talent was a capacity for resenting accomplishments that were beyond his own power.[34]

These literary fisticuffs were unedifying and unfortunate, for the antagonists were really in agreement on the major issues of their time. If Young Germans had not been so self-important and so jealous of their exclusive claim to modernity, they might have noticed that Lenau was no less modern than they and that the poet who wrote songs of the reeds and the waters was also capable of writing about the railroad and of speculating about its services to humanity.[35] And if they had been less insistent upon the superiority of prose over poetry as a weapon in the fight for freedom,they might have discovered that in Lenau they had a political poet who on occasion could be as eloquent as Byron and Heine and who therefore deserved their respect.

Certainly a modern reader who reviews the output of the Young German school is apt to be impressed less by their noble motives than by the way in which they blunted their potential effectiveness by shrillness and exaggeration and an indiscriminate participation in good causes. In contrast, Lenau is impressive because of his relative reticence on political subjects and his controlled force when he speaks out. Nothing that the Young Germans ever wrote against the

Metternich system was more incisive and prophetic than Lenau's "To the Unrepentent" (1838), written, as Turóczi-Trostler reminds us, years before the political poetry of Heine, Herwegh, and Freiligrath.[36] Here, in lines that breathe a democratic conviction that should have stilled the gibes of his critics, the poet hints at a coming overthrow of the system that will be elemental in its fury and revolutionary in its result.

> Funken sind des Feuers Boten,
> Funken jagen durch das Land,
> Und den großen Gottesbrand
> Dämpft ihr nicht mit euren Pfoten.
>
> Zitternd seht ihr und erschrocken
> Funken, die der Witz gefacht,
> Die das Volk, indem es lacht,
> Haucht in tote Aschenflocken;
>
> Aber nicht wollt ihr erschrecken,
> Wenn es blitzt im Herzensgrund,
> Wenn die Sklaven, kettenwund,
> Doch den Gott in sich entdecken.
>
> Hört, es kann die Stunde kommen,
> Wo das Lamm ein Löwe heißt,
> Wo es brüllend euch zerreißt;
> Laßt euch Gottes Zeichen frommen![37]
>
> [Sparks are fire's harbingers,
> Sparks race through the land,
> And God's great conflagration
> You will not extinguish with your fingers.
>
> You quiver and look startled
> At sparks which wit has fanned
> And which the people, as it laughs,
> Exhales as dead flakes of ash.
>
> But you do not become frightened
> When there is a flash in the depths of the heart,
> And the slaves, galled by their chains,
> Discover the god in them.
>
> Listen! The hour may come
> When the lamb becomes a lion
> And tears you roaring into pieces;
> See that you make the most of God's warning!]

The decade of the 1840s was marked by a heightening of political agitation in Germany, but these were years of increasing emotional complications for Lenau, and long before the great upheaval that he had himself predicted, the poet's mental balance had broken down irretrievably. Before that happened, however, he made at least one more poetic contribution to the fight for freedom. The *Albigensians*, a violent and luridly colored epic poem about Innocent III's crusade against the dissenting sect in southern France, is usually considered to be merely another illustration of Lenau's romantic interest in the middle ages. The brutal realism of his approach to the subject makes this view untenable; and, when one remembers that Lenau had, from his youth onward, detested both feudalism and clericalism and regarded them as the chief pillars of the Metternich system, one is forced to conclude that the poet was thinking as much of his own age as he was of the thirteenth century. This is apparent in the opening lines, where he imagines himself, like an ancient Chinese, adopting a tiger as his guardian spirit and as his supporter in his attacks upon the foes of freedom.

> Send' ich ein Lied auf die Tyrannenfratzen,
> So hilf ihm, Tiger, nach mit deinen Tatzen![38]
>
> [If I send a song to those rascals of tyrants,
> Help it along, Tiger, with your paws!]

And it is doubly apparent in the last lines, when, having concluded the bloody tale of repression, Lenau speaks to his own revolutionary generation and, with an almost Hegelian confidence, tells it that in the end the cause of freedom must triumph since the dialectic of history demands it.

> Das Licht vom Himmel läßt sich nicht versprengen,
> Noch läßt der Sonnenaufgang sich verhängen
> Mit Purpurmänteln oder dunklen Kutten;
> Den Albigensern folgen die Hussiten
> Und zahlen blutig heim, was jene litten;
> Nach Hus und Ziska kommen Luther, Hutten,
> Die dreißig Jahre, die Cevennenstreiter,
> Die Stürmer der Bastille, und so weiter.[39]
>
> [The light from heaven does not allow itself to be dispersed,
> Nor does the sunrise permit itself to be draped
> With purple cloaks and dark cowls.
> The Hussites follow the Albigensians

And pay back in blood for what those suffered,
After Hus and Ziska follow Luther, Hutten,
The thirty years, the fighters in the Cevennes,
Those who stormed the Bastille, and so forth.]

The poet's mental collapse made him incapable of understanding the next phase in that historical process or of commenting upon the illusory victory and ultimate collapse of the revolutionary effort in 1848. Yet even if he had been at the height of his powers, it is impossible to believe that his faith in the inevitable victory of liberty would have been destroyed by that disappointment or that he would not have continued "when it pleased [him], to make up songs of freedom." However much he insisted that politics was not the poet's real business, Lenau found it impossible to remain silent in the face of tyranny. His poetry of protest deserves more recognition than it has received.

9

Heinrich Heine and the Germans

It is difficult to think of a more charming companion for a plane trip or a vacation than Heinrich Heine, or one who wears so well. For the serious mood or the sentimental he is equally congenial; his comments on the world and its ways are penetrating and provocative; and he is philosopher enough to see a meaning in history and historian enough to place philosophy within its social context. His characterization of the great actors on the world's stage are as deft as they are often malicious, and he is never at a loss for a good story. Who could resist his comparison of the mind of Alexandre Dumas to "an inn where sometimes good ideas put up but stay no longer than overnight and which very often stands empty,"[1] or his story of Napoleon commissioning a French scholar to make a *précis* of Kant's philosophy and, having read it, declaring, "All this has no practical value, and the world is little advanced by people like Kant, Cagliostro, Swedenborg und Philadelphia."[2]

Why have these attractive qualities been lost upon so many of Heine's own countrymen in the century and a half since his death, and how are we to account for their repeated failure to accept Heine as one of their own and to pay him the honors usually accorded to great artists? This is a puzzling question but not an idle one, for the search for an answer to it cannot but illuminate the psychological and political attitudes of Germans toward literature and its social functions.

I

Modern society has devised numerous ways of honoring the illus-
trious dead, among them the erection of statuary of one kind or
another in public parks, portraiture on postage stamps, and the
dedication of institutions, most frequently schools and universities, to
their memory. Heine has not done well with this kind of tribute. In
1887, when the writer Paul Heyse took up the suggestion of the
Empress Elizabeth of Austria, a great admirer of Heine's poetry, and
campaigned for the erection of a monument to Heine in his birthplace
Düsseldorf, there were angry objections from local patriotic organi-
zations, *Gesangvereine*, and student unions, who protested against
the idea of erecting what they called "a column of shame" to this
"*Schmutzfink* [dirty slob] in the grove of German poesy," and the
municipal government finally turned down the proposal on the
grounds that the site designated for the monument was too close to an
already existing war memorial. The statue that had been built for
Heine was subsequently offered to and rejected by the cities of Mainz
and Hamburg, the Catholic press in the former city leading the
agitation against accepting it and the Hamburg Senate turning it down
on the grounds that it was "used." It finally made its way to the New
World, where, thanks to Carl Schurz, it found a home in the Bronx.
Inspired by these humiliating events, the sixteen-year-old Heinrich
Mann wrote:

> Ihr wollt Ihm kein Denkmal setzen,
> Ihr lieben, braven Leut?
> So dumm, wie ihr wart, als Er lebte,
> So dumm seid ihr noch heut.[3]
>
> [So, you honest, worthy people,
> You wouldn't honor his name?
> You were stupid when he was living,
> And today you're just the same.]

During the Weimar Republic, a second attempt was made to erect a
monument in Düsseldorf. Once more this led to vicious attacks by
right-wing organisations, and again the city fathers became fright-
ened and refused to take decisive action. Although a statue was built
(one called "Young Man Rising" by Georg Kolbe), it had not been
erected before the Nazis took control of the country, and was subse-

quently hidden in Düsseldorf's art museum until after the war, when it was quietly put up in a public park, without, however, any mention of the poet's name.[4]

Nothing was done, of course, to honor Heine during the Nazi period. The country's new masters showed their feelings for the poet by burning his books in 1933 and by encouraging a movement to find writers of new lyrics for the music composed for Heine's poems by Schubert and Schumann. This was an idiotic enterprise, as even its party sponsors were forced to admit. (The poet Borries von Münchhausen wrote an article objecting to this nonsense but felt obliged to end his remarks by saying, "As far as I'm concerned, Heinrich Heine was a son of a bitch."[5]) Their embarrassment did not prevent them, however, from using the funds collected for the Heine memorial to build a new town hall in 1937.

After the Nazis had gone their way, a third, and this time rather timid, campaign was started in Düsseldorf to do belated justice to the poet. Its result was the erection in the Hofgarten of a female figure designed by the French sculptor Maillol which was officially designated as a Heine memorial although it was difficult to discover why, particularly in view of the fact that Maillol had played an ambiguous role during the Nazi occupation of France. In any case, some people found themselves thinking of it more as a kind of female garden gnome than as an appropriate tribute to the poet.

As far as postage stamps were concerned, Heine was hardly more successful. The government of the Federal Government of Germany after 1949 was reasonably liberal in its choice of the persons who would be memorialized by having their faces placed upon stamps. They honored great conservative figures of the past, like Bismark and Hardenberg and Ranke; they printed series of postage stamps to commemorate the women's liberation movement of the nineteenth century and the resistance to Hitler; and they did not hesitate to put Friedrich Lassalle's head on a twenty-pfennig stamp (the same denomination accorded to Bismarck) and that of Karl Marx upon one for thirty pfennig. But, in a series dedicated to *Dichter und Denker* in 1962-63, Heine was given no place, although Annette von Droste Hülshoff and Gerhart Hauptmann were, and it was not until 1971, and then only because of the strenuous efforts of the Social Democrat leader Carlo Schmid, that the postal authorities finally gave Heinrich Heine membership in their exclusive circle.

As for institutional commemoration, after Düsseldorf's Medical Academy had been transformed in 1965 into a university, the suggestion was made that it be named after Heine, as the university in Mainz was named after Gutenberg and the one in Frankfurt am Main after Goethe. This proposal was immediately scotched by the Rektor and Senate of the university and, when its supporters continued their campaign, defeated overwhelmingly by a plebiscite of the students. In January of the year 1973 the question was raised again, and this time the Senate voted fifty-six to twenty-one, with two abstentions, to confirm their previous decision. And there the question stood for sixteen years, when at long last Heine's supporters had their way, although, as we shall see, in circumstances that can hardly be described as a triumph for the poet.

II

This persistent snubbing of Heinrich Heine can hardly be explained on the grounds that his literary achievement does not warrant recognition. The critical assaults by Karl Kraus and Hugo von Hofmannstahl upon his literary style were essentially elitist attacks upon a man who had spoken in plain terms to a large audience,[6] and Theodor Adorno's involved critique of the *Gedichte* surely merits the acerbic comment of Jeffrey L. Sammons, who has written that, when Adorno insists that "Heine's poetry is the application of the industrial technique of mass production to Romantic archetypes, or that his colloquial style is assimilationist and 'the excessive imitative zeal of the excluded,' or that Heine's theme of unrequited love is not what it seems to be at all but rather a simile for his rootlessness in society, then the literary critic must stand up and say, with all due respect to Adorno's great intellectual gifts and achievements, that this is absurd and tends to bring the sociological enterprise into disrepute."[7] The fact of the matter is that Heine was the most popular and most widely read poet of his time and that his poems entered into the national consciousness to such an extent that, when the Nazis tried to expunge them from anthologies and school instruction, they found that this was impossible and were forced to resort to the expedient of attributing them to *Dichter unbekannt*, an unconscious tribute that raised them to the level of the traditional and mythical. As for Heine's prose, it has won the admiration of such rigorous critics as Nietzsche and Thomas Mann, both of whom regarded Heine as one of the few real masters of the German prose style.[8]

Yet, from the beginning even people who were dazzled by Heine's gifts were disturbed by the way in which he used them, and as early as the 1830s the fatal verdict of being un-German was being leveled against the poet. Jost Hermand, in a brilliant essay on Heine's early critics, summed the matter up concisely:

> Because Heine presented himself so subjectively, he appeared to his critics as footloose and unconventional. Because he was so unconventional, he was regarded as being frivolous and immoral. Because he inclined to the immoral, he was put down as a Saint-Simonian. Whoever adhered to such a doctrine must naturally be regarded by conservative eyes as "Frenchified." One who was Frenchified was immediately suspected of wandering around the world in a rootless fashion. But anyone who was rootless could only be a Jew. And as a Jew one was burdened even in those days with the stigma of Grub Street and falseness—et cetera ad libitum in infinitum.[9]

The nature of Heine's writing and the circumstances of his life laid him open to this kind of criticism. In his prose writing, but also in much of his poetry, particularly in the two great epics *Atta Troll* and *Deutschland: Ein Wintermärchen* (Germany: A Winter's Tale), he was a satirist, intent upon using the weapons of exaggeration and irony and ridicule to expose German faults and, by doing so, to persuade his fellow-countrymen to correct them. The Germans have never taken kindly to satire. Erich Kästner, Heine's great successor in the Weimar period, once wrote:

> The satirical writer pillories stupidity, malice, laziness, and related qualities. He holds a mirror up to people, generally a distorted mirror, so that by looking they will attain understanding. It is hard for him to understand that they are annoyed with him. He wants them to be annoyed with *themselves*. To become more intelligent. More sensible.[10]

The great public did not like to have its writers expect too much of it. Nor did most people regard satire, which deals with everyday life, as a legitimate form of literature. As Robert Minder has written, Germans tended (this is far less true today than it was in the nineteenth century) to place writers in two categories. Those who dealt, in

generally exalted terms, with eternal values were regarded with
reverence as *Dichter*; on the other hand, those who descended from
these heights and insisted upon discussing mundane things and commenting on contemporary politics were regarded with condescen-
sion, if not contempt, as mere *Literaten*.[11] Hence, the difference
between the reputations of a Goethe and a Spielhagen. In this scheme
of things, Heine was clearly a *Literat*, and more suspicious than most,
for not only was politics never very far under the surface of everything he wrote, but his satirical vein shocked people who expected
literature to be serious and respectful of things that demanded respect. What was one to do with a writer who apparently didn't even
take his own writing seriously? – who could write in his fourth series
of *Reisebilder*:

> There is nothing more boring on this earth than having to read an
> Italian travel account – except perhaps having to write one – and the
> only way in which the author can make it to some extent tolerable is
> for him to talk about Italy itself as little as possible. Despite the fact
> that I make full use of this technique, I cannot promise you, dear
> reader, much entertainment in the chapters that follow. If you
> become bored with the tiresome stuff that appears in them, comfort
> yourself with the thought of me, who have to write all this
> rubbish."[12]

Earnest readers found that sort of thing distasteful, and vaguely
subversive. They were even more annoyed by Heine's habit of leading
them into sentimental moods and then opening trap doors beneath
them. Engels once pointed out that Heine delighted in using the
weapon of irony to destroy bourgeois illusions about the harmony of
life, and one of his favorite tricks was to play upon his readers'
Schwärmerei and then, when their defenses were down, to confront
them brutally with reality. He was here, as in other aspects of his
writing – not least of all in his political reports from France[13] – a
disturber of the peace, a *Ruhestörer*, reminding the complacent of the
possibility, if not the imminence, of change.[14]

Nor did they appreciate Heine's irreverent sallies against established institutions like universities and churches. Consider the
celebrated opening to *Die Harzreise*, for example: "The city of
Göttingen, famous for its sausages and university, belongs to the
King of Hannover and contains 999 hearths, diverse churches, a
lying-in hospital, an observatory, a lock-up, a library, and a *Rat-*

skeller where the beer is very good."[15] Surely this demonstrated a very perverted sense of values. And how could one respect a writer who could not mention religion without being either jocular or blasphemous, as in the passage in *Die Stadt Lucca* in which he uses the liturgy of the church to celebrate a passing amour—

> Oh the beautiful, holy Catholic night! I lie in your arms; I believe, with strict Catholicism, in the heaven of your love; from our lips we kiss the blessed confession; the word becomes flesh; faith is sensualized, in form and appearance—what a religion!"[16]—

or that in *Zur Geschichte der Religion und Philosophie in Deutschland* in which he notes that St. Peter's Church in Rome was built with the monies raised by selling indulgences and thereby became "so to speak a monument to fleshly love, . . . like that pyramid which an Egyptian prostitute built with money that she gained by her trade"— going on to contrast this southern carnality with the sobriety of the north, where

> on the 31st of October 1517, as Luther nailed his theses against indulgences on the doors of the Augustiner Church, the city moat of Wittenberg was perhaps already frozen, and people could already skate upon it, which is a very cold pleasure and therefore not a sin.[17]

Finally, how could one tolerate a writer who wrote of his countrymen with good-natured contempt as "a very big fool, enormously big, who calls itself the German people,"[18] who made fun of German ambitions, who jeered at German impotence in comparison with other nations—

> Franzosen und Russen gehört das Land,
> Das Meer gehört den Briten,
> Wir aber besitzen im Luftreich des Traums
> Die Herrschaft unbestritten.[19]
>
> [The French and the Russians rule the land,
> Great Britain rules the sea,
> But we're supreme in the realm of dreams,
> Where there's no rivalry.]—

and who expressed contempt both for its rulers and for the subjects who revered them despite their broken promises?[20] It was easy for Heine's early critics to attribute this frivolous irreverence to the fact that he had been corrupted by an unhealthy admiration of France, which he openly admitted in his writings, beginning with his prose masterpiece *Ideen: Buch le Grand*, and by his fascination for Paris, where he resided continuously after 1831. Heine provided his enemies, in this respect, with all the ammunition they needed, announcing in 1828:

> Freedom is a new religion, the religion of our time. But the French are the chosen people of the new religion, in their language the first gospels and dogmas are inscribed, Paris is the new Jerusalem, and the Rhine is the Jordan which separates the consecrated land of freedom from the land of the Philistines.[21]

Even so, it was forgotten that Heine's protracted exile was not entirely voluntary. When he chose it, his hope of securing a governmental or academic position in either Berlin or Munich had been disappointed[22] and, although he was already famous, he could not hope to live off his writings, given the advanced nature of his political views and the pervasive obscurantism in his native land. If he was not actually driven to leave his country by Metternichian persecution, he was effectively prevented from returning to it after the Austrian chancellor persuaded the Bundestag to issue the decrees of 1835 that proscribed his books. Metternich enjoyed Heine's poetry and is said to have wept copiously over the *Buch der Lieder* (Book of Songs), but he had nevertheless believed that the ban of 1835 was necessary to preserve "the political structure of the state,"[23] and that meant that Heine would not have been able to earn a living in Germany without compromising his political principles and changing his literary style.

But all of that meant nothing to Heine's enemies, who made the most of the fact that he had, in order to subsist in Paris, been forced to accept a pension from the French government. They accused him of working against the national interest and spread the rumor that he had become a naturalized French subject, a charge that he indignantly repudiated.

> The marriage that I have had with our dear Frau Germania, the beautiful bear-skinner, has never been a happy one. I still remember well several beautiful moonlit nights when she pressed me tenderly to her great bosom with the virtuous nipples. But these sentimental nights could be counted on one's fingers and toward morning a peevish yawning coolness always intervened and the endless nagging began. And in the end we lived separated in bed

and board. But it never came to a real divorce. The stone mason who has to decorate our last resting place with an inscription will have to reckon with no objection if he engraves there the words, "Here lies a German writer."[24]

In addition, of course, there was the fact that Heine was a Jew, which gave his critics an explanation for everything that they disliked about him. Historians of German anti-Semitism have argued that, until relatively late in the nineteenth century, there was nothing racial about anti-Jewish prejudice and that only those Jews who refused to be baptized were the subject of criticism. If one reads what was said about Heinrich Heine in the 1830s and 1840s, one finds it difficult to support this thesis. In 1831, in an attack upon Heine and his fellow exile in Paris, Ludwig Börne, Eduard Meyer wrote,

> Baptized or not, it's all the same. It's not the faith of the Jews that we hate, but the many hateful characteristics of these Asiatics, among them so often impudence and arrogance, immorality and wantonness, their forward manner and their so often common mentality. They belong to no people, no state, no community; they roam around the world as adventurers, sniffing around everywhere . . . and remain where they find lots to manipulate. Where it is quiet and lawful, they don't feel comfortable in their skins."[25]

Even more vituperative was the editor of the *Stuttgarter Literaturzeitung*, Wolfgang Menzel, a respected critic with a university chair, who professed to be shocked by Heine's *Reise von München nach Genua* and wrote: "We see there the Jewish youth standing insolently with his hands in his pockets before paintings of Madonnas" and went on to talk of "young Jews coming from Paris, dressed in the latest mode but *blasé* and enervated by dissipation, and with a characteristic smell of musk and garlic."[26]

As Jost Hermand has written, this is language that would not have been out of place in Julius Streicher's *Der Stürmer* a hundred years later.

III

Even before his death, then, Heine was being attacked by his fellow countrymen as frivolous, immoral, French, and Jewish, and hence un-German, charges that are to be explained partly by the provincialism and lack of urbanity of German literature, the prudery of German moral attitudes, the long and baleful history of anti-Semitism, and the inferiority and sensitivity to criticism that Germans felt in the days when they lived in an atomized nation that enjoyed little political respect in the world. This became, if anything, more virulent after his death, when his country finally became united and strong. During the Bismarckian Reich, Heine became a favorite whipping boy for self-designated guardians of the purity of the language, such as Adolf Bartels, for unprincipled men with political ambitions, such as Court Preacher Stöcker, and for adulators of the pure Teutonic past, such as Richard Wagner (who, nevertheless, borrowed the plot of *Der fliegende Holländer* from the version that Heine gave of the legend in *Aus den Memoiren des Herren Schnabelowopski*).

But the most important and implacable of his foes after 1871 was Heinrich von Treitschke. This is significant because Treitschke fancied himself, and was regarded by many, as a kind of official spokesman for the new Germany, and his *German History*, which began to appear in the 1870s, was, in the words of Erich Marcks, "the outstanding book in the national literature of this decade above all, next to the speeches of Bismarck the most sublime and powerful expression of the culminating and leading forces, the most significant product of that period of all-pervasive national politics, whose herald Treitschke had now become."[27] In that work, which was designed to explain to the Germans what and who had made them great, the historian was careful to deny to Heine any share in Germany's rise to nationhood, although he was generous in writing of the contributions of other writers. He could not deny that Heine's poetry in particular had enjoyed wide popularity and still did, but he insisted that

> It was a long time before it was acknowledged that German hearts were not easy with Heine's witticisms. Purely and simply, he was the only one of our lyricists who never wrote a drinking song. His heaven was full of almond cakes, purses of gold and street girls. Of carousing in the German way the oriental was incapable. It took still longer before people discovered that Heine's *esprit* was by no means *Geist* in the German sense.[28]

Treitschke was a historian of some distinction, and it is disconcerting to find him writing as if he were seeking to disqualify Heine from membership in a student fraternity. Nor is what he writes strictly accurate, for if Heine did not write drinking songs, he once wrote a rather good poem about a drinking bout in Bremen which ends:

> Du braver Ratskellermeister von Bremen!
> Siehst du, auf den Dächern der Häuser sitzen
> Die Engel und sind betrunken und singen;
> Die glühende Sonne dort oben
> Ist nur eine rote, betrunkene Nase,
> Die Nase des Weltgeists;
> Und um die rote Weltgeistsnase
> Dreht sich die ganze, betrunkene Welt.[29]

> [You worthy master of the Ratskeller of Bremen!
> Look! On the roofs of the houses sit
> The angels, and they're drunk and singing;
> The glowing sun up there in heaven
> Is nothing but the red drunken nose
> That the Spirit of the World sticks out,
> And around the red World Spirit's nose
> Revolves the whole drunken world.]

Such objections, however, would have had no power to deter a person who could write of Heine's great satirical masterpiece, *Germany: A Winter's Tale*: "Particularly this poem, one of the most brilliant and characteristic works from Heine's pen, must show Germans what separated them from this Jew. The Aryan peoples have their Thersites and their Loki; but a Ham, who uncovers his father's shame, is known only to the sagas of the orientals."[30]

Perhaps the anti-Semitism of these two statements should not be exaggerated. Treitschke was, to be sure, in great part responsible for giving a spurious respectability to anti-Semitism in Germany by writing a notorious article in the *Preußische Jahrbücher* in 1879 which began with the words, "The Jews are our national misfortune." He was not invariably hostile to Jews and was capable of praising those who were, in his eyes, good Germans, as he did in the case of Felix Mendelssohn-Bartholdy. But this did not fit the case of Heine, who had been an incisive critic of German failings and whose criticisms had not lost their force with his death. Treitschke was entirely correct in seeing that the poet's greatest political works — the long poems *Atta Troll* and *Deutschland: Ein Wintermärchen* and the essay *Zur Geschichte der Religion und Philosophie in Deutschland* — exposed Germany's nakedness.

IV

Heine had once used the same biblical figure employed against him by
Treitschke when he wrote:

> Ah! I don't want to be another Ham, lifting the covers from the
> shame of the fatherland, but it is dreadful how people among us
> have understood how to make even slavery a matter of polite
> conversation and how German philosophers and historians torture
> their brains in order to defend any despotism, no matter how silly
> or clumsy it may be, as sensible and authentic."[31]

Atta Troll, a lengthy *jeux d'esprit* which Heine wrote in 1841 for a
Young German magazine edited by his friend Heinrich Laube, was an
elaboration on that statement. The story of a dancing bear who
escapes from his keeper and returns to his den in the high Spanish
mountains, only to be hunted down and killed by the zombie-like son
of a witch with the aid of magic bullets and secret spells, it is a
magnificent example of Heine's irrepressible romanticism and is, as
he said himself,

> . . . viellecht das letzte
> Freies Waldlied der Romantik.[32]
>
> [. . . perhaps the last
> Free forest song of romanticism.]

But it is also a profoundly political work, a slashing attack upon all
those liberal intellectuals who, in the wake of the crisis of 1840, when
a French setback in the Middle East aroused fears that France might
seek compensation on the Rhine, had succumbed to a paroxysm of
superheated nationalism without troubling to analyze the issues at
stake or the nature of German capabilities and interests. In 1846, in a
new introduction to his poem, Heine wrote:

> There arose, in the German grove of poetry particularly, that
> vague, unfruitful pathos, that unprofitable vapor of enthusiasm,
> which plunges, scorning death, into an ocean of generalizations
> and which always reminds me of the American sailor who was so
> enraptured by General Jackson that he once sprang from the top-
> mast into the sea, crying, "I die for General Jackson!" Yes, al-
> though we Germans possessed no fleet, we had lots of sailors who
> died for General Jackson in verse and prose.[33]

Heine, a democrat and a socialist, whose gifts of social analysis, as revealed in his reports from Paris in the '30s and '40s, were far in advance of his time, was contemptuous of this empty tub-thumping and caricatured it in a seris of stanzas in which Atta Troll lectures his children about freedom and unity and hatred of the national enemy.[34]

At the same time, Heine recognized that behind all the brave gestures was a deep-seated philistinism and a petty bourgeois timidity that would prevent these heroes of the word from accomplishing anything. For all his revolutionary speeches, Atta Troll secretly longed to be dancing again in chains, and it was only logical that his revolutionary ardor would be snuffed out by the dark forces of the past, to which he was drawn by the witch's seductive call. The bear was the symbol, in short, of the foolish German people and the intellectuals, equally foolish, who played at politics without real conviction; and Heine's poem was a kind of prevision of what was to happen to them in 1848 and 1866 and 1871. His epitaph was more scornful than kind:

> Atta Troll, Tendenzbär; sittlich
> Religiös; als Gatte brünstig;
> Durch Verführtsein von dem Zeitgeist,
> Waldursprünglich Sanskulotte;
>
> Sehr schlecht tanzend, doch Gesinnung
> Tragend in der zott'gen Hochbrust;
> Manchmal auch gestunken habend;
> Kein Talent, doch ein Charakter.[35]
>
> [Atta Troll, trend-conscious bear, respectably
> Religious, passionate as a mate,
> Through seduction by the Spirit of the Age
> A *sansculotte* of the primeval forest.
>
> A very bad dancer, yet with
> Conviction in his shaggy bosom.
> Also pretty smelly on occasion.
> No talent, but a character.]

Written in 1844, *Deutschland: Ein Wintermärchen* is a satirical account of a trip that Heine made to Germany in the previous year. Of all of Heine's poems, it is perhaps the most unrestrained in its attacks upon the things that he most detested in his native land—its provincialism, its romantic and ineffectual nationalism, the Prussian militarism that held it in its grip, the federal censorship that stifled independent thought, and the medieval obscurantism that still shackled it to the past. In a famous passage the traveller, passing the Kyffhäuser, visits the sleeping Barbarossa, who is waiting to rise and liberate Germany. He jeers at King Redbeard as a creature of fable who has turned the heads of the credulous and urges him to foreswear his mission.

> Das beste wäre, du bliebest zu Haus,
> Hier im den alten Kyffhäuser—
> Bedenk ich die Sache ganz genau,
> So brauchen wir keinen Kaiser.[36]

> [The best thing would be for you to remain at home,
> Here in the old Kyffhäuser.
> When I consider the matter carefully,
> It's clear that we don't need an Emperor.]

In another, often cited by critics who accused Heine of delighting in filth, he meets the goddess Hammonia, guardian spirit of Hamburg, and is told that, if he looks into a large box that stands in the corner of her room, he will be able to see Germany's future. The box is a commode and, when he looks into it, he is overwhelmed by a stink as if from thirty-six graves, the separate states of Germany, and sees no future at all.[37] An angry poem and a defiant one, which begins by reminding its readers that

> Die Jungfer Europa ist verlobt
> Mit dem schönen Geniusse
> Der Freiheit, sie liegen einander im Arm,
> Sie schwelgen im ersten Kusse.

> Und fehlt der Pfaffensegen dabei,
> Die Ehe wird gültig nicht minder . . . [38]

> [The maiden Europa is affianced
> To the handsome genius
> Of freedom. They lie embraced
> And luxuriate in their first kiss.

> And if this is without benefit of clergy,
> The marriage is nonetheless valid.],

the poem ends with a warning to the German rulers who are depriving their subjects of the benefits of that union to beware of poets, for it is they who will expose their obliquities and blacken their reputations for all future time.

Atta Troll and *Deutschland: Ein Wintermärchen* made uncomfortable reading after 1871, precisely because the conditions that they portrayed still existed, often in more brutal forms. The marriage with freedom had not been consummated in Germany; the prosperity engendered by the new industrialism had deepened the pervasive materialism of society; politically, the Germans were as ill-educated as ever; and Prussian militarism had become a way of life. It is understandable that Treitschke would not want people to read these attacks upon the Germany he loved, and that he would depreciate them as the immoral and unpatriotic scribblings of a Frenchified Jew.

It is likely that he was even more disturbed by Heine's remarkable *Zur Geschichte der Religion und Philosophie in Deutschland*, although it cannot be described as unpatriotic, since it is, throughout most of its length, a glowing tribute to the German spirit and the achievements of those who expressed it, such as Luther, Lessing and Kant. It is essentially an unfinished history of Germany, which focuses on two revolutions—the Reformation, which liberated the Germans from the tyranny of a foreign religion, and the Enlightenment, which freed them from a narrow deism—and which forecasts a third, which will bring political freedom and enable the Germans to play an honorable role in Europe. But it is precisely in dealing with the last revolution that Heine betrays doubts about its outcome, in a prophetic passage that must have enraged Treitschke and can surely not be read by Germans even today without discomfort.

Heine had always felt that one of the signs of his country's political backwardness was a tendency towards what he called Teutomania, the practice of idealizing Germany for its own sake, which was practiced by the so-called Old Germans, by eccentrics like Father Jahn and Turnmeister Massmann, and by the more reactionary branches of the Burschenschaft. In his book on Ludwig Börne, Heine attacked this disease by writing of the famous Wartburg ceremony of 1817:

> On the Wartburg the past croaked its notorious raven's song, and stupidities were said and done by torchlight that were worthy of the most imbecilic parts of the middle ages. Dominant there was that Teutomania that shed so many tears over love and faith, but whose love was no different than hatred of the foreigner and whose faith

lay only in stupidity and could, in its ignorance, find nothing better
to do than to burn books![39]

The poet was under no illusions about the possibility that veneration
of the remote past might lead to imitation of its more brutal forms,
and he noted that, among the Old Germans, the victory of Hermann
the Cherusker over Quintilius Varus in the Teutoburger Forest was
regarded as a symbol of a future victory over France. Heine had
always dreaded a Franco-German war because he felt it would halt the
progress Europe was making towards freedom. His fears found their
extremest formulation in the conclusion of *Zur Geschichte der Religion und Philosophie* where he foresaw that the next revolution might
take unexpected forms and be characterized by a revival of "the
senseless berserker rage about which the nordic bards sing and say so
much." He warned the French against a revolution inspired by German philosophers.

> The thought precedes the deed as the lightning the thunder. The
> German thunder is, to be sure, German and not very nimble and
> comes rolling rather slowly, but come it will, and when you once
> hear it crash, as it has never crashed before in world history, then
> you will know that the German thunder has finally reached its goal.
> At that sound the eagle will fall dead from the sky, and lions in the
> most distant deserts of Africa will put their tails between their legs
> and creep into their royal huts. And a piece will be played in
> Germany, compared with which the French Revolution will look
> like a harmless idyll. . . . Be careful! I mean well by you, and
> therefore I tell you the bitter truth. You have more to fear from a
> liberated Germany than from the whole Holy Alliance together
> with all of the Croats and Cossacks. . . . Once, in a beer cellar in
> Göttingen, a young Old German said that one must take revenge on
> the French for Conradin von Hohenstaufen, whom they beheaded
> in Naples. You have certainly long forgotten that. But we forget
> nothing.[40]

V

One might have thought that this powerful essay would have com-
mended itself, if not to Treitschke and his power-obsessed society,
then at least to the republican regimes that came into existence in 1919
and 1949, after two explosions of berserker Teutomania had con-

firmed Heine's wildest fears. But the leaders of the Weimar Republic could not be expected to recognize Heine as one of the spiritual leaders of their state after they had compromised with all of the forces that the poet had detested and fought against, and the Germany of 1919–1933 was in any case too filled with people who rejected any responsibility for the tragedy of the First World War to accept as their own a man whose writings were a standing reproach to them.

In the divided Germany after 1945, Heine's position was ambivalent at best. It is true that he found a measure of recognition in the German Democratic Republic because of his association with Marx and Engels and his supposed sympathy with communism in Paris in the 1840's.[41] It is doubtful that the poet would have been entirely happy with these eastern credentials, which took the form of making *Deutschland: Ein Wintermärchen* compulsory reading in schools. That he recognized the proletariat as a vital new force in politics and was fascinated by the growth of communism is true, but it is equally so that he viewed these developments with a kind of dread.[42] Peter Demetz has written that his attitude to communism moved from an aesthetic repugnance to a metaphysical opposition. In the French edition of *Lutézia*, which was published in 1855, Heine wrote:

> It is with fear and horror only that I think of that age when these somber iconoclasts will come to power; with their calloused hands they will smash unmercifully all the marble statues of beauty so dear to my heart; they will shatter all the fantastic baubles and bangles of art that the poet loves so well; they will destroy my forests of laurel and plant potatoes there. . . . The nightingales, those useless singers, will be chased away, and, alas!, my *Book of Songs* will serve my grocer for paper bags into which he will pour coffee or snuff for the old ladies of posterity.[43]

Communist ideologues have been at pains to take this as a kind of joke (although anyone who visited the Mark Brandenburg after 1990 could see how closely the government of the German Democratic Republic had lived up to Heine's prediction). He was, in any case, beneath the flippant tone, entirely serious and, having suffered under one kind of absolutism, had no hankering after another.

Meanwhile, the Federal Republic of the West showed no great desire to pay belated homage to the poet. It may be that the memory of Auschwitz and its refusal to go away rendered Heine less than *salonfähig*;[44] and perhaps the *Wirtschaftswunder* contributed its part.

Certainly, the younger generation seemed to have little knowledge of him. One of the most shocking commentaries upon political culture in the West was a remark of the leader of the Düsseldorf student government in 1973 at the time of the debate over naming the university for Heine: he said that most students didn't know enough about Heine to vote intelligently on the issue. Even that was better than what happened in December 1988 when Heine won on the same issue by a default, the bestowal of his name on the university attracting virtually no interest or comment in the national press.[45] To all intents and purposes, Harry Heine was still languishing in exile.

VI

And yet, of course, it may turn out differently. In the introduction of *Deutschland: Ein Wintermärchen*, Heine, anticipating the criticism that he knew the poem would elicit, wrote:

> I already hear your beery voices: "You defame our colors, you scorner of the fatherland, you friend of the French, to whom you want to hand over the free Rhine!" Calm yourselves! I will respect and honor your colors when they deserve it, when they no longer represent an idle and obsequious form of playacting. Plant the black-red-gold on the height of German thought, make it the standard of a free humanity, and I will give my heart's blood for it. Calm yourselves! I love the fatherland just as much as you do. Because of this love I have spent thirteen years of my life in exile, and it was because of this love also that I go back into exile, perhaps for ever.[46]

Forever is a long time. It would be good to think that the new unification of Germany will change things, and that the citizens of the new *Länder* will learn to know and admire the Heine whom their old leaders hid from them, while their fellow Germans in the old *Bundesrepublik* discover the Heine whom they have never known or have forgotten.

10

Gervinus and German Unity

On 17 June 1871, the recently crowned Emperor of Germany returned triumphantly from the battlefields of France and led his armies into his capital. Three days later, George Bancroft, the United States Minister to Berlin, sent a report on the attendant ceremonies to Secretary of State Hamilton Fish. He wrote.[1]

The *via triumphalis* was about three miles long, through streets as wide and in some places thrice as wide as Broadway. Lines of cannon captured from the French were ranged in close order on each side of the way, and the whole line of march was through an *allée* of flag-staffs garlanded and festooned with oak-leaves and evergreens. The flags, as they represented Germany and its several States, were of all colors, and all harmoniously contrasted and blended. The best talent of the sculptors and painters of Berlin was called into requisition, and under the hands of men of genius, the coarsest linen, stuffed with straw and covered with gypsum, produced in the distance the effect of marble, and, near at hand, that of casts of beautiful statues. At the starting point of the march, a gigantic image, representing the city of Berlin, gave the welcome to the returning troops. Midway on the line of march a colossal victory, having on her right hand and left statues of Strasburg and Metz, in sitting posture, was much admired. At the end, a Germania receiving back into her arms Alsace and Lorraine, on a pedestal encircled by *bas-reliefs*, was generally thought a design worthy of being perpetuated in bronze or marble. In the street *Unter den Linden* skillfully executed historical and allegorical pictures, of enormous dimensions, hung across the avenue along which the army was to pass. The Academy of Arts was conspicuous by well-executed full-length portraits of the Emperor, Bismarck, and the generals. Altogether the decorations were never paltry or common-place, but the designs showed, on the part of the artists, felicity and fertility of invention. The Emperor, now in his seventy-fifth year, rode out to his troops at 10 o'clock, returned at the head of forty thousand men, and, in the scorching sun, received the salutations of all the regiments as they passed by him, and then superintended the unveiling of the statue of his father, remaining on horseback more than six hours, and in all that time showing no sign of fatigue. The spectacle was not inferior to the Roman triumphs of old, except, indeed, that prisoners did not form a part of the procession, and that no other spoils were exhibited beyond captured eagles and banners, and trophies gained in battle. The pageant had for its spectators, besides the citizens of Berlin, three or four hundred thousand strangers, gathered from Germany and almost every part of the civilized world.

Conspicuously absent from this throng was the figure of Georg Gottfried Gervinus, a fact that may have surprised some people who had followed his early career. As a historian and a political activist, Gervinus had tried as hard as any individual, and more than most, to shake Germany out of the provincialism and atomization that were characteristic of the years that followed the Vienna settlement of 1815 and to awaken a new national consciousness and a desire to give it political expression. Nevertheless, in the 1860s, when the unity movement won its first impressive successes, he stood aside; and in 1871, the year of his death, he repudiated the new Empire that was proclaimed in Versailles. Because he—virtually alone among German *Wissenschaftler* (one must at least take note of Nietzche's dark forebodings)[2]—believed that Germany had taken a false turn in 1871, and because (in the sense that he meant this) he was right, he deserves our attention, the more so because both his original work for the unity movement and his later rejection of it were prompted by his conception of the role of the historian in society and his duty to his country.

I

It has often been said that the besetting sins of the Germans in the modern period has been *Innerlichkeit*, the tendency to retreat from the problems of the real world into the safety of private contemplation and to sacrifice civil liberties and the responsibilities that go with them for the security promised by authority. Of Gervinus it may be said that he spent his life fighting that attitude and that in the end it proved too much for him. His first historical works were appeals for the assumption of political responsibilities by his people; his last were vain attempts to prevent a new surrender to authoritarian government.

It will be apparent from this that Gervinus was not the kind of historian who was content to spend his time investigating the problems of the past for their own sake. He had first become interested in the study of history at Heidelberg, where he sat at the feet of Friedrich Schlosser, perhaps the most influential writer and teacher of history in the first thirty years of the nineteenth century. Schlosser was always more of a moralist than a historian, believing, as Henry St. John, Viscount Bolingbroke had believed, that history was "philosophy teaching by examples" and that its first purpose was "to teach and inculcate the general principles of virtue." His never flagging didactic purpose and his disdain of colleagues who sacrificed their teaching function to their research made a lasting impression on the young Gervinus.[3] He was soon writing, with a contempt equal to that of his master, of "the usual spiritless *Faktensammler*, who merely puts things together like a chronicler and yet wants to be considered a historian."[4] A real historian, he was convinced, had a responsibility to instruct his contemporaries, either by teaching moral lessons validated by past experience or by bringing them something else from history.

What that something else might be, he learned from his early researches on Machiavelli, the great pragmatist who had taught that the historian must be "a master of knowledge and a master of life" and that his role in guiding the political fortunes of his people was analogous to that of the statesman.[5] Gervinus was inspired by this without taking it too literally. At no time in his career did he aspire to high office, and he never succumbed to the kind of fantasies that ruined the career of Johannes von Müller, the historian of the Swiss Confederacy who had dissipated his energies in fruitless attempts to make himself the counselor of princes.[6] But his admiration for Machiavelli led him to ask himself what a historian should be doing about the conditions prevailing in the Germany of his time. He had soon convinced himself that he was required to make himself the political preceptor of his people—

indeed, more than that, a kind of tribune who called his people to action, since "the active life . . . is the focus of all history. All the forces of mankind concentrate on action."[7]

At least they should do so, but one would never think so by looking at Germany, a land in which inertia had become a law of life. Gervinus defined the German question, as he saw it, in an essay written in 1836, a fragment of a largely and sadly abortive work on *The Art of Drinking*. A discussion of this subject, he wrote, was probably too earthy, too much a part of the actual world, to be taken seriously by Germans. "In our case life has retreated into books, and our books know little or nothing about real life. For centuries we have neglected action and lived in a world of ideas. . . . We bury ourselves in sweet play with sensibilities, in self-indulgent toying with thought, in ego-gratifying games with emotions, in order to escape the necessity of having anything to do with activity or the life of action."[8] To change this lamentable situation was a challenge worthy of the historian, but it required him, if he was to be successful, to abandon the aridities of antiquarian research and to "make art fruitful for the present situation by writing books based on ideas that can serve the time and its needs."[9]

It was with this motivation that Gervinus embarked upon his most ambitious work, the *Geschichte der poetischen Nationalliteratur*, or as it is usually called, the *Geschichte der deutschen Dichtung* (History of German Literature). Politics aside, this was a work of great erudition and originality. The first modern history of its kind and the first complete account of the evolution of German literature from its origins to the author's own time, it was distinguished by its avoidance of lengthy disquisitions on aesthetics and by its concentration on the relationship between literature on the one hand and social and political history on the other.

Stylistically, the work leaves something to be desired. Heinrich von Treitschke complained, justifiably, of its "barbaric formlessness" and wrote: "The critic, who made judgments about the style of all of the German writers, even Goethe, couldn't write German himself. After struggling for a while through the brambles of Gervinus's sentences, his readers come into the open again panting, disheveled and tattered." But Treitschke also praised the work as the first serious attempt "to comprehend the evolution of literature in its relationship to the destinies, the achievements, and the sentiments of the nation, that is, in its necessity."[10] This judgment was subscribed to by the noted Socialist critic, Franz Mehring, and by Wilhelm Dilthey, who later wrote that Gervinus's work revealed to him for the first time the possibility of finding a connection between cultural history and philosophical thought.[11]

But Gervinus's main purpose was political: to convince his readers that the time had come for them to break out of the world of aesthetic contemplation and prepare themselves for political action. The five volumes of the *German Literature* were written not only as a tribute to Germany's literary past, but also as a valedictory to the age of literature as such. Gervinus's argument was that with the high achievement of the classical period of Goethe and Schiller, the Germans had accomplished everything they could in the world of the arts and must turn their energies elsewhere, lest their vital energy falter and die. The sharp decline in artistic excellence since the death of Schiller, as typified in the carping negativism of the Young German movement and the scurrilities of Heinrich Heine and Ludwig Börne, proved that literature had become corrupt and could only have a negative influence upon German youth. "Our *belles lettres* have become a stagnant swamp," Gervinus wrote to his friend Friedrich Dahlmann in a preface to the fourth volume, "filled with such poisonous substances that one must sigh for a hurricane from without. . . . Our literature has had its day, and, if German life is not to stand still, then we must entice the talents that now have no real goal to turn toward the real world and the State, where new spirit waits to be poured into the new material."[12]

In the last volumes of his work Gervinus leveled his sternest criticism against writers who had been oblivious to the necessity of this change or who had stood in its way. These included that arch embodiment of German philistinism and *Innerlichkeit*, the poet Johann Wilhelm Ludwig Gleim, "who had sympathy only for private life and family existence and whose ideals reached no further than the thought that we should sit nice and quiet (*hübsch still*) under the protection of the law and live peacefully with our muses and our wives,"[13] and cosmopolitans like Johann Gottfried Herder and Christoph Martin Wieland and Jean Paul, who had no sense of the needs or opportunities of the nation. (His judgment of the last of these writers was probably too strongly influenced by Jean Paul's sentimental, and immensely popular, portraits of "little people", like *Schulmeisterlein*

Wutz, and too little by Jean Paul's ambitious political novels, *Die unsichtbare Loge, Hesperus*, and *Titan*.)

Gervinus's heroes, on the other hand, were people like Lessing, who had constantly attacked the narrow vision and petty-mindedness of his compatriots, and Georg Forster, the natural historian and essayist who had founded the Mainz republic in 1793 and died during the Terror in Paris. Gervinus praised Forster as "a man who made the hard transition from the idea to the deed, from the principle to its implementation, from knowledge to action."[14] Above all others, Schiller was Gervinus's hero. In contrast to Goethe, whom he criticized sharply for his indifference to the great issues of politics, Schiller was, in his view, an intensely political man, whose ideal of an aesthetic education was in part designed to teach his fellow citizens to respond more flexibly and intelligently to the political demands of the new age. "The last of the poets of unquestionable stature," Gervinus declared, Schiller showed the fatherland "the direction that must bring the rhythm of our time to its fruition" in the developed political society of freedom.[15] How soon the nation would be ready to travel that road, Gervinus wrote in his last pages, "how well equipped an aesthetic people will be, by virtue of its harmonious education, to move forward towards a harmoniously articulated political system," it was still too soon to say. The German people were confronted now with the necessary transition from the world of fantasy to the world of reality. This would not be an easy change. But if sensitivity and power of the imagination could facilitate this passage to a rational use of life, then perhaps the transfer had already begun.[16]

II

It is, of course, impossible to guess how effective this kind of exhortation, which was also the substance of Gervinus's university lectures, was in influencing the thinking of the reading public and of academic youth. It seems safe to say that its effect was not inconsiderable, for it was enhanced, in 1837 and intermittently for more than a decade thereafter, by Gervinus's public activities. He became, in fact, a political activist.

In a sense, the role was forced upon him. In 1837, the new ruler of Hanover abrogated the constitution which his predecessor had granted to the kingdom and ordered all civil servants to revoke the oath which they had given to support it. Gervinus was one of seven professors at the University of Göttingen who refused to obey and who signed a declaration, drafted by the historian Friedrich Dahlmann, which said in part, "The success of our activities is dependent just as much upon our personal integrity as upon the scientific worth of our teaching. As soon as the students can regard us as persons to whom oaths are trifles, the value of our work comes to an end."[17] The signatories were dismissed immediately, an event that aroused national attention and led them to be hailed as the Göttingen Seven. Over night Gervinus became a figure in public life whose name was in every mouth.

He became in fact an acknowledged leader of that liberal movement which, during the 1840s, worked for the attainment of national unity and constitutional liberty and whose efforts culminated and failed in the revolution of 1848. Even without the impulse of the events in Göttingen, he would probably have taken this road. As early as 1835, he had been associated with leading liberals in the publication of the *Deutsche Jahrbücher*, a journal of literary criticism which devoted itself also to history and politics; and in 1837, in his *Principles of History*, he had made explicit avowal of his own liberal principles by writing that the reflective historian "must be a natural friend of progress and can hardly escape the suspicion of *always* sympathizing with freedom."[18] Now he became more active, devoting the time he could spare from university work to writing pamphlets on the politics of the day,[19] taking a leading role in the founding and editing of a new journal, the *Deutsche Zeitung*, which became the party organ for moderate liberalism in both northern and southern Germany, serving at the Bundestag as agent for the Hansa cities, and finally, in 1848, becoming a deputy both in the *Vorparlament* and in the National Assembly in Frankfurt.

The program of the *Deutsche Zeitung*, before and during the events of 1848, was the exclusion of Austria from Germany and the union of other states in a federation of constitutional rulers under the leadership of Prussia. But Gervinus seems always to have been more realistic and hardheaded than other advocates of these ideas; he was also less sanguine about the possibility of effecting the program and more stubborn in insisting that nothing less than the whole program would do. He repeatedly pointed out that success would depend upon a uniform acceptance of constitutional principles by all German states and particularly by Prussia, which, if unreformed, would defeat all liberal hopes. As early as March 1848, he predicted that, unless the initial momentum of the forces that gathered in the Paulskirche in Frankfurt were maintained, reaction would triumph, and warned that it would be a mistake to place any trust in Frederick William IV of Prussia. At a later date, he was among the first to see that Austria's success or failure in the Hungarian war would determine the fate of liberalism in central Europe for decades.[20] And when all of his presentiments were justified, he refused to relapse into that cheerful resignation that was adopted by so many liberals, including his friend Dahlmann, who concluded amid the ruins of their hopes that they had been foolish to insist upon principle in a world in which only power counted and that they should, therefore, adjust their program to the *Realpolitik* of the day. When the liberals made the turning that transformed them, in the end, into allies of Bismarck, Gervinus stubbornly turned the other way. He moved towards democracy.

In a brilliant essay written at a critical moment in the fortunes of the Weimar Republic, Hans Rosenberg charted Gervinus's progress from the moderate liberalism of the *Deutsche Zeitung* to the democratic conviction that he held for the rest of his life. He pointed out that, as early as December 1848, Gervinus believed that both the German people and their governments had proven their unreadiness for unity and liberty. The weakness of insight and will that had been revealed in the events of the past year indicated that there was no hope for Germany "without the nation's being shaken and shocked to its very depths, so that a new generation may come forth that is born with the iron nerves that belong to the creation of a new state life." The age of literature that had been the subject of the *History of German Litera-ture* and the aesthetic education of which Schiller had written so eloquently had not left the Germans prepared to meet reality, but had, in fact, incapacitated them for action. This must be corrected, if necessary by drastic means. "The enfeebled limbs," Gervinus wrote, "will not escape revolution's Medean cauldron and, if they are really to be rejuvenated, they should not."[21] A few months later, after Frederick William IV had refused the imperial crown which the National Assembly had offered to him, Gervinus concluded that the cause of monarchy was bankrupt—"Whatever Prussian bayonets may achieve, its cause is wholly lost in Germany"—and, not long after that, in a letter to his friend Rudolf Haym, he suggested that the time had come to begin working for the establishment of a national German republic.[22]

He was too clear-sighted to believe that this could be effected soon or—in view of what had happened in Hungary in 1849—that it could ever be realized except by a massive and successful crusade against Russian absolutism.[23] This was hardly practical in the circumstances of 1850. What then was a historian to do? Gervinus determined to make one more effort to overcome the spiritless inertia of his compatriots, this time by revealing to them the forces of movement in history and the goal to which they were tending. Out of this resolve grew his plan for a history of Europe in the nineteenth century and—a matter of greater consequence—his decision to write a prolegomena to it.

III

It never occurred to Gervinus to question the legitimacy of the historian's setting himself up as a prophet, although he disliked the term. At the end of his life, he wrote:

> It isn't the historian, but time and history that are the prophets. He listens to their oracles with humility and proclaims them . . . when they are clear to him. [When they are not,] he keeps them to himself, waiting for enlightenment. His eye, bent upon the past, discerns its patterns; turned upon the present, it detects forms of the future. And when he sees these last in firm delineation, like a seer in a vision, these shapes have already begun to take on the substance of history. The historian stands at the gates through which the future comes into the present.[24]

And, in a less complicated figure, he likened the historian to a doctor who, guided by his past experience and his knowledge of the laws of life, makes diagnoses from the pulse beats of the present.[25]

Feeling this way, Gervinus did not hesitate, before embarking upon his projected multivolume history of Europe since 1815, to write an introduction that was designed specifically to reveal the pattern of the past and the shape of the future. He hoped that such a demonstration might restore the confidence of the German people in their

destiny and help them chart the course that would realize it.[26] The
Introduction to the History of the Nineteenth Century, which gave
expression to this intention, was a remarkable book on many counts.
It was almost entirely free of the clotted prose that disfigured
Gervinus's other works. In an age in which historians had little regard
for brevity, it managed to survey the course of European history since
the middle ages with lucidity and authority in less than two hundred
small pages. It demonstrated an understanding of the movement of
political and social forces and of the emergence of a mass society of
which no other historian of the age, with the exception of Karl Marx,
was capable. And finally, and not least remarkable, it led to the
suspension of its author's right to teach *(venia legendi)* at the University of Heidelberg and his trial before a court in Baden on charges of
high treason and endangering the public order.

This legal action and the preliminary verdict (later set aside) which
ordered the confiscation of all copies of the book and the imprison-
ment of its author for two months were shameful illustrations of what
the forces of reaction were capable of in the decade that followed the
1848 revolution. One might become highly exercised about the case
were it not for the fact that the verdict later passed upon Gervinus
by his fellow historians was infinitely more disgraceful. As it was,
he was more pleased than outraged by the charges brought against
his book, for they advertised his views. The government's case
was argued in specific rather than general terms, and its brief singled
out as objectionable those passages in which the historian had described, as natural and inevitable, the passing of power from monarchy and aristocracy to the fourth estate. It also denounced his claim
that the British and American constitutions, particularly the latter,
were models to which the dissatisfied, the oppressed, and the progressive elements of all nations aspired. It objected to his attack on
reactionary governments and his argument, illustrated with historical
examples, that their methods could no longer halt "the forces of
movement of the age" which "were borne by the instinct of the
masses." And it found especially reprehensible his clearly expressed
belief that democracy was the wave of the future, providential and
irresistible.[27] In its attempts to convince the court that the exposition
of such views was equivalent to incitation and hence treasonable, the
government did more to spread them abroad than Gervinus's publisher had done. And when it was made to realize this by the rallying

of public opinion to the historian's side, it allowed the case to come to an inconclusive end. Gervinus had every reason for satisfaction and for hope that the purposes for which the book had been written would soon be realized.

And yet, as he sat down with his usual diligence to write his *History of the Nineteenth Century*, a work which, even in its unfinished state, was to comprise eight volumes, Gervinus discovered that, in the short run at least, his predictions about the shape of the future were false. It was not democracy that triumphed in Germany in the 1860s, but the monarchical-military power that he despised; and the people, whom he had described in the *Introduction* as being no longer willing to accept revolution from above,[28] showed every indication of doing precisely that. The Prussian victories over Denmark and Austria seemed to corrupt the principles even of men whom he had once admired and trusted; and, in April 1867, in a letter to a friend, he spoke of those who deprecated Bismarck's methods but accepted them because "the fraudulent desire for German power" blinded them to the consequences and permitted them to excuse crimes of the present in the name of problematical future glories.[29] During the war against France, he was disgusted equally by the chauvinism of his academic colleagues and the measureless Gallophobia that revealed itself in a people who had in the past been all too prone to Gallomania.[30] He could not help but feel now that all his attempts to educate the German people for reasoned political action had failed. And, if that was true, what would be the future of the new German Empire? The establishment of a military-absolutist state in the middle of Europe in this age of industrial and material progress was not only anachronistic but dangerous.[31] What evils might not stem from this combination of caesarism and political naiveté?

In 1849, with some of the worst excesses of revolution still fresh in his mind, Gervinus had written a book on Shakespeare in which he had compared the German people to Hamlet, lost in dreams and self-doubt, averse to action and ill-trained in the uses of power, and, when forced into activity, immoderate and violent. In an unconscious echo of the concluding pages of Heine's *History of Religion and Philosophy*, he had warned of the crimes—the cruelty, vengefulness, bloodlust and murder—of which his countrymen, these "heroes of the word," these impractical aesthetes, were capable.[32] Perhaps the comparison touched his mind again in 1871. Certainly his resistance to the form in which unification was finally achieved and his plea that a continuation of German *Kleinstaaterei* would be the safest basis for national political development—an idea that tickled the risibilities of all of the Bismarck adulators and the super-heated patriots—were animated by a presentiment that his country-men were not ready for the imperial role they were assuming and that their arrogant immaturity might one day wreak havoc on a potentially democratic Europe. It is difficult to argue that his fears were exaggerated.

IV

Gervinus died in March 1871. A few months later, Leopold von Ranke, speaking at the twelfth plenary session of the Historical Commission, made brief reference to his passing. No one who reads his remarks today will doubt that he came to bury Gervinus, not to praise him. He described his attitude in the Göttingen affair of 1837 as "manly" and granted that he had shown considerable talent as a publicist in the days of the *Deutsche Zeitung*. But he made no attempt to hide his complete rejection of his historical work, finding it flawed on the one hand by the belief that history has laws that historians can discover (a theory that Ranke rejected as a kind of barren determin-ism that would discourage historical research) and, on the other, by the insistence that *Wissenschaft* must be made relevant to life. "Very true," Ranke said, "but in order to be effective in this respect, it must, first and foremost, *be Wissenschaft*, for it is impossible to adopt a point of view in life and then carry it over into scholarship, because then it is life that is influencing scholarship, and not scholarship life. . . . We can only have a real influence on the contemporary world if we first turn our eyes away from it and lift ourselves to the plane of free objective scholarship."[33] Apart from this, Ranke said in conclusion, Gervinus had been a man of the 1830s and 1840s, who was "overtaken by events." It was a pity that he had sought to hold on to outworn ideas and that he was incapable of appreciating the new Empire, of whose establishment Ranke spoke with unstinted gratification.

This cold and unappreciative judgment became the accepted one in Germany, and Gervinus was relegated to an oblivion from which he is only now beginning to emerge. Carefully avoiding his example, academic historians during the Bismarck and Wilhelmine periods, and in the Weimar and Hitler years as well, followed Ranke's prescriptions for success. They turned their eyes away from contemporary life in order to profess a disciplined, specialized, and supposedly objective kind of scholarship, and they rarely ever turned them back again. They retreated into a heightened form of *Innerlichkeit* that was broken only by intermittent acts of ritual obeisance to the Empire that had been founded in 1871, or, as the case might be, the Nazi Reich of 1933. And in doing this, they helped to make Gervinus's dark forebodings come true, while giving us all reason to ask ourselves whether his kind of history was not, all things considered, rather better than Ranke's.

V

Meanwhile, Germany is united again and, while it would be unscientific to speculate about what Gervinus would think of that, it is certainly permissible to hope that he would be more sympathetic to it than he was to the founding of the Reich in 1871. Perhaps he would have found the modesty and simplicity of the ceremonies in Berlin at midnight on the third of October 1990 reassuring when compared with the blatant arrogance and self-satisfaction that characterized what went on in the Hall of Mirrors in Versailles and the streets of Berlin in 1871. Perhaps he might be inclined to agree that, if the unification of 1871 was a false start, with its ultimate failure already programmed by everything that had happened since 1849, the democratic progress made in West Germany since 1949 gave Germans reason to regard the unification of 1990 as a new and promising beginning. Even the thought that there were still millions of Germans in the east who were not democrats, had no notion of how to be democrats or to use democratic procedures, and had been living, some of them quite happily, under authoritarian regimes for the past fifty-seven years might not concern Gervinus unduly. He knew, and had always argued, that with a good constitution and a good legal system and able leaders to show the way, democracy is something that can be learned. And, in any case, were not these latecomers to democracy the same people who had in

October 1989 started the revolution in the streets that swept away the East German government? A hundred years earlier, the course of events had convinced Gervinus that the German people had proven their unreadiness for unity and liberty. He would now, one hopes, be inclined to believe that things were different, and one hopes that he would be right.

Notes

Introduction

1. Thomas Mann, *Betrachtungen eines Unpolitischen* (Stockholmer Ausgabe, Frankfurt am Main, 1956), p. 103.
2. *Ibid.*, p. 251.
3. Thomas Mann, *Dr. Faustus* (Stockholmer Ausgabe, Frankfurt am Main, 1947), p. 731.
4. Felix Gilbert, *Machiavelli and Guicciardini: Politics and History in Sixteenth Century Florence* (Princeton, 1963), pp. 199 f.
5. *Betrachtungen*, p. 253.
6. Robert Minder, *Kultur und Literatur in Deutschland und Frankreich: Fünf Essays* (Frankfurt am Main, 1962), p. 9.
7. Wilhelm von Humboldt, *Werke in fünf Bänden*, herausgegeben von Andreas Flitner und Klaus Giel, I (Darmstadt, 1960), pp. 56-233 (*Ideen zu einem Versuch die Grenzen der Wirksamkeit des Staats zu bestimmen* [1792]
8. *Faust, Erster Teil*, lines 2091-92.

1. Goethe as Statesman

1. Johann Peter Eckermann, *Gespräche mit Goethe in den letzen Jahren seines Lebens* (Berlin and Weimar, 1982), pp. 579 f.
2. See below, Chapter 7.
3. Eckermann, *Gespräche*, p. 440.
4. Frederic-Jean Soret, *Zehn Jahre bei Goethe*, ed. H. H. Houben (Leipzig, 1929), p. 590.
5. Friedrich Nietzsche, *Menschliches Allzumenschliches: Ein Buch für freie Geister* (Stuttgart, 1972), p. 235.

6. Wilhelm Mommsen, *Die politischen Anschauungen Goethes* (Stuttgart, 1948), p. 22.

7. Goethe, *Werke*, Weimar ed., section 3, I, 8 f. (Hereafter cited as WA.)

8. *Goethes Briefe*, ed. Karl Robert Mandelkow, I, (3rd ed., Munich, 1986), 205.

9. *Ibid.*, p. 209 (6 March 1776).

10. On Möser's influence on Goethe, see Mommsen, *Politische Anschauungen*, pp. 29–34.

11. *Goethes Werke*, Hamburg Edition in 14 Vols., ed. Erich Trunz, V (München, 1982), 90. (*Torquato Tasso*, First Act, Scene 4, lines 639–643. (Hereafter cited as HA.)

12. *Briefe*, I, 231. (To Johann Heinrich Merck, 5 January 1777.) Goethe's letters to Merck were often filled with sarcasms and exaggerations.

13. Richard Friedenthal, *Goethe. Sein Leben und seine Zeit* (Munich, 1963), p. 228.

14. See, for instance, Carl August's firm rejoinder in May 1776 to Jakob Friedrich von Fritsch when he threatened to resign from the State Council if Goethe were appointed to it. *Goethe in vertraulichen Briefen seiner Zeitgenossen*, ed. von Wilhelm Bode (3 vols. Berlin and Weimar, 1979), I, 176–180. (Hereafter cited as Bode.)

15. *Briefe*, I, 319.

16. *Ibid.*, p. 320.

17. Bode, I, 190.

18. *Briefe*, I, 344.

19. Fritz Hartung, *Das Großherzogtum Sachsen unter der Regierung Carl Augusts 1775–1828* (Weimar, 1923), pp. 12 ff.

20. See Nicolas Boyle, *Goethe, the Poet and the Age* (Oxford, 1991), 252.

21. See *Briefe*, I, 249 ff.

22. *Ibid.*, p. 784.

23. *Ibid.*, p. 204. (To Herder, 2 January 1776.)

24. Bode, I, 283.

25. Mommsen, *Politsche Anschauungen*, pp. 39 f.

26. Hartung, *Großherzogtum Sachsen*, p. 58–60.

27. Boyle, *The Poet and the Age*, p. 254.

28. Hartung, *Großherzogtum Sachsen*, p. 87.

29. *Ibid.*, p. 92.

30. *Briefe*, I, 320.

31. *Ibid.*, p. 457. (To Herzog Carl August, 26 December 1784.) See also., *ibid.*, p. 482. (To Charlotte von Stein, 5 September 1785.)

32. Hartung, *Großherzogtum Sachsen*, p. 125.

33. *Ibid.*, p. 119.

34. HA, I, 119. ("Ilmenau," lines 176–191.)

35. Boyle, *The Poet and the Age*, p. 242.

36. *Ibid.*, pp. 19 f.

37. *Briefe*, I, 346 f.

38. *Ibid.*, p. 378. (To Charlotte von Stein, 10 December 1781.)

39. Mommsen, *Politische Anschauungen*, p. 43.

40. *Ibid.*, p. 44.

41. Katharina Mommsen, "Der politische Kern von Goethes 'Elpenor,' " *Jahrbuch des Freien Deutschen Hochstifts, 1991* (Tubingen 1991).

42. *Briefe*, I, 512. (To Charlotte von Stein, 25 June 1786.)

43. *Ibid.*, p. 518. (To Carl August, 24 July 1786.)

44. *Ibid.*, II (2 Aufl., 1968), 84 ff.

45. Hartung, *Großherzogtum Sachsen*, p. 26.

46. HA, I, 180. ("Venetianische Epigramme," 22.)

47. *Briefe*, II, 153. (To Christian Gottlob Voigt, 10 September 1792.)

48. HA, X, 235. (*Campagne in Frankreich, 1792* [1822])

49. *Briefe*, II, 159. (To Voigt, 10 October 1792.)

50. HA, X, 695.

51. Eckermann, *Gespräche*, p. 471 f.

52. *Briefe*, II, 181.

53. *Ibid.*, p. 184.

54. HA, II, 514. (*Hermann und Dorothea*, canto 9, lines 305–307.)

55. See Dolf Sternberger, *Gut und Böse* (Frankfurt am Main, 1988), pp. 227 ff. ("Parabel von der Verfolgung: Uber Goethes 'Natürliche Tochter.' ")

56. HA, V, 290. (*Die Natürliche Tochter*, Act 5, scene 6, lines 2617–2623.)

57. HA, X, 495. (Tag und Jahreshefte, 1806.)

58. Bode, II, 332. (Koes, *Tagebuch*, 13 October 1806.)

59. HA, X, 496. (Tag und Jahreshefte, 1806.)

60. Erich Weniger, *Goethe und die Generale der Freiheitskriege* (revised edition, Stuttgart, 1959), pp. 49 f.

61. *Briefe*, II, 30. (To Cotta, 24 October 1806.)

62. HA, X, 363.

63. Katharina Mommsen, "Faust II als politisches Vermächtnis des Staatsmannes Goethe," *Jahrbuch des Freien Deutschen Hochstifts, 1989* (Tubingen 1989).

64. HA, III, especially 184, 196 ff., 311 ff., 314, 323 f., 341 f.

65. See Eckermann, *Gespräche*, p. 300.

66. *Wilhelm und Caroline von Humboldt in ihren Briefe*, ed. Anna von Sydow, IV (Berlin, 1910), 163, 167, 188.

67. Mommsen, *Politische Anschauungen*, p. 166.

68. Eckermann, *Gespräche*, p. 169.

69. *Ibid.*, p. 418 (italics mine).

70. *Ibid.*, p. 440 (March, 1832).

2. A German Jacobin: Georg Forster

1. Klaus Harpprecht, *Georg Forster oder die Liebe zur Welt* (Reinbek bei Hamburg, 1987). In the United States there is a study in preparation by Hugh West entitled *From Tahiti to the Terror: Georg Forster and the Sociological Imagination*, which will be published by the University of North Carolina Press.

2. Friedrich Schlegel, "Georg Forster: Fragment einer Characteristik der deutschen Klassiker," in *Meisterwerke der deutscher Literaturkritik: Aufklärung, Klassik, Romantik*, ed. Hans Mayer (Stuttgart, 1962), pp. 560 f.

3. Robert Minder, "Die Literaturgeschichten und die deutsche Wirklichkeit," in *Sind wir noch das Volk der Dichter und Denker?*, ed. Gert Kalow (Berlin, 1962), pp. 23 ff.

4. See the account of the 1964 Tutzing conference of *Germanisten* in *Die Welt* (Hamburg), 27 May 1964.

5. Georg Forster, *Ansichten vom Niederrhein, von Brabant, Flandern, Holland, England und Frankreich in April. Mai und Junius 1790*, in *Georg Forsters Werke*, ed. Akademie der Wissenschafter der Deutschen Demokratischen Republik (Berlin, 1985 ff.), IX, 236 (hereafter cited as *Werke*).

6. Schlegel, *loc. cit.*, p. 562, comments: "If his voyage with Cook was the cell from which that free aspiration, that broad outlook later developed to their full extent, then one might wish that young friends of the truth might be able more frequently to choose, instead of school, a voyage around the world, not only to add riches to their drawings of plants, but to develop wisdom in themselves." See also Harpprecht, *Georg Forster*, pp. 77–124, and the thoughtful essay by Hugh West, "The Limits of Enlightenment Anthropology: Georg Forster and the Tahitians," *History of European Ideas*, X, No. 2 (1989), 147–60.

7. *Werke*, XVI, 366; Kurt Kersten, *Der Weltumsegler: Johann Georg Adam Forster. 1754–1794* (Bern, 1957), pp. 247 f.

8. *Werke*, XVII, 334; Harpprecht, *Forster*, pp. 497 ff.

9. *Werke*, XVII, 383; Gustav Landauer, *Briefe der Revolutionszeit* (Berlin, 1919), II, 261.

10. Wolfgang Rödel, *Forster und Lichtenberg: Ein Beitrag zum Problem deutscher Intelligenz und Französiche Revolution* (Berlin, 1960), p. 106.

11. *Ibid.*, p. 108. See his letter of 6 June 1793 to his friend Samuel Thomas Sömmerring in *Werke*, XVII, 299.

12. Rodel, *Forster und Lichtenberg*, p. 145.

13. Landauer, *Briefe*, II, 245.

14. Georg Forster, *Kleine Schriften und Briefe*, ed. Claus Träger (Leipzig, 1961), p. 20 (hereafter cited as FKS).

15. *Musenalmanach für das Jahr 1797*, ed. Friedrich Schiller (Tubingen, 1796.)

16. K. Klein, *Georg Forster in Mainz* (Gotha, 1863), pp. 260 ff., 263 ff.

17. Kersten, *Weltumsegler*, pp. 274 f. Cf. Harpprecht, *Forster*, pp. 543 ff.

18. Reinhold Aris, *History of Political Thought in Germany from 1789 to 1815* (London, 1936), pp. 45 f.

19. See the speeches cited in Georg Forster, *Über die Beziehung der Staatskunst auf das Glück der Menschheit und andere Schriften*, ed. Wolfgang Rödel (Frankfurt am Main, 1966), pp. 75–83, and the wider selection in *Werke, X (Revolutionsschriften)* (1990).

20. Kersten, *Weltumsegler*, p. 290.

21. Rodel, *Forster und Lichtenberg.*, p. 150.

22. Aris, *History*, p. 44.

23. *Werke*, V, 295.

24. G.G. Gervinus, *Geschichte der deutschen Dichtung*, 4th ed., V (Leipzig, 1853), 354 f.

25. *Ibid.*, p. 335; Edgar Bonjour's introduction to Johannes von Müller, *Schriften in Auswahl*, 2d ed. (Bern, 1955), pp. 13 ff.; Aris, *History*, pp. 61 ff.

26. Kersten, *Weltumsegler*, p. 77; Harpprecht, *Forster*, pp. 218 ff.

27. Rödel, *Forster und Lichtenberg*, p. 62.

28. See Georg Lukacs, *Der junge Hegel* (Berlin, 1964), especially pp. 40 ff., 121.

29. *Werke*, XV, 24.

30. *Ibid.*, XVI, 319.

31. *Ibid.*, p. 328.

32. Harpprecht, *Forster*, pp. 422 f.

33. *Werke*, IX, 123 f.

34. *Ibid.*, XVII, 279 f.; *Georg Forsters Briefe an Ch. Fr. Voss*, ed. Paul Zincke (Dortmund, 1915), pp. 173 f.

35. *Werke*, XVII, 123.

36. *Ibid.*, p. 93; Harpprecht, *Forster*, p. 491.

37. *Werke*, XVII, 126.

38. Rödel, *Forster und Lichtenberg*, p. 51.

39. *Werke*, XVII, 234.

40. *Ibid.*, pp. 241 f.

41. *Ibid.*, p. 250.

42. Johannes von Müller, *Sämtliche Werke*, ed. Johann Georg Müller (Stuttgart, 1835), XXXI, 51 ff.

43. *Werke*, XVII, 296.

44. *Ibid.*, p. 334.

45. *Ibid.*, p. 342 f.

46. *Ibid.*, p. 349.

47. *Ibid.*, p. 376.
48. *Ibid.*, p. 375.
49. *Ibid.*, p. 424.
50. *Ibid.*, p. 395, 402, 404, 466; Kersten, *Weltumsegler*, pp. 315–321; Harpprecht, *Forster*, pp. 575–578.
51. Kersten, *Weltumsegler*, pp. 327 ff., 344 ff.
52. Forster, *Über die Beziehung, passim,* but especially pp. 142, 149, 151.
53. *Werke*, XVII, 398.
54. "Pariser Umrisse," in *Über die Beziehung*, p. 88.
55. *Werke*, IX, 134.
56. *Ibid.*, XVII, 379.
57. *Ibid.*, p. 338.
58. "Pariser Umrisse," in *Über die Beziehung*, p. 93.
59. *Werke*, XVII, 338.
60. *Ibid.*, p. 478.
61. *Ibid.*, p. 464.
62. Forster, *Kleine Schriften*, p. 29.
63. Gervinus, *Deutsche Dichtung*, V, 365, quoted by Träger in FKS, p. 29.
64. G.G. Gervinus, *Einleitung in die Geschichte des neunzehnten Jahrhunderts*, ed. Walter Boehlich (Frankfurt am Main, 1967), pp. 210 f.

3. Friedrich Schiller and the Police

1. Address of 12 November 1859, in St. Peter's Church, Zürich. Cited in Gordon A. Craig, *Geld und Geist: Zürich im Zeitalter des Liberalismus, 1833–1869* (Munich, 1988), p. 180.
2. Benno von Wiese, *Schiller. Festschrift 1959* (Cologne, 1960), p. 7.
3. *Ibid.*, p. 8.
4. Friedrich Schiller, *On the Aesthetic Education of Man in a Series of Letters*, ed. and trans. Elizabeth M. Wilkinson and L. A. Willoughby (Oxford, 1967), pp. xi, xv, xviii, xx, 30–43; Derik Regin, *Freedom and Dignity: The Historical and Philosophical Thought of Schiller* (The Hague, 1965), pp. 118 ff.
5. To Goethe, 5 January, 1798, in *Goethe-Schiller Briefwechsel*, ed. Ernst Beutler with an afterword by Emil Staiger (Frankfurt am Main, 1950), p. 279.
6. "Was kann eine gute stehende Schaubühne eigentlich wirken?" in Friedrich Schiller, *Sämtliche Werke*, ed. Gerhard Fricke and Herbert G. Göpfert (2nd ed., Munich, 1960), V, 828.
7. See W. Emrich "Schiller und die Antinomien der menschlichen Gesellschaft," in *Schiller: Reden im Gedenkjahr 1955* (Stuttgart, 1956), pp. 240–241.

8. *Wallensteins Lager*, Prologue, lines 65–66.

9. See Georg Witkowski, *Aus Schillers Werkstatt: Seine dramatischen Pläne und Bruchstücke* (Leipzig, 1910), pp. 94–102; and *Schillers Sämtliche Werke*, ed. Conrad Höfer (22 vols., Horen ed., Munich, Leipzig and Berlin, 1910–1926) XXII, 78–86.

10. See especially Melitta Gerhard, *Schiller und die griechische Tragödie* (Weimar, 1919), p. 84 n.

11. This is true even of so extended a study as Manfred Schunicht. "Schillers Fragmente 'Die Polizei' und 'Die Kinder des Hauses,' " *Wirkendes Wort*, xiv (1964) 196–208.

12. Witkowski, *Aus Schillers Werkstatt*, p. 100.

13. Saint-Simon, *Mémoires* (Paris, 1955), p. 910.

14. Jacques Saint Germain, *La vie quotidienne en France à la fin du grand siècle, d'après les archives, en partie inédites, du lieutenant-général de police Marc-René d'Argenson* (Paris, 1965), p. 267.

15. *Schillers Sämtliche Werke* (Horen ed.), XXII, 79–86.

16. In Schiller's two later sketches for a police play, the role of the police is diminished and d'Argenson disappears. See Schiller, *Sämtliche Werke* (Horen ed.) XXII, 86–128.

17. *Une ténébreuse affaire*, in Honoré de Balzac, *La Comédie humaine*, (11 vols., Gallimard ed., Paris, 1950–1959) VII. 497.

18. Willy-Paul Romain, *Le Dossier de la police* (Paris, 1966), pp. 64–66, 83–85; and, at greater length, Louis Madelin, *Fouché, 1759–1820* (Paris, 1900), Part 2. Like d'Argenson's face, Fouché's had a great influence on his reputation. "Grand, maigre, osseux et un peu vouté, il était d'une paleur étrange, qui étonnait et parfois terrifiat; cette face exsangue ne pouvait ni rougir ni palir . . . ce visage apparraissait comme fermé, mort, impénétrable. . . ." *Ibid.*, p. 379.

19. See Viktor Bibl, *Die Wiener Polizei* (Leipzig and Vienna, 1927), p. 274 and, on the Franciscan system in general, chap. 6.

20. See August Fournier, *Die geheime Polizei auf dem Wienerkongress* (Vienna, 1913).

21. "Ideen zu einem Versuch die Grenzen der Wirksamkeit des Staats zu bestimmen" (1792), in *Wilhelm von Humboldts Werke*, ed. Albert Leitzmann (15 v., Royal Prussian Academy ed., Berlin, 1903–1918), I, 97–254 and particularly 106–133.

22. "Die Gesetzgebung des Lykurgus und Solon," in *Sämtliche Werke*, ed. Fricke and Göpfert, IV, 815.

23. Schiller, *Aesthetic Education*, p. 35.

24. See Walter Muschg, "Schiller—Die Tragödie der Freiheit," in *Schiller: Reden im Gedenkjahr 1959* (Stuttgart, 1961), pp. 228–239.

25. Ses Schunicht, "Fragmente," p. 197.

26. *Wallensteins Tod*, Act 2, lines 799–800.
27. Schiller, *Aesthetic Education*, introduction, p. cx.

4. Johannes von Müller: The Historian in Search of a Hero

1. Herbert Lüthy, "What's the Point of History?", *Journal of Contemporary History*, III, no. 2 (April, 1968), pp. 13 f.
2. A good selection from the letters can be found in Johannes von Müller, *Briefe in Auswahl*, ed. Edgar Bonjour (2nd edition, Basel, 1954) (cited hereafter as Müller, *Briefe*). See also *Johannes von Müllers sämmtliche Werke*, ed. Johann Georg Müller (41 vols., Stuttgart and Tübingen, 1834), (cited hereafter as *S.W.*), vols. XXIX-XL. Perhaps the most interesting of the letters from a political point of view are in *Briefwechsel zwischen Friedrich von Gentz und Johannes von Müller*, ed. Gustav Schlesier (Mannheim, 1840).
3. Wilhelm Hoffner (Wilhelm Dilthey), "Deutsche Geschichtschreiber: Johannes von Müller", *Westermanns Jahrbuch der Illustrirten Deutschen Monatshefte*, XIX (1866), 246.
4. Heinrich Ritter von Srbik, *Geist und Geschichte, vom deutschen Humanismus bis zur Gegenwart*, I (Munich, 1950), 161.
5. He was ennobled by the Emperor of Austria in 1791 in recognition of diplomatic services in connection with the imperial elections of 1790 while he was in the service of the Archbishop-Elector of Mainz, and he took the title Johannes, Edler von Müller zu Sylvelden, H. R. R. Ritter. See *S.W.*, XXXVI, 14, 191 f.
6. On Schlözer, see Srbik, *Geist und Geschichte*, I, 124–126.
7. *S.W.*, XXIII, 205 ff. It was published in 1772 and translated into German in 1810.
8. Kurt Wehrle, *Die geistige Entwicklung Johannes von Müllers* (Basler Beiträge zur Geschichtswissenschaft, XCVIII) (Basel, 1965), pp. 13 f. Niebuhr was no great admirer of Müller, and this praise of his first work may have been intended to depreciate what came later.
9. This was Carl Victor von Bonstetten, the son of a patrician family in Geneva. Müller's letters to him, published by Friederika Brun in 1802 under the title *Briefe eines jungen Gelehrten an seinen Freund*, won him almost as much attention and praise from his contemporaries as his historical work. They are included in *S.W.*, vols. XXXIV-XXXVI. An exception to the general chorus of admiration was Franz Grillparzer, who found the letters affected. See Grillparzer, *Sämtliche Werke*, ed. Peter Frank and Karl Pörnbacher, (4 vols., Munich, 1960–65), III, 1011. On the friendship between Müller and Bonstetten, see W. Kirchner, *Studien zu einer Darstellung Johannes von Müllers* (Heidelberg, 1927), pp. 22 ff.
10. See *S.W.*, vols. VII-XXII.

11. See, *inter alia*, G.P. Gooch, *History and Historians in the Nineteenth Century* (new impression, London, 1935), pp. 11, 445 f.

12. Johannes von Müller, *Geschichten schweizerischer Eidgenossenschaft*, sel. and ed. Friedrich Gundolf (Leipzig, 1923), p. 28. See also "Geschichtswerk als große Prosa: Johannes von Müller", *Die Welt der Literatur*, 26 October 1967.

13. See the analysis in Kirchner, *Studien*, pp. 47 ff.

14. See Edgar Bonjour's introduction to his edition of Johannes von Müller, *Schriften in Auswahl* (2nd edition, Basel, 1955), p. 28. Schiller acknowledged his debt in the first scene of his play's last act where Stauffacher says

> "Es ist gewiß, bei Bruck fiel König Albrecht
> Durch Mörders Hand – ein glaubenwerter Mann,
> Johannes Müller, bracht' es von Schaffhausen."
>
> ["It is true, at Bruck King Albrecht fell
> By the hand of a murderer – a trustworthy man,
> Johannes Müller, brought the news from Schaffhausen."]

Wilhelm Tell, Act 5, lines 2946–2948.

15. Albert Leitzmann, "Goethes Beziehungen zu Johannes von Müller", *Historische Zeitschrift*, CLII (1935), 518.

16. Even before the publication of his first volume, Voltaire had introduced him to an acquaintance with the words: "This young man with the face of a fifteen year old boy is *the* historian of Switzerland". Dilthey in *Westermanns Jahrbuch*, XIX, 248.

17. Kirchner, *Studien*, pp. 54 ff.

18. *S.W.*, XXX, 139.

19. Müller, *Briefe*, pp. 43 f.

20. *S.W.*, XXXV, 161.

21. *Oeuvres de Frédéric le Grand*, XXV (Berlin, 1854), 176. It was d'Alembert who confused Müller's name (*ibid.*, p. 174) and the King followed suit.

22. *S.W.*, XXXV, 229 ff., 301.

23. See, for instance, *ibid.*, XXX, 171 ff.; Müller, *Briefe*, p. 177.

24. Müller, *Briefe*, pp. 73 ff.

25. On Montesquieu's influence on Müller, see Kirchner, *Studien*, pp. 33 ff.; on Machiavelli's, *ibid.*, pp. 36 f., and Wehrle, *Geistige Entwicklung*, p. 29.

26. In the twenty-third book of his *Vier-und-zwanzig Bücher allgemeiner Geschichten besonders der europäischen Menschheit* (1797), Müller described the partition as the "strongest blow against the principles and treaties upon which depended the existence and balance of the state system" that had painfully evolved since the collapse of the western empire. *S.W.*, VI, 214.

See also Paul Stauffer, *Die Idee des europäischen Gleichgewichts im politischen Denken Johannes von Müllers* (Basel, 1960), p. 36.

27. Müller's interest in America had probably been aroused by Francis Kinloch of South Carolina, a close friend of his in the 1770s. His works abound with interesting and sometimes prophetic passages about America's future. See, for instance, *S.W.*, VI, 270 and XXIX, 209; and Müller, *Briefe*, p. 133.

28. *S.W.*, XXV, 305.

29. Müller, *Briefe*, p. 133.

30. *S.W.*, XXXV, 174.

31. The post of librarian he relinquished in 1788 to the natural philosopher Georg Forster, whom he had known in Kassel and who was later to become the leading spirit in the Rhenish Republic when the French took Mainz in 1792. See Chapter 2 above; and *Briefe an Johann von Müller*, ed. Maurer-Constant (6 vols., Schaffhausen, 1839–40), VI, 243–316.

32. In 1787 he carried out a successful mission to Rome in connection with the appointment of Freiherr Karl Theodor von Dalberg as *Koadjutor* in Mainz, and in 1790 he was active in the negotiations in Frankfurt preceding the election of Emperor Leopold II. See Müller, *Briefe*, p. 158; and Johann von Müller, *Geschichten schweizerischer Eidgenossenschaft*, (new improved edition with a biography of the author). (4 vols., Reutlingen, 1824–25), I, ix–x.

33. On Müller's interview with Custine, see *ibid.*, pp. x–xi, and his letter of 9 November 1792 in *S.W.*, XXXI, 51 ff.

34. On his publicistic activities in Vienna, see Müller, *Eidgenossenschaft* (Reutlingen edition), p. xi; Stauffer, *Gleichgewicht*, pp. 53 ff; *S.W.*, XXXI, 128 f.

35. "Darstellung des Fürstenbundes" (1787), *S.W.*, XXIV, 8–258. See also Stauffer, *Gleichgewicht*, pp. 13 ff., 40, 43, 46; Wehrle, *Geistige Entwicklung*, pp. 117 ff.

36. "Teutschlands Erwartungen von Fürstenbunde" (1788), *S.W.*, XXIV, 259–284.

37. *Ibid.*, XXX, 222.

38. *Ibid.*, XXXI, 64.

39. *Ibid.*, XXXVIII, 178.

40. *Ibid.*, p. 167.

41. *Ibid.*, XXXI, 128 f.; Stauffer, *Gleichgewicht*, pp. 50 f.

42. *S.W.*, XXXI, 88.

43. *Ibid.*, XXXII, 79.

44. Müller, *Briefe*, pp. 230 f.

45. *S.W.*, XXXII, 198 f.

46. The official censorship held up the publication of the Swiss history because it seemed to be a glorification of revolutionary principles. See Müller, *Briefe*, pp. 301 f.

47. On the mission to Dresden and the talks in Weimar and Berlin, see August Fournier, *Gentz und Cobenzl* (Vienna, 1880), pp. 124 ff.; Willy Andreas, "Johannes von Müller in Weimar 1804" *Historische Zeitschrift*, CXLV (1932), 69 ff.; and Paul R. Sweet, *Friedrich von Gentz: Defender of the Old Order* (Madison, Wisconsin, 1941), pp. 88 ff. The last work is over-critical of Müller and sometimes resorts to adjectival abuse without supplying supporting evidence.

48. *Briefwechsel zwischen Gentz und Müller*, p. 38.

49. These include essays on Frederick II, the Cid, the decline of freedom among the ancient peoples, and the calculation of time in the prehistorical period. See *S.W.*, XXV, 78 ff., 93 ff., 101 ff., 152 ff.

50. Marwitz's brother, Friedrich August Ludwig, disapproved of Alexander's friendship with Müller, and it is to him that we owe the following unflattering portrait of the historian in his Berlin period: "Johann von Müller was a small, thoroughly ugly fellow with a paunch and little short legs and a fat face that was always glowing from much gobbling and boozing, and with goggle eyes that stuck away out of his head and were perpetually rimmed with red." Theodor Fontane, *Wanderungen durch die Mark Brandenburg*, II (Nymphenburg edition, Munich, 1960), 225.

51. See Paul Bailleu, "Prinz Louis Ferdinand: eine historisch biographische Studie", *Deutsche Rundschau*, XLV (1885), 35 ff. The prince was a commanding and mercurial person who treated Müller, depending on his mood, either as a great scholar or as a figure of fun. See Henriette Herz, *Lebenserinnerungen* (n. d.), p. 202.

52. See, for instance, the reviews included in *S.W.*, XXVII, 1–21, 21–28; and, for Gentz's reaction, *Briefe von und an Friedrich von Gentz*, edited by Friedrich Carl Wittichen (2 vols., 1909–10), I, 277, II, 190.

53. Bailleu in *Deutsche Rundschax*, XLV, 45 ff.

54. Müller, *Briefe*, pp. 315 ff.

55. Wehrle, *Geistige Entwicklung*, pp. 195–1948; Stauffer, *Gleichgewicht*, pp. 66–68.

56. Gerhard Ritter, *Stein: eine politische Biographie* (3d ed., Stuttgart, 1958), pp. 146 f., 160; Bailleu in *Deutsche Rundschau*, XLV, 221.

57. See Müller, *Briefe*, pp. 304, 312 ff., 315 ff.

58. *Ibid.*, p. 326.

59. *S.W.*, XXXIII, 169.

60. Müller, *Briefe*, pp. 331.

61. *S.W.*, XXXIII, 111 ff. (To his brother, 25 November 1806).

62. *Ibid.*, p. 113. See also Werner Kirchner, "Napoleons Unterredung mit Johannes von Müller", *Jahrbuch der Goethe-Gesellschaft*, XVI (1930), 108–120; and Heinz Gollwitzer, *Europabild und Europagedanke: Beiträge zur deutschen Geistesgeschichte des 18 und 19. Jahrhunderts* (Munich, 1964), p. 100.

63. The address is to be found in *S.W.*, XXV, 274–285, and Müller, *Schriften in Auswahl*, pp. 285–294.

64. See Leitzmann in *Historische Zeitschrift*, CLII, 507 ff.

65. Sweet, *Gentz*, pp. 135 f. Adam Müller shared Gentz's opinion (*Briefe von und an Gentz*, II, 416) but Alexander von Humboldt and Karl August Bötticher were sympathetic. *Ibid.*, I, 213 f.; Edgar Bonjour, *Studien zu Johannes von Müller* (Basel, 1957), p. 198. One of the most balanced judgements of the address was that of Clausewitz. See *Karl und Marie von Clausewitz: Ein Lebensbild in Briefen und Tagebuchblättern*, ed. Karl Linnebach (Berlin, 1917), pp. 90–91.

66. Müller, *Briefe*, p. 364.

67. Wehrle, *Geistige Entwicklung*, pp. 238 f.

68. *Wilhelm und Caroline von Humboldt in ihren Briefe*, ed. Anna von Sydow (7 vols., Berlin, 1906–16), II, 19.

69. Bonjour, *Studien*, pp. 260 f.

70. *S.W.*, XXXI, 165.

71. Wehrle, *Geistige Entwicklung*, p. 239.

72. Müller, *Briefe*, p. 417. See also Bonjour, *Studien*, pp. 281 ff.

73. *Correspondance de Napoleon I*, XVI (Paris, 1864), 272.

74. Müller, *Briefe*, p. 366. Compare Rahel Varnhagen's formulation, in a letter of 30 November 1819 to Karl Gustav von Brinckmann: "Among other things, I forgot to tell you that many of our friends have become ministers of state and that is also a kind of death." *Rahel Varnhagen im Umgange mit ihren Freunden: Briefe, 1793–1833*, ed. Friedhelm Kemp (Munich, 1967), p. 116.

75. See his own statement in the conclusion of *Vier-und-zwanzig Bücher allgemeiner Geschichten* in *S.W.*, VI, 350 f.

76. Dilthey in *Westermanns Jahrbuch*, XIX, 246.

5. Heinrich von Kleist and the Duel Against Napoleon

1. *Heinrich von Kleists Nachruhm: Eine Wirkungsgeschichte in Dokumenten*, ed. Helmut Sembdner (Bremen, 1967), p. 468.

2. See, for instance, his letters to Christian Ernst Martini in Heinrich von Kleist, *Sämtliche Werke und Briefe*, ed. Helmut Sembdner (2 vols., Munich, 1961), II, 472–86. (Hereafter cited as *SW*).

3. Michael Hamburger, *Reason and Energy: Studies in German Literature* (New York, 1957), p. 113.

4. Eugene Newton Anderson, *Nationalism and the Cultural Crisis in Prussia, 1806–1815* (New York, 1939), pp. 123, 127, 133.

5. *SW*, II, 719.

6. See for instance, *SW*, II, 718–21; and Hans Mayer, *Heinrich von Kleist: Der geschichtliche Augenblick* (Pfullingen, 1962), p. 38.

7. *SW*, II, 735, 737; Mayer, *Kleist*, p. 34; Joachim Maas, *Kleist: die Fackel Preussens*, pp. 92 f.

8. Hans M. Wolff, *Heinrich von Kleist als politischer Denker* (University of California Publications in Modern Philology, Volume 27, No. 6, Berkeley, 1947), p. 459.

9. *SW*, II, 760–61.

10. Günter Blöcker, *Heinrich von Kleist oder das absolute Ich* (Berlin, 1960), pp. 87 f.

11. Anderson, *Nationalism and the Cultural Crisis*, p. 127; and Hans Kohn, *Prelude to Nation-States: The French and German Experience, 1789–1815* (Princeton, 1967), p. 195.

12. Gottfried Benn, *Das gezeichnete Ich: Briefe aus den Jahren 1900–1956* (Hamburg, 1962), pp. 32, 35; Manfred Delling, "Irrtum und Fehltritt des Gottfried Benns," *Die Welt* (Hamburg), May 30, 1963.

13. *SW*, II, 771.

14. *Ibid.*, p. 815.

15. On Humboldt and Müller, see, *inter alia*, Edgar Bonjour, *Studien zu Johannes von Müller* (Basel, 1957), p. 198; on Voss, see Klaus Epstein, *The Genesis of German Conservatism* (Princeton, 1966), p. 669, and Jacques Droz, *Le romantisme allemand et l'État: Résistance et collaboration dans l'Allemagne napoléonienne* (Paris, 1966), pp. 98 f., III.

16. *Heinrich von Kleists Lebensspuren*, ed. Helmut Sembdner (2nd ed., Bremen, 1964), p. 165.

17. *SW*, II, 782.

18. *Kleists Lebensspuren*, pp. 285 f.

19. It had, indeed, been further inflamed by the fact that, as a result of one of the absurd incidents that recur in Kleist's life, he had been arrested by the French during a trip from Königsberg to Berlin early in 1807, and imprisoned for four months at Chalons-sur-Marne on suspicion of espionage, a charge of which he was entirely innocent.

20. *SW*, II, 782.

21. See J. G. Fichte, *Reden an die deutsche Nation*, ed. by Herman Schneider (Leipzig, 1924), especially Addresses 8 and 12.

22. *SW*, I, 585 (*Die Hermannsschlacht*, lines 1496–1503).

23. See *ibid.*, II, 675 (To Adolfine von Werdeck, July 28 / 29, 1801).

24. Wolff, *Kleist als politischer Denker*, p. 474 ff.

25. See *Kleists Nachruhm*, p. 356. The critic was Arthur Eloesser.

26. *SW*, I, 585 (*Die Hermannsschlacht*, lines 1482–89).

27. *Ibid.*, p. 593 (lines 1698–99).

28. *Ibid.*, p. 615–21 (Scenes 15–19). Kleist explained to Dahlmann that Thusnelda was a good girl, somewhat simple and vain, like many of those who were at first taken in by the French, whose reaction was violent when the scales

fell from their eyes. *Kleists Lebensspuren*, p. 301. One can imagine that "the young country girl from the Mark," about whom Kleist wrote in the second of his *Satirical Letters*, would act in the same way as Thusnelda. See *S. W.*, II, 368 ff.

29. As was the anonymous reviewer in the *Times Literary Supplement*, Aug. 21, 1953, who described Hermann and Thusnelda as "slyer and more brutal than those whose badness was supposed to be demonstrated." Cited in *Kleists Nachruhm*, p. 474.

30. *SW*, I, 608 (*Die Hermannsschlacht*, lines 2096–98).

31. *Ibid.*, pp. 28–31.

32. *Ibid.*, p. 28.

33. *Ibid.*, p. 26 f.

34. *SW*, II, 354 f.

35. *Ibid.*, pp. 380–82.

36. *Kleists Lebensspuren*, pp. 293 f. On the Emperor's jealousy of his brother, see Gordon A. Craig, *War, Politics and Diplomacy: Selected Essays* (New York, 1966), pp. 6–8.

37. Maas, *Kleist*, p. 218.

38. *SW*, II, 828.

39. *SW*, I, 32, ("Das letze Lied").

40. *Berliner Abendblätter*, ed. Heinrich von Kleist (Facsimile edition, with epilogue by Helmut Sembdner, Stuttgart, 1965), issues of Oct 1 and 22, 1810.

41. Maas, *Kleist*, pp. 239–53; *Kleists Lebensspuren*, pp. 370, 382 f., 385 f., 416. On Hardenberg's policy at this time, see Peter Gerrit Thielen, *Karl August von Hardenberg, 1750–1822* (Cologne, 1967), pp. 245 ff.

42. *SW*, II, 857.

43. The story of the *Berliner Abendblätter* is told with great detail, but often with tendentious interpretation, in Reinhold Steig, *Heinrich von Kleists Berliner Kämpfe* (Berlin, 1900). More accurate is Helmut Sembdner, *Die Berliner Abendblätter Heinrich von Kleists* (Berlin, 1939). See also Helmut Rogge, "Heinrich von Kleists letzte Leiden," *Jahrbuch der Kleist-Gesellschaft* 1922 (Berlin, 1923) pp. 34–50.

44. *SW*, II, 871.

45. Heinrich von Kleist, *Prinz Friedrich von Homburg*, ed. Richard Samuel in collaboration with Dorothea Coverlid (Berlin, 1964), introduction, pp. 26–28.

46. *SW*, I, 704 (*Prinz Friedrich von Homburg*, lines 1750–52).

47. *Ibid.*, p. 707, line 1830.

48. For his earlier views on these things, see *SW*, II, 584 f., 626 f., 681; Wolff, *Kleist*, p. 363 f.; and Curt Hohoff, *Heinrich von Kleist in Selbstzeugnissen und Dokumenten* (Hamburg, 1958), p. 38.

49. See Droz, *Le romantisme allemand*, p. 232.

50. *Prinz Friedrich von Homburg* (Samuel ed.), introduction, p. 10.

51. Blöcker, *Kleist*, p. 202.
52. *Kleists Nachruhm*, p. 330.
53. *SW*, I, 698 (*Prinz Friedrich von Homburg*, lines 1575–87).
54. *Historische Zeitschrift*, LXXXVI (1901), 89 ff.; and the comments of Gerhard Ritter, *Stein: Eine politische Biographie* (3rd ed., Stuttgart, 1958), pp. 336 f.
55. *SW*, I, 545 (*Die Hermannsschlacht*, lines 332–35).
56. G.H. Pertz and H. Delbrück, *Das Leben das Feld-Marschalls Grafen Neidthardt von Gneisenau* (5 vols., Berlin, 1864–80), II, 112 ff.
57. *Kleists Lebensspuren*, pp. 441–43; *SW*, II, 879.
58. Thielen, *Hardenberg*, p. 272.
59. See below, Chapter 6.
60. Pertz, *Gneisenau*, II, 191 ff.
61. *SW*, II, 878.
62. *Ibid.*, p. 884.
63. *Wallensteins Lager*, "Prolog," lines 65–66.
64. Hamburger, *Reason and Energy*, p. 113. Compare Anderson, *Nationalism and the Cultural Crisis*, pp. 141–42.
65. Bertolt Brecht, *Gesammelte Werke* (Suhrkamp ed., 20 vols., Frankfurt am Main, 1967), IX, 723 ("An die Nachgeborene," lines 6–8).
66. See, for instance, his letter of late November 1805 to Rühle von Lilienstern, where he asks: "Where is the freshness of mind that is so absolutely indispensable to come from in times when, as Pfuel would say, misery grabs you by the neck?" *SW*, II, 761.
67. See Droz, *Le romantisme allemand*, pp. 231 f.
68. On the Expressionists, see Gordon A. Craig, "Engagement and Neutrality in Weimar Germany," *Journal of Contemporary History*, II, No. 2 (1967), 49–63.

6. Wilhelm von Humboldt as Diplomat

1. *American Foreign Service Journal*, June 1956, p. 21.
2. Occasionally the brothers were confused by contemporaries. On 13 December 1813, Wilhelm von Humboldt wrote to his wife from Darmstadt that, at a recent dinner with the grand duke, some of the female guests had thought he was Alexander and that he had not corrected this impression until they became too pressing about crocodiles and tigers. *Wilhelm und Caroline von Humboldt in ihren Briefe*, ed. Anna von Sydow (Berlin, 1910), IV, 196. (Hereafter cited as *Briefe*.)
3. C. K. Webster, *The Foreign Policy of Castlereagh, 1812–1815* (London, 1931), especially p. 334.

4. Harold Nicolson, *The Congress of Vienna* (New York, 1946), Henry A. Kissinger, *A World Restored*, (new ed., New York, 1964.)

5. August Fournier, *Die Geheimpolizei auf dem Wiener Congress*, (Vienna, 1913), p. 386.

6. Bruno Gebhardt, *Wilhelm von Humboldt als Staatsmann*, (Stuttgart, 1899), II, p. 172.

7. *Ibid.*, I, p. 116.

8. Siegfried Kaehler, *Wilhelm von Humboldt und der Staat*, (new ed., Göttingen, 1963), p. 206.

9. Compare Bismarck's letter to his wife in 1851: "In the art of saying absolutely nothing with lots of words I am making raging progress, and I write dispatches of many pages which read just as plain and blunt as any leading article, and if Manteuffel [the minister president] can say what's in them after he has read them, then he can do more than I." *Briefe an seine Frau und Gattin*, (Stuttgart, 1900), p. 281.

10. *Briefe*, IV, p. 70.

11. Carl von Clausewitz, *Politische Schriften und Briefe*, ed. Hans Rothfels, (Munich, 1922), p. 84.

12. Peter G. Thielen, "Karl August von Hardenberg", in *Männer der deutschen Verwaltung*, (Cologne, 1963), p. 29.

13. To Hardenberg, 13 January 1813, Gebhardt, *Humboldt*, I, 398 ff.

14. *The Practice of Diplomacy*, being an English rendering of Francois de Callières's "De la manière de négocier avec les souverains," presented with an introduction by A. F. Whyte (London, 1919), p. 23.

15. The best expression of this, as well as Humboldt's most extensive appraisal of Metternich's personality and policy, is in his dispatch of 17 February 1811. *Wilhelm von Humboldts Gesammelte Schriften*, ed. Königliche Preußische Akademie der Wissenschaften, XI (Berlin, 1903), 5–8.

16. Gebhardt, *Humboldt*, I, 388 n.

17. See *Gesammelte Schriften*, vol. XI, pp. 9–10, 13 ff.; Gebhardt, *Humboldt*, I, pp. 375 ff.; Friedrich Schaffstein, *Wilhelm von Humboldt: Ein Lebensbild*, (Frankfurt am Main, 1952), pp. 240 ff.

18. On Austro-Russian relations in 1811, see Enno E. Kraehe, *Metternich's German Policy: I. The Contest with Napoleon, 1799–1814*, (Princeton, 1963) pp. 139 f.

19. H. Ritter von Srbik, *Metternich: Der Staatsmann und der Mensch*, (Munich, 1925 ff.), I, p. 400.

20. *Gesammelte Schriften*, XI, 17 ff.

21. *Ibid.*, XI, 23 f.; Gebhardt, *Humboldt*, I, 410.

22. Gebhardt, *Humboldt*, I, 404.

23. See, for instance, *Briefe*, IV, 201, and Schaffstein, *Humboldt*, p. 245.

24. Gebhardt, *Humboldt*, I, 423.

25. *Gesammelte Schriften*, XI, 32 f.
26. *Ibid.*, XI, 29 f.
27. Gebhardt, *Humboldt*, I, 429 f.
28. *Ibid.*, I, 433.
29. *Briefe*, IV, 27.
30. *Ibid.*, IV, 38 ff., 54; Gebhardt, *Humboldt*, I, 446 n.
31. *Gesammelte Schriften*, XI, 67 ff., 82.
32. On the Prague conference, which Humboldt called "our singular and bizarre congress", see Gebhardt, *Humboldt*, I, 471 ff.; and Kraehe, I, pp. 181-5.
33. Kraehe, *Metternich's German Policy*, I, 184.
34. *Briefe*, IV, 93.
35. Gebhardt Humboldt, I, 438. See also *Briefe*, V, 94.
36. *Briefe*, IV, 76 ff.
37. *Aus dem Nachlaß Varnhagens von Ense. Tagebücher von Friedrich von Gentz*, V (Leipzig, 1873), 265.
38. See Gordon A. Craig, "Problems of Coalition Warfare: The Military Alliance Against Napoleon, 1813-1814," *Harmon Memorial Lectures*, No. 7, (U.S. Air Force Academy, 1965) especially pp. 9 ff.
39. Kaehler, *Humboldt*, p. 265; Gebhardt, *Humboldt*, II, 4 ff.; Schaffstein, *Humboldt*, pp. 250 ff.; *Briefe*, IV, 163, 167, 188; Kraehe, *Metternich's German Policy*, I, 268.
40. *Briefe*, IV, 194, 217.
41. Gebhardt, *Humboldt*, II, 12-14.
42. Schaffstein, *Humboldt*, p. 260.
43. *Briefe*, IV, 314.
44. For instance, the famous memorandum of 9 December 1813. *Gesammelte Schriften*, XI, 91-95.
45. Gebhardt, *Humboldt*, II, 14 ff.
46. On the First Peace of Paris, see Heinrich von Treitschke, *Deutsche Geschichte*, (6th ed., Leipzig, 1897), I, 563-5.
47. See his letter of 1 August 1814, *Briefe*, IV, 367.
48. *Ibid.*, IV, 400.
49. See *Gesammelte Schriften*, XI, 163-172; Webster, *Castlereagh*, p. 338.
50. Treitschke, *Deutsche Geschichte*, I, 610.
51. See *Gesammelte Schriften*, XI, 145-159.
52. Treitschke, *Deutsche Geschichte*, I, 583 f.
53. Gebhardt, *Humboldt*, II, 63, 96; H. Freiherr von Egloffstein, *Carl August auf dem Wiener Kongress*, (Leipzig, 1915), p. 11.
54. See Fournier, *Geheimpolizei*, p. 260.
55. Gebhardt, *Humboldt*, II, 105 ff.; *Briefe*, IV, 418; *Gesammelte Schriften*, XI, 189-97. Compare Srbik, *Deutsche Einheit*, I, 189 and Webster,

Castlereagh, p. 349, both misleading with respect to Humboldt's position. Humboldt, an ardent champion of Jewish rights at the congress, had in fact been offered financial rewards by the Jewish community in Prague, but had, to Gentz's astonishment, declined them. *Briefe*, IV, 565 f.

56. *Briefe*, IV, 572.

57. See, for instance, *Gesammelte Schriften*, XII, 2–18.

58. Webster, *Castlereagh*, p. 319.

59. Talleyrand, *Mémoires* (Paris, 1889), III, 58. See also *Briefe*, IV, 484.

60. See, *inter alia*, Craig, "Coalition Warfare," pp. 17–20; Gerhard Ritter, *Staatskunst und Kriegshandwerk*, 1 (Munich, 1954), 110–11, 115–16; and H. G. Schenk, *The Aftermath of the Napoleonic Wars*, (New York, 1947), pp. 116 f.

61. *Briefe*, V, 21.

62. *Ibid.*, V, 43.

63. *Ibid.*, V, 56 ff.

64. *Ibid.*, IV, 243 f.

65. In the subsequent period Gneisenau was most caustic in his criticisms of Humboldt, calling him "immoral, cowardly and spiritless". See Srbik, *Deutsche Einheit*, I, 229; Gebhardt, *Humboldt*, II, 237; and G. H. Pertz and Hans Delbrück, *Das Leben des Feld-Marschalls Grafen Neithardt von Gneisenau*, (Berlin, 1864–80) V, 395 f.

66. James Joll, *Three Intellectuals in Politics: Blum, Rathenau, Marinetti*, (New York, 1960), p. xi.

67. *The Practice of Diplomacy*, p. 62.

68. See, for instance, *Briefe*, IV, 133.

7. Hölderlin and the Barbarians

1. Seamus Heaney, "The Redress of Poetry," *Times Literary Supplement*, 22–28 December 1989, pp. 1412, 1413, 1418.

2. See above, Introduction, p. x f.

3. Friedrich Hölderlin, *Sämtliche Werke und Briefe*, ed. Günter Mieth (2 vols., Munich, 1970), I, 313. ("Brot und Wein.")

4. *Ibid.*, II, 822. (To his brother, 4 July 1799.)

5. *Ibid.*, I, 332–34. The English translation is that of David Constantine in his *Hölderlin* (Oxford, 1988), p. 375.

6. See, in general, the brilliant essay of Robert Minder, "Hölderlin unter den Deutschen," in his *Dichter in der Gesellschaft: Erfahrungen mit deutscher und französischer Literatur* (Frankfurt am Main, 1966).

7. Georg Lukács, *Goethe and His Age* (London, 1968), p. 136.

8. William Hazlitt, "Observations on Mr. Wordsworth's Poem 'The Excursion'," *The Round Table* (Everyman edition, 1936), pp. 119 f.

9. See *S.W.*, II, 575.

10. *Ibid.*, p. 554.

11. *Ibid.*, p. 571.

12. *Ibid.*, pp. 716–17.

13. Walther Harich, *Jean Paul* (Leipzig, 1925), p. 698.

14. Hölderlin, *S.W.*, I, 415.

15. Lukács, *Age of Goethe*, p. 138.

16. A measured view of Hölderlin's political interests and activities can be found in M. Delorme, *Hölderlin et la Révolution francaise* (Monaco, 1959). Pierre Bertaux, in *Hölderlin, Essai de Biographie intérieur* (Paris, 1936) and *Hölderlin und die französische Revolution* (Frankfurt am Main, 1969) and other works is inclined to attribute more importance to Hölderlin as a political conspirator, without always being persuasive. See also W. Kirchner, *Der Hochverratsprozeß gegen Sinclair* (Marburg, 1949).

17. Hölderlin, *S.W.*, I, 224.

18. Constantine, *Hölderlin*, pp. 223 f.

19. See Hölderlin, *S.W.*, II, 866 ff. (To Susette Gontard, beginning of November, 1799.)

20. Lukács, *Age of Goethe*, pp. 154 f.

21. On the *citoyen* as distinct from the *Bürger*, see Ernst Bloch, *Das Prinzip Hoffnung* (Frankfurt am Main, 1973), III, 1095, 1557 f.

22. See the passage, late in the novel, where he takes his lute and sings a "Schicksalslied" that he had written in his youth. Hölderlin, *S.W.*, I, 726 f.

23. *Ibid.*, p. 607.

24. *Ibid.*

25. *Ibid.*, p. 677.

26. *Ibid.*, pp. 737–38.

27. Constantine, *Hölderlin*, pp. 140, 150.

28. E. M. Butler, *The Tyranny of Greece Over Germany* (Cambridge, 1935), p. 224.

29. Hölderlin, *S.W.*, II, 39.

30. *Ibid.*, p. 65.

31. Georg Herwegh, *Literatur und Politik*, ed. Katharina Mommsen (Frankfurt am Main, 1969), pp. 62 ff. ("Ein Verschollener.")

32. Ferdinand Freiligrath, "Der gute Bürger," in Hein und Oss, *Deutsche Lieder, 1848–1849* (Gustav-Heinemann-Preis für die Schuljugend, 1974).

33. Friedrich Theodor Vischer, *Kritische Gänge*, second series, III, 197.

34. Friedrich Theodor Vischer, *Aesthetik oder die Wissenschaft der Schöne*, II, 1. Abt., "Die Lehre vom Naturschönen."(Leipzig, 1847).

35. Cosima Wagner, *Die Tagebücher*, I (Frankfurt am Main, 1976), entry for 23 December 1873.

36. Norbert von Hellingrath, "Hölderlins Wahnsinn," in *Deutscher Geist: Ein Lesebuch aus zwei Jahrhunderten*, ed. Oskar Loerke (enlarged new ed., Berlin and Frankfurt am Main, 1953), II, 879.

37. *Ibid.*

38. See Stefan George, *Werke*, ed. Robert Boehringer (Stuttgart, 1983), II, 298 ff. ("Lobrede auf Hölderlin"); Rainer Maria Rilke, *Der ausgewählte Gedichte anderer Teil*, selected by Katharina Kippenberg (Wiesbaden, 1958), pp. 45 f. ("Hölderlin").

39. George, *Werke*, II, 236 f. ("Norbert").

40. *Ibid.*, p. 301.

41. Hölderlin, *S.W.*, II, 62.

42. *Ibid.*, I, 301.

43. Martin Heidegger, *Die Selbstbehauptung der deutschen Universität* (Breslau, 1933).

44. Minder, *Dichter in der Gesellschaft*, p. 81. ("Hölderlin unter den Deutschen").

45. *Ibid.*, p. 251. ("Heidegger und Hebel, oder die Sprache von Meßkirch").

46. Martin Heidegger, *Hölderlins Hymne 'Andenken'* (Vorlesungen, Freiburg, 1941–1942) (Frankfurt am Main, 1982), pp. 6, 21.

47. Josef Wulf, *Literatur und Dichtung im Dritten Reich: Eine Dokumentation* (Gütersloh, 1963), p. 174.

48. Constantine, *Hölderlin*, p. 257 and note.

49. Carl Petersen, *Der Seher deutscher Volkheit Friedrich Hölderlin* (Kiel, 1934).

50. Hans Gottschalk, *Das Mythische in der Dichtung Hölderlins* (Stuttgart, 1943), p. 9.

51. Hajo Jappe, *Jugend deutschen Geistes* (Berlin, 1939), p. 414.

52. Julius Richter, *Hölderlins Christusmythos und die deutsche Gegenwart* (München, 1941), p. 48.

53. See *Iduna: Jahrbuch der Hölderlin-Gesellschaft*, ed. Friedrich Beissner and Paul Kluckhohn, I (Tübingen, 1944).

54. Hölderlin, *S.W.*, I, 390.

55. *Ibid.*, p. 257. The English translation of this poem, "An die Deutschen," is by Constantine. See his *Hölderlin*, p. 372.

8. Lenau as Political Writer

1. Theodor Fontane, *Werke* (Nymphenburg edition, vol. XV), *Von Zwanzig bis Dreißig*, ed. Kurt Schreinert and Jutta Neuendorff-Fürstenau (Munich, 1967), p. 36. Fontane's admiration for Lenau continued through his life and is illustrated by the fact that one of his most attractive heroines, Lene

Nimptsch in *Irrungen, Wirrungen*, is named after the poet. See Hans-Heinrich Reuter, *Fontane* (2 vols., Munich, 1967), I, 137.

2. Nikolaus Lenau, *Sämtliche Werke*, ed. Eduard Castle, (6 vols., Leipzig, 1911), III, 146.

3. *Ibid*, p. 24.

4. József Turóczi-Trostler, *Lenau*. Translated from the Hungarian by Bruno Heilig (Berlin, 1961), pp. 22–23. Rembold was lecturing, not on Austrian politics, but upon Kant. The impression he made on Lenau may be judged by the poet's letter of 28 June 1820 to his mother, in which he speaks of "the teaching of a wise man, the professor of philosophy", who is helping him to become "an independent man" *Sämtliche Werke*, III, 14.

5. Charles Sealsfield, *Österreich, wie es ist*. Trans. from the English and ed. Viktor Klarwill (Vienna, 1919), p. 197.

6. Turóczi-Trostler, *Lenau*, p. 15. On the censorship, see also Julius Marx, *Die österreichische Zensur im Vormärz* (Munich, 1959), and Donald E. Emerson, *Metternich and the Secret Police: Security and Subversion in the Habsburg Monarchy, 1815–1830* (The Hague, 1968), pp. 136–175.

7. Frnz Grillparzer, *Werke* (3 Bände, Munich, 1971), III, 608 ff.

8. Ludwig Börne, *Werke*, (2 vols., Berlin, 1964), I, 226.

9. *Sämtliche Werke*, III, 62.

10. See Anastasius Grün [Anton Alexander Graf Auersperg] *Spaziergänge eines Wiener Poeten* (1831). ("Salonszcene")

11. See Byron's *Don Juan*, canto I, stanzas xi–xiv, preface to cantos 6, 7, and 8, canto 9, stanza xlix; canto 10, stanza lix; *Epigrams; The Irish Avatar*. See Shelley's *The Mask of Anarchy*, stanza II, III.

12. It was published in 1832 with the title "At the Grave of a Minister" *Sämtliche Werke*, I, 122 f.

13. See, for instance, "Der geldgierige Pfaffe" and the posthumously published "Protest". Lenau's bitterest attack upon the aristocracy, "Des Teufels Lied vom Aristokraten," came in the last years of his life but reflected earlier feelings.

14. "In der Schenke". See also "Die polnischen Flüchtlinge", "Maskenball", "Abschied von Galizien" (a translation of a poem by Bolosz von Antoniewicz), and the later poem "Die nächtliche Fahrt" (1838).

15. Nikolaus Lenau, *Werke in cinem Bande*, ed. Egbert Hoehl (Hamburg, 1966), p. 495.

16. "Fragmente" (1832).

17. "Abschied" (1832).

18. *Sämtliche Werke*, III, 145.

19. See the poem "Der Urwald" (1832).

20. *Sämtliche Werke*, III, 193.

21. See "Der Indianerzug" (1834).

22. "Das Blockhaus" (1838).
23. *Gedichte*, published by Cotta in 1832.
24. *Faust*, "Die Lektion", "Das Lied"; *Sämtliche Werke*, IV, 311.
25. Heine and Börne are often regarded as members of this group, but their connection was tenuous in view of their absence from Germany, and they do not seem to have concerned themselves with Lenau.
26. Cited in *Das Junge Deutschland: Texte und Dokumente*, ed. Jost Hermand (Stuttgart, 1966), pp. 365–366.
27. See Karl Vietor, *George Büchner* (Bern, 1949), pp. 274, 276.
28. *Sämtliche Werke*, III, 85.
29. Hermand in *Das Junge Deutschland*, p. 375.
30. In his novel *Wally, die Zweiflerin*, cited in *Das Junge Deutschland*, p. 109.
31. See Engels's criticism, *ibid.*, p. 357.
32. *Ibid.*, p. 101.
33. *Sämtliche Werke*, I, 366 f.
34. Turóczi-Trostler, *Lenau*, p. 231 ff.
35. "An den Frühling 1838" (1838).
36. Turóczi-Trostler, *Lenau*, p. 158.
37. *Sämtliche Werke*, I, 318 f.
38. *Die Albigenser* (1842), "Nachtgesang."
39. *Ibid.*, "Schlußgesang."

9. Heinrich Heine and the Germans

1. *Insel Heine* (Frankfurt am Main, 1968), III, *Schriften über Frankreich*, ed. Eberhard Galley, *271 (Uber die französische Bühne*, Sechster Brief).
2. *Ibid.*, p. 465 (*Lutézia*, Zweiter Teil, 2 June 1842).
3. Richard Winston, *Thomas Mann, The Making of an Artist* (New York, 1973), p. 49.
4. On this and the following four paragraphs, see F. Hellendall, "Heinrich Heine and Düsseldorf—A City Afraid of its Great Son," *Monatshefte für deutsche Unterricht*, LXIII, No. 1, (1971), 56–59, *Der Spiegel* (Hamburg), 1969/9, 85 ff. ("Nur nix"), and Barbara Glauert, "Heinrich Heine und Deutschland: Ein bio-bibliographischer Ruckblick," *Börsenblatt für den deutschen Buchhandel* (Frankfurt ed., Nr. 8 (30 January 1973).
5. Jeffrey L. Sammons, *Heinrich Heine, the Elusive Poet* (New Haven, 1969), p. 372 n.
6. See Karl Kraus, "Heine und die Folgen," in *Auswahl aus dem Werk*, ed. Heinrich Fischer (Frankfurt am Main, 1961), pp. 138 ff.
7. See Theodor K. Adorno, "Die Wunde Heines," in Adorno, *Noten zur Literatur*, I (Frankfurt am Main, 1958), pp. 144–153; and Sammons, *The Elusive Poet*, p. 24.

8. Friedrich Nietzsche, *Götzendämmerung; Der Antichrist, Ecce Homo, Gedichte* (Stuttgart, 1964), p. 323; Thomas Mann, *Reden und Aufsätze* (Stockholm ed., Oldenburg, 1965), II, 680.

9. Jost Hermand, "Heines frühe Kritiker," in *Der Dichter und seine Zeit: Politik im Spiegel der Literatur*, ed. Wolfgang Paulsen (Heidelberg, 1970), pp. 118 f.

10. Erich Kästner, *Gesammelte Schriften* (7 Bde., Zürich, Berlin, 1959), V, *Vermischte Beiträge* ("Eine kleine Sonntagspredigt," August 1947).

11. Robert Minder, *Kultur und Literatur in Deutschland und Frankreich* (Frankfurt am Main, 1962), p. 10.

12. Heinrich Heine, *Werke*, ed. Martin Greiner (2 Bde., Köln, 1962), II, 37 (*Die Bäder von Lucca*, Kapitel IX). [Hereafter cited as *Werke* (Greiner)].

13. See the remarkable reports on the larger implications of the social question and of the situation in the Near East in the 1840's in *Insel Heine*, III, 326, 370 ff., 406 (*Lutézia*, Erster Teil, 30 April and the months following.)

14. See Marcel Reich-Ranicki, *Über Ruhestörer: Juden in der deutsche Literatur* (München, 1973), p. 59.

15. *Werke*, (Greiner ed.), I, 768.

16. *Ibid.*, II, 94.

17. *Ibid.*, p. 407.

18. *Ibid.*, p. 208 (*Französiche Zustände*, Vorrede).

19. *Ibid.*, I, 711 (*Deutschland: Ein Wintermärchen*, Caput 7).

20. See his remarks on Frederick William III of Prussia in *Französiche Zustände*, Vorrede (*Ibid.*, II, 204 f.) and his attacks on Frederick William IV in his political verse of the 1840's (*Ibid.*, I, 292, 544–47).

21. *Ibid.*, II, 195 (*Englische Fragmente*, XIII).

22. See Fritz J. Raddatz, *Heine: Ein Deutsches Märchen* (Hamburg, 1977), pp. 30 f., 89 ff.

23. Sammons, *The Elusive Poet*, p. 11. On Heine's exile, see also Carl Zuckmayer, "Heinrich Heine, der liebe Gott und ich: Ein Dreipersonenspiel," *Die Zeit*, Nr.50, 19 December 1972.

24. *Insel Heine*, III, 537 f. (*Lutézia*, Zweier Teil, "Retrospektive Aufklärung," August 1854).

25. Jost Hermand, "Heines frühe Kritiker," *Der Dichter und seine Zeit*, p. 129.

26. *Ibid.*, p. 130.

27. Erich Marcks, *Heinrich von Treitschke: Ein Gedenkblatt* (Heidelberg, 1906), p. 64.

28. Heinrich von Treitschke, *Deutsche Geschichte im neunzehnten Jahrhundert*. IV (Leipzig, 1890), 423.

29. *Werke* (Greiner), I, 185 (*Die Nordsee*, Zweiter Zyklus, IX).

30. Treitschke, *ibid.*, V (Leipzig, 1894), 381.

31. *Werke* (Greiner ed.) II, 119 (*Die Stadt Lucca*, Kapitel XVII).
32. *Ibid.*, I, 684.
33. *Ibid.*, p. 612.
34. *Ibid.*, p. 635.
35. *Ibid.*, p. 678.
36. *Ibid.*, p. 732.
37. *Ibid.*, pp. 754 f.
38. *Ibid.*, p. 697.
39. *Ibid.*, II, 752 (*Heinrich Heine uber Ludwig Börne*, Viertes Buch).
40. *Ibid.*, pp. 499 f.
41. See Dolf Sternberger, *Heinrich Heine und die Abschaffung der Sünde* (Hamburg, 1972), where it is strongly argued that, in his Paris years, Heine was interested in the doctrines of Saint-Simonianism and in the moral regeneration of mankind more than he was in communism or political parties.
42. See *Insel Heine*, III, 406 (*Lutézia*, Erster Teil, XXVIII).
43. Peter Demetz, *Marx, Engels and the Poets* (Chicago, 1967), p. 80.
44. Reich-Ranicki, *Über Ruhestörer*, p. 57.
45. *Der Spiegel*, for example, had lots to say about universities in its issues of 26 December 1988 and 30 January 1989 but mentioned nothing about either Düsseldorf or Heine.
46. *Werke*, (Greiner ed.), I, 694.

10. Gervinus and German Unity

1. *Papers Relating to the Foreign Relations of the United States. Transmitted to Congress with the Annual Message of the President. December 4, 1871* (Washington, 1871), pp. 397 f.
2. See, for instance, the introduction and early pages of *Unzeitgemäße Betrachtungen* (Leipzig, 1873).
3. On Schlosser and his influence on Gervinus, see G.P. Gooch, *History and Historians in the Nineteenth Century* (rev. ed., London, 1952), 101–102.
4. *Grundzüge der Historik* (1837), in Georg Gottfried Gervinus, *Schriften zur Literatur*, edited, with an introduction, by Gotthard Erler (Berlin, 1962), p. 56.
5. *Ibid.*, p. 99; Gooch, *History*, p. 102.
6. See above, Chapter 6.
7. Quoted in Gooch, *History*, p. 103.
8. "Geschichte der Zechkunst" (1836), in G.G. Gervinus, *Gesammelte kleine historische Schriften* (Karlsruhe, 1838), pp. 170 f.
9. "Einleitung in die *Deutschen Jahrbücher*" (1835), in *ibid.*, p. 322.
10. Heinrich von Treitschke, *Deutsche Geschichte im Neunzehnten Jahrhundert*, V (Leipzig, 1894), 418.

11. Franz Mehring, *Gesammelte Schriften* (15 vols., Berlin, 1960–1967), IX, 49; K. Höfele, *Geist und Geschichte der Bismarckszeit, 1870–1890* (Göttingen, 1967), p. 345.

12. *Geschichte der deutschen Dichtung* (5th ed., 5 vols., Leipzig, 1871–1874), IV, v. See also Johannes Dörfel, *Gervinus als historischer Denker* (Inaugural dissertation, Gotha, 1903), pp. 31 ff.

13. *Deutsche Dichtung*, V, 429 ff.

14. See especially, Mehring, *Gesammelte Schriften*, IX, 48; and Gervinus, *Deutsche Dichtung*, V, 356.

15. Gervinus, *Deutsche Dichtung*, V, 356, 468 ff.

16. *Ibid.*, p. 473.

17. Treitschke, *ibid*, IV (Leipzig, 1890), 658.

18. "Einleitung in die *Deutschen Jahrbücher,*" *Kleine historische Schriften*, 329; Gervinus, *Schriften zur Literatur*, introduction, pp. 86, 102.

19. See Treitschke, *ibid.*, V, 688 ff.

20. Gervinus, *Hinterlassene Schriften* (Wien, 1872), pp. 51 ff.

21. Hans Rosenberg, "Gervinus und die deutsche Republik: Ein Beitrag zur Geistesgeschichte der deutschen Demokratie," *Die Gesellschaft*, VI (1929), 124 ff.

22. *Ibid.*, pp. 127 f.

23. *Ibid.*

24. *Hinterlassene Schriften*, p. 48.

25. *Ibid.*, p. 52.

26. Gervinus, *Einleitung in die Geschichte des neunzehnten Jahrhunderts*, ed. Walter Boehlich (Frankfurt am Main, 1967), p. 9.

27. *Ibid.*, pp. 96, 128, 149, 154, 162, 164–165, 170–171; *Der Hochverratsprozeß gegen Gervinus*, ed. Walter Boehlich (Frankfurt am Main, 1967), pp. 7, 54–59; Rosenberg in *Die Gessellschaft*, VI, 129–133.

28. *Einleitung*, pp. 128, 149.

29. *Schriften zur Literatur*, introduction, p. lxxi.

30. *Hinterlassene Schriften*, pp. 97 ff.

31. Rosenberg in *Die Gesellschaft*, VI, 134.

32. *Shakespeare* (4th ed., Leipzig, 1872), II, 132 f. The comparison of Germany to Hamlet was, of course, not original with Gervinus. Among others to whom it occurred was his *béte noir* Börne. See Ludwig Börne, *Gesammelte Schriften* (10 vols. Hamburg, 1832–1935), II, 198. See also Freiligrath's poem, *Hamlet* (1844).

33. *Historische Zeitschrift*, XXVII (1872), 134 ff.

Index

183